HOUGHTON MIFFLIN

Imagine

INVITATIONS
TO LITERACY

Houghton Mifflin Company • Boston

Atlanta • Dallas • Geneva, Illinois • Palo Alto • Princeton

HOUGHTON MIFFLIN

Imagine

Senior Authors

J. David Cooper
John J. Pikulski

Authors

Kathryn H. Au
Margarita Calderón
Jacqueline C. Comas
Marjorie Y. Lipson
J. Sabrina Mims
Susan E. Page
Sheila W. Valencia
MaryEllen Vogt

Consultants

Dolores Malcolm
Tina Saldivar
Shane Templeton

INVITATIONS TO LITERACY

Houghton Mifflin Company • Boston

Atlanta • Dallas • Geneva, Illinois • Palo Alto • Princeton

Introductory Selection

Themes

CONTENTS

School's Open: Check It Out!

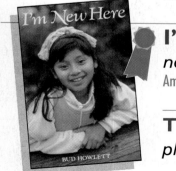

PRESERVE AND EARTH PATROL PROTECT

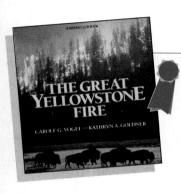

Get Involved: Preserve and Protect!

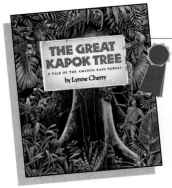

PAPERBACK **PLUS**

A River Ran Wild
nonfiction
by Lynne Cherry

In the same book . . .
more about river pollution
and how to clean it up

Misty of Chincoteague
fiction
by Marguerite Henry

In the same book . . .
more about Misty and other
kinds of horses

SUPER SLEUTHS

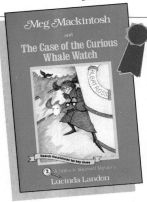

PAPERBACK **PLUS**

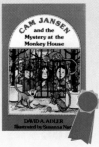

CONTENTS

PAPERBACK **PLUS**

Radio Man/ Don Radio: A Story in English and Spanish
fiction by Arthur Dorros

In the same book . . .
more about migrant farm workers and radio

Justin and the Best Biscuits in the World
fiction
by Mildred Pitts Walter

In the same book . . .
more about African American cowboys and cowboy life

CONTENTS

Meet the Challenge

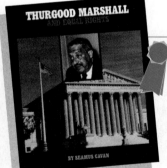

COULD IT REALLY HAPPEN?

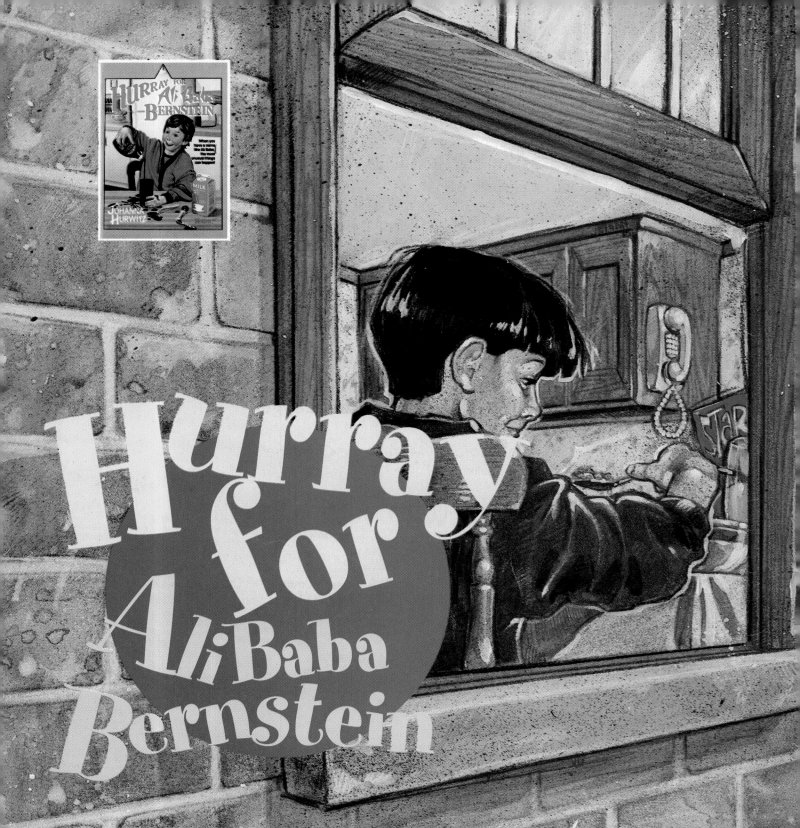

Hurray for Ali Baba Bernstein

by JOHANNA HURWITZ

Ali Baba and the Mystery of the Missing Circus Tickets

On the Sunday morning when Ali Baba was nine years, eleven months, and four days old, his best friend, Roger Zucker, was ten years old. As a birthday treat, Roger's parents had bought three tickets to the circus. Originally the plan was for both parents to take Roger. But then Roger's little sister, Sarah, who was nicknamed Sugar, got the chicken pox. So Mrs. Zucker said that she would stay home with Sugar instead of leaving her with a baby-sitter. And that meant there was an extra ticket. Roger phoned at nine-thirty in the morning and invited Ali Baba to go with him and his father.

"Super!" shouted Ali Baba into the telephone. What great luck that Sugar had gotten the chicken pox!

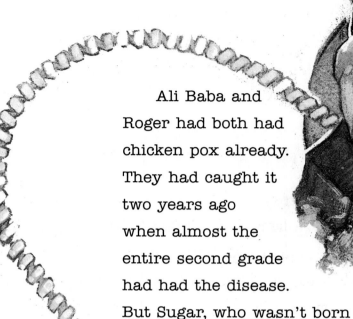

Ali Baba and Roger had both had chicken pox already. They had caught it two years ago when almost the entire second grade had had the disease. But Sugar, who wasn't born at the time, had not caught it then. Ali Baba did a happy little dance around the kitchen. He loved the circus and couldn't wait till the afternoon.

Then the phone rang again. It was Roger.

"You didn't change your mind, did you?" asked Ali Baba nervously. Perhaps Roger was going to invite someone else instead. Or maybe Sugar had miraculously recovered.

"No, but something terrible has happened," said Roger. "My mother can't find the tickets. She said they were in her pocketbook, but they aren't there now."

"Maybe she put them some-place else," suggested Ali Baba.

"No. She says she's certain that she put them right in her pocketbook when she bought them a couple of days ago. And she called the ticket office and they told her they've sold out all the tickets. This is the last performance, so we can't go to the circus after all." Roger sounded miserable. "This is turning out to be a rotten birthday," he said.

"Wait," said Ali Baba. "I'm coming over. We'll search your house. If they weren't stolen, we'll find them."

He hung up the phone and raced to get his jacket. "I'm going over to Roger's house," he informed his mother. And then, without any further explanation, he rushed out.

Ali Baba wanted to go to the circus very much. But there was something that he loved even more than the circus. He loved mysteries. And here were both at the same time. A mystery about the tickets, which if he solved it would mean that he would get his afternoon entertainment, too. But he had to work fast. It was already after ten o'clock. The circus was scheduled to begin at two. He had less than four hours to locate the missing tickets.

"Are you sure you put the tickets in your pocketbook?" he grilled Mrs. Zucker when he got to Roger's house. Mrs. Zucker was sitting at the kitchen table with the entire contents of her pocketbook spilled onto the table. There were her keys, sunglasses, wallet, a small notebook, a makeup case, and a package of sugarless gum. There were no circus tickets.

"I know!" said Ali Baba suddenly. "You were carrying a different pocketbook when you bought the tickets!"

It was a good idea on his part. His mother had several different pocketbooks, and which one she carried depended on which outfit she was wearing. (And Ali Baba noticed that her keys were almost always in a pocketbook that she wasn't carrying.)

Mrs. Zucker shook her head. "The handle just came off my other bag," she said. "I have to get it repaired or replaced. This is the only pocketbook I've used for the past two weeks."

Roger sighed.

"Where do you leave your pocketbook when you are at home?" asked Ali Baba. "Did anyone touch it? Could Sugar have taken the tickets out? I don't mean she stole them, but she could have taken them to play with, couldn't she?" he asked.

"I keep my pocketbook on a shelf in the closet. She can't reach it," explained Mrs. Zucker. "Besides, even if she could, she wouldn't be able to open the clasp on the bag."

Ali Baba sighed.

"I'm looking to see if there is a good movie playing," called Mr. Zucker from the next room. He had the newspaper open before him and had promised the boys to take them to a film as a consolation. But neither boy wanted a movie. What was a movie compared to the circus?

"Could you have put the tickets in your pocket?" Ali Baba suggested. "Did you look in your coat pocket?"

Mrs. Zucker gasped. "I think you're right!" she said, jumping up. "I think I stuffed the tickets into my raincoat pocket. How silly of me to forget." She jumped up and went to the closet. "See, here they are," she said, pulling an envelope out of the pocket. However, the envelope did not contain circus tickets. There were grocery coupons to get fifteen and twenty cents off on cat food and coffee and things like that.

"How did these get into my pocket?" Mrs. Zucker asked. She

inspected the coat closely. "This isn't my coat," she exclaimed.

"Whose coat is it?" asked Ali Baba excitedly. This mystery was getting more and more mysterious.

Mrs. Zucker shrugged her shoulders. "I don't know,"
she said. "I guess someone took my coat from the closet
and left this one instead."

"How can we find out who it was?"
asked Roger.

Just then the telephone rang. Mrs.
Zucker went to answer it as Roger and
Ali Baba stood looking at each other
helplessly.

"It's here! I have it!" Mrs. Zucker
shouted happily into the phone. "I'll
have Roger bring it over to you right
away."

She hung up the receiver and smiled
brightly. "Your worries are over," she
said. "That was Rosie Relkin. She was here
last night with some of our friends for coffee
and dessert. And she accidentally took the wrong raincoat when she went home. So all you have to do is drop off
this one at her apartment and get mine."

"Did you ask her if there were circus tickets in the
pocket?" asked Roger.

"Don't be silly," said his mother. "Of course the tickets
are in the pocket. You'll see for yourself as soon as you get
the coat."

"Let's get going," said Ali Baba. "Where does Rosie Relkin live?"

It was only two blocks to Rosie Relkin's apartment. She opened the door as soon as the boys rang the bell. She had been waiting for them.

"Here," said Roger, exchanging the tan raincoat in his arms for the one Rosie Relkin held out. Roger put his hands into the pockets and immediately pulled out an envelope addressed to Kit Conners and a subway token. But there were no circus tickets.

"Where are the tickets? They're not in either pocket," said Roger, mystified. "And what is this letter doing in my mother's pocket?"

"That can't be your mother's coat," Ali Baba said. "It must belong to someone named Kit Conners."

"This isn't my coat, either," said Rosie Relkin, handing back the coat that Roger had given her. "Mine has a red plaid lining. This is blue."

Roger took one raincoat, and Ali Baba took the other. "Who do they belong to?" Ali Baba asked.

"And what about the circus tickets?" asked Roger.

25

"I bet Kit Conners took my coat," said Rosie Relkin. "She was at the Zuckers' apartment last night, too."

"What about Mrs. Zucker's coat?" asked Ali Baba. "Where do you think that is?"

Rosie Relkin shook her head. "I don't know," she said.

"This is quite a tangle. But I'd really appreciate it if you took this over to Kit Conners's apartment and brought my coat to me. Kit only lives a block away."

"I wonder if we'll ever get to the circus?" Roger sighed as the two boys and the two raincoats went off in the direction of Kit Conners's apartment.

"Maybe Kit Conners has your mother's coat," said Ali Baba. "We've got to find those tickets before two o'clock."

"And we still have to find Rosie Relkin's raincoat for her, too," Roger said.

"You know something?" said Ali Baba. "If I were president of the United States, I would make a law against these tan raincoats. Why does everyone wear the same kind of coat?"

Kit Conners was delighted to see the boys. "Rosie Relkin phoned to tell me you were coming. She said you had my coat. I didn't realize that I had taken the wrong one last night. But I looked now, and sure enough, I've got someone else's."

She took the coat that Roger gave her. "It's mine, all right," she said. "I wonder whose coat I wore home last night?"

"It must be my mother's," said Roger.

"It might belong to Rosie Relkin," Ali Baba reminded his friend. "Her coat is still missing, too."

Kit Conners handed Roger a coat that was a clone of the one that he had given her. However, on closer inspection, the lining was different. "It's not Rosie Relkin's raincoat," said Ali Baba. The lining was green plaid.

"I never noticed what color lining my mother's coat had," said Roger. "Up until today it never mattered. But I sure hope the lining of her coat is green plaid and that this is it." He put his hands inside the pockets of the coat that Kit Conners had handed him. "What's this?" he asked.

"Let's see," demanded Ali Baba.

Roger handed Ali Baba a baby's pacifier.

"Does your sister still use one of these?" asked Ali Baba.

"No," said Roger with disgust. "She outgrew it ages ago."

"Margie and George Upchurch were at your house last night," Kit Conners told Roger. "They have a six-month-old baby. I bet this coat belongs to Margie. Let me give you her address."

"Your parents have too many friends," complained Ali Baba.

A minute later the boys were off looking for the street where the Upchurch family lived.

"That can't be my coat," said Margie Upchurch when Ali Baba and Roger Zucker tried explaining about the mix-up of the raincoats the night before. "I wore my coat home," she shouted above the wails of a crying baby.

In the background Ali Baba could see Mr. Upchurch, unshaven and still in his bathrobe, trying to comfort the infant.

"It must be your coat," said Ali Baba. "There was a pacifier in the pocket, and we can see you have a baby."

Mrs. Upchurch looked surprised at this piece of information. "A pacifier?" she asked with delight. "We've been looking all over the house for one of the baby's pacifiers, and they've all disappeared." She examined the object that Roger handed her.

"Let me just go and wash it," she shouted above the baby's cries. A minute later the clean pacifier was in the baby's mouth and all was quiet. Then Margie Upchurch went to her closet and took out still another tan raincoat.

"I don't know who this one belongs to," she said.

Roger looked at the coat hopefully. "You look," he told Ali Baba. "I'm scared."

Ali Baba wasn't scared at all. He was confident that they had finally tracked down the correct coat. He put his hands into the pockets and triumphantly pulled out a small envelope from one of them. Inside there were three tan tickets for that afternoon's circus performance. The tickets were the same color as all of the coats.

"Hurray! We did it! We found the tickets!" he began shouting. Of all the mysteries he had ever attempted to solve, this had been the most successful.

But there was still one small mystery before the boys.

"Whose raincoat is this?" asked Margie Upchurch, pointing to the other one that was still unclaimed.

"We don't know. It isn't Rosie Relkin's," said Roger. He pulled the envelope with the grocery coupons out of the mystery raincoat. "These could belong to anyone."

"Not just anyone," Ali Baba pointed out. "They must belong to someone who has a cat."

"Muriel and Alfred Thomas were at your house last night," Margie Upchurch told Roger. "And they have a cat," she added. "I can't ever go to their house because I have an allergy to cats. They make my eyes tear and make me sneeze, too." She went off to check the exact address where the Thomases lived.

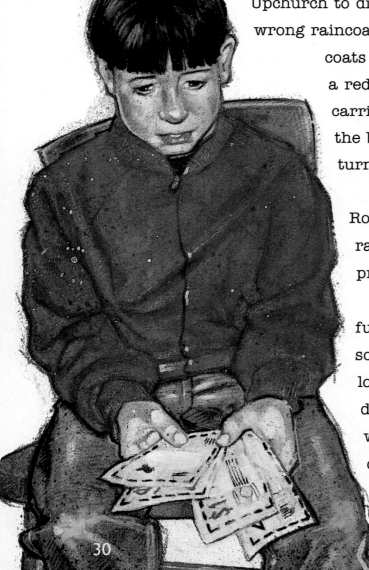

Muriel Thomas was just as surprised as Mrs. Upchurch to discover that she had taken the wrong raincoat the evening before. She traded coats with Roger, giving him a coat with a red lining in exchange for the one he carried with a blue lining. And then the boys retraced their steps and returned to Rosie Relkin's apartment.

"Thank goodness you found it!" Rosie Relkin said, clutching her raincoat as if it were a very precious item.

Ali Baba thought that was very funny. It wasn't as if she had lost something unique. All the coats looked the same — what difference did it make what color the lining was? Once you put the coat on, no one could see the lining inside.

To the boys
the unique coat
was the one with
the circus tickets in
the pocket. Ali Baba
and Roger Zucker ran
all the way back to the
Zucker apartment.

"I'm glad you got my
coat from Rosie Relkin,"
said Mrs. Zucker when she saw
the boys.

"We didn't get it from Rosie Relkin,"
announced Roger.

"What do you mean?" asked Mrs. Zucker.

"It will take too long to explain," said Roger. "We've got
to hurry if we're going to get to the circus on time."

But there was still enough time for Ali Baba to phone
home and tell his parents that he was going off to the circus with Roger. They also had time enough to admire
Sugar's chicken pox and to eat a quick lunch. And finally
Mr. Zucker, Roger, and Ali Baba were off to the circus.

"How does it feel being ten?" Mr. Zucker asked his son as the three of them rode downtown on the bus.

"I don't know," Roger complained. "I've been too busy this morning to think about it."

"We sure solved a big mystery," said Ali Baba proudly. He felt like a real private eye. Imagine, a mystery and a circus all on the same day. **It was super!**

Johanna Hurwitz

John Dunivant

Books and stories played a big part in Johanna Hurwitz's life even before she was born — her parents met each other in a bookstore in New York City. Hurwitz grew up in an apartment stuffed with books and says that some of her "happiest early memories are of being read to by my parents." When Hurwitz was eight, she began telling stories to her two-year-old brother William. William's interest in her stories, Hurwitz says, was important in "sparking my writing career." Hurwitz also loved the public library, and at the age of ten decided to be a librarian. At the same time, she decided to become a writer.

She did succeed in becoming a librarian by the age of twenty-two, but she was almost forty before she published her first book, *Busybody Nora.*

Hurwitz has written more than thirty books for young people. You may have read or heard of *School Spirit, Class Clown,* and *The Adventures of Ali Baba Bernstein.*

Meet the Illustrator

John Dunivant has been drawing ever since he can remember. When he was six, he saw the movie *Star Wars* and began to concentrate on drawing creatures and spaceships. Later, when he received a book of the paintings and drawings that were used to plan the film, he says, "I realized 'grown-ups' do this too," and began to think of art as "my destiny."

When Dunivant does illustrations, such as the ones he did for this selection, he tries to imagine himself in the situations described in the story. He usually listens to music when he works, often the soundtrack from — you guessed it — *Star Wars.*

That's the

Draw a Map

Which Way Did He Go?

Use the details from the story to help you draw a map of Ali Baba's neighborhood. Label all the places where he and Roger stopped in their search for the tickets. Then draw the route that the boys followed as they went from one house to the next.

Write a Letter

You Do the Explaining

When Mrs. Zucker asked Ali Baba and Roger how they found her coat, Roger replied, "It will take too long to explain." How would you explain what happened? Write a letter to Mrs. Zucker telling her how Roger and Ali Baba found her coat with the tickets.

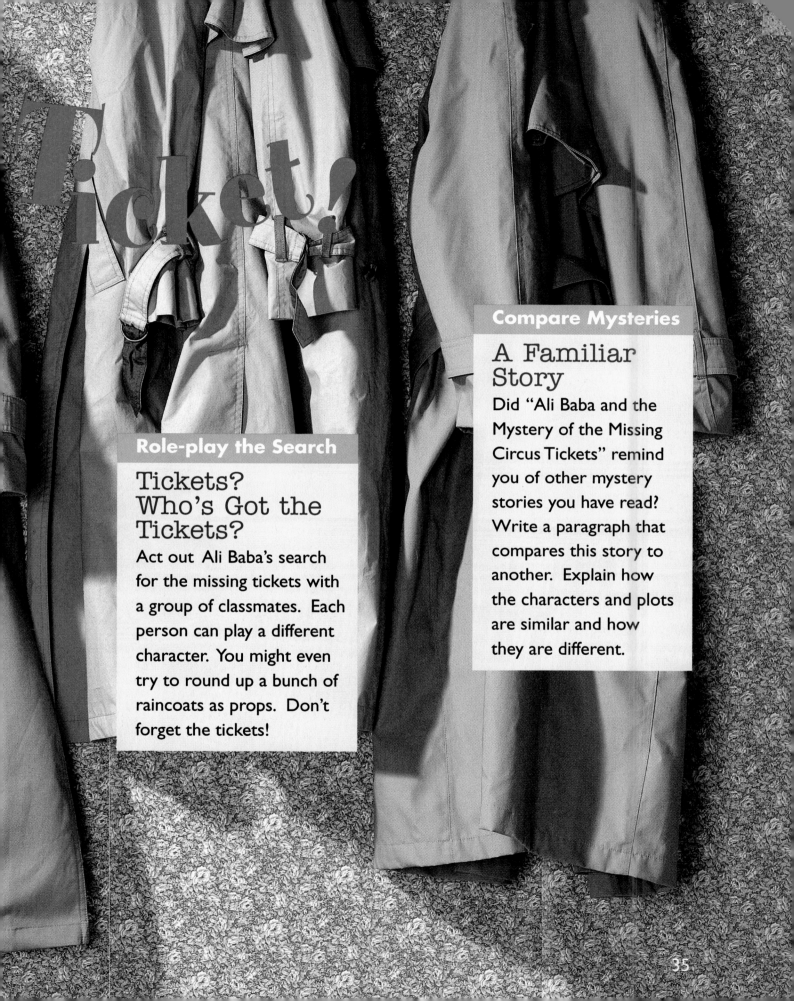

Ticket!

Tickets? Who's Got the Tickets?

Act out Ali Baba's search for the missing tickets with a group of classmates. Each person can play a different character. You might even try to round up a bunch of raincoats as props. Don't forget the tickets!

A Familiar Story

Did "Ali Baba and the Mystery of the Missing Circus Tickets" remind you of other mystery stories you have read? Write a paragraph that compares this story to another. Explain how the characters and plots are similar and how they are different.

CONTENTS

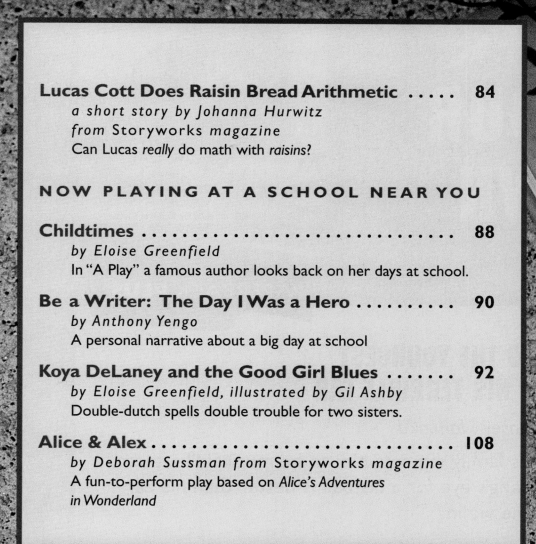

READ ON YOUR OWN

Lensey Namioka

Yang the Youngest and His Terrible Ear

Illustrated by Kees de Kiefte

PAPERBACK PLUS

YANG THE YOUNGEST AND HIS TERRIBLE EAR

by Lensey Namioka

Yang's family expects him to be musical like them, but Yang's eye for a fastball is better than his ear for the violin.

In the same book ...

Lots more about making music and playing baseball and experimenting with the science of sound.

JUDY BLUME
FRECKLE JUICE

Illustrated by
Sonia O. Lisker

PAPERBACK **PLUS**

FRECKLE JUICE

by *Judy Blume*

Andrew will do almost anything to have freckles.

In the same book . . .

More about freckles and school, as well as a hands-on science experiment for making marvelous mixtures.

MORE COOL BOOKS

My Name Is María Isabel
by *Alma Flor Ada*
María Isabel Salazar López is not pleased when her new teacher shortens her name to Mary López.

Wayside School Is Falling Down
by *Louis Sachar*
Imagine going to class on the thirtieth floor in a school with no elevators! It doesn't bother Mrs. Jewls and her unusual students.

Earthquake in the Third Grade
by *Laurie Myers*
What a day! John knocks over the class ant farm, and then his class learns their teacher is leaving. How can they make her stay?

Author's Day
by *Daniel Pinkwater*
When a children's book author shows up for a classroom visit, he gets more than he bargained for.

Muggie Maggie
by *Beverly Cleary*
How can Maggie go back on her refusal to learn cursive writing without losing face?

As a child, Judy Blume liked movies, radio shows, and the children's room of her library. "But," she says, "I didn't find real satisfaction in reading until I was older . . . there weren't any books with characters who felt the way I felt, who acted the way I did . . . ." So, when Blume grew up, she decided to write books for children about real life.

In 1966, Blume started writing children's stories, thinking about them while she washed the dinner dishes. For two years her stories were rejected, and she almost gave up. Then she took a course on how to write for children. She loved the course so much she took it twice! Finally her career took off.

Blume has written novels for both children and adults. She won awards for *Tales of a Fourth Grade Nothing* and *Superfudge,* among others. Blume says about her writing that "until you pull it out of your own heart, it doesn't really work."

Betsy James grew up in Salt Lake City, Utah. She liked hiking and camping with her family, and she also liked to read. "I could usually be found up in a pine tree or with my nose in a book," she says. When not reading or hiking, James was drawing. In her family, the children always made their own greeting cards and gifts for relatives.

James went from creating books as gifts to writing and illustrating books for publication. To prepare to illustrate this selection, James read lots of stories by Judy Blume, who lives only fifty miles away from her in New Mexico.

Tales of a
Fourth
Grade
Nothing

In January our class started a project on The City. Mrs. Haver, our teacher, divided us up into committees by where we live. That way we could work at home. My committee was me, Jimmy Fargo, and Sheila. Our topic was Transportation. We decided to make my apartment the meeting place because I'm the only one of the three of us who's got his own bedroom. In a few weeks each committee has to hand in a booklet, a poster, and be ready to give an oral report.

The first day we got together after school we bought a yellow posterboard. Jimmy wanted a blue one but Sheila talked him out of it. "Yellow is a much brighter color," she explained. "Everything will show up on it. Blue is too dull."

Sheila thinks she's smarter than me and Jimmy put together — just because she's a girl! So right away she told us she would be in charge of our booklet and me and Jimmy could do most of the poster. As long as we check with her first, to make sure she likes our ideas. We agreed, since Sheila promised to do ten pages of written work and we would only do five.

After we bought the yellow posterboard we went to the library. We took out seven books on transportation. We wanted to learn all we could about speed, traffic congestion, and pollution. We arranged to meet on Tuesday and Thursday afternoons for the next two weeks.

Our first few committee meetings turned out like this: We got to my place by three-thirty, had a snack, then played with Dribble for another half hour. Sheila gave up on cooties when Fudge lost his front teeth. But it still isn't much fun to have her hanging around. She's always complaining that she got stuck with the worst possible committee. And that me and Jimmy fool more than we work. We only put up with her because we have no choice!

Sheila and Jimmy have to be home for supper before five-thirty. So at five o'clock we start cleaning up. We keep our equipment under my bed in a shoebox. We have a set of Magic Markers, Elmer's glue, Scotch tape, a really sharp pair of scissors, and a container of silver sparkle.

Sheila carries our committee booklet back and forth with her. She doesn't trust us enough to leave it at my house! The posterboard fits under my bed, along with our supplies. We stack the library books on my desk. The reason I make sure we clean up good is that my mother told me if I left a mess we'd have to find some place else to work.

By our third meeting I told Jimmy and Sheila that I'd figured out the solution to New York City's traffic problems. "We have to get rid of the traffic," I said. "There shouldn't be any cars or buses or taxis allowed in the city. What we really need is a citywide monorail system."

"That's too expensive," Sheila said. "It sounds good but it's not practical."

"I disagree!" I told Sheila. "It's very practical. Besides getting rid of traffic it'll get rid of air pollution and it'll get people where they're going a lot faster."

"But it's not practical, Peter!" Sheila said again. "It costs too much."

I opened one of my books on transportation and read Sheila a quote. "'A monorail system is the hope of the future.'" I cleared my throat and looked up.

"But we can't write a report just about the monorail," Sheila said. "We'll never be able to fill twenty written pages with that."

"We can write big," Jimmy suggested.

"No!" Sheila said. "I want a good mark on this project. Peter, you can write your five pages about the monorail system and how it works. Jimmy, you can write your five pages about pollution caused by transportation. And I'll write my ten pages on the history of transportation in the city." Sheila folded her arms and smiled.

"Can I write big?" Jimmy asked.

"I don't care how big you write as long as you put your name on your five pages!" Sheila told him.

"That's not fair!" Jimmy said. "This is supposed to be a group project. Why should I have to put my name on my five pages?"

"Then don't write BIG!" Sheila shouted.

"Okay. Okay . . . I'll write so small Mrs. Haver will need a microscope to see the letters."

"Very funny," Sheila said.

"Look," I told both of them, "I think all our written work should be in the same handwriting. That's the only fair way. Otherwise Mrs. Haver will know who did what. And it won't be a group project."

"Say, that's a good idea," Jimmy said. "Which one of us has the best handwriting?"

Me and Jimmy looked at Sheila.

"Well, I do have a nice even script," Sheila said. "But if I'm going to copy over your written work you better give it to me by next Tuesday. Otherwise, I won't have enough time to do the job. And you two better get going on your poster." Sheila talked like she was the teacher and we were the kids.

Me and Jimmy designed the whole poster ourselves. We used the pros and cons of each kind of transportation. It was really clever. We divided a chart into land, sea, and air and we planned an illustration for each — with the airplane done in silver sparkle and the letters done in red and blue Magic Marker. We got halfway through the lettering that day. We also sketched in the ship, the plane, and the truck.

When Sheila saw it she asked, "Is that supposed to be a train?"

"No," I told her. "It's a truck."

"It doesn't look like one," she said.

"It will," Jimmy told her, "when it's finished."

"I hope so," Sheila said. "Because right now it looks like a flying train!"

"That's because the ground's not under it yet," Jimmy said.

"Yeah," I agreed. "See, we've got to make it look like it's on a street. Right now it does kind of look like it's up in space."

"So does the ship," Sheila said.

"We'll put some waterlines around it," I told her.

"And some clouds around the plane," Sheila said.

"Listen," Jimmy hollered, "did anybody ever tell you you're too bossy? This poster is ours! You do the booklet. Remember . . . that's the way you wanted it!"

"See . . . there you go again!" Sheila said. "You keep forgetting this is a committee. We're supposed to work together."

"Working together doesn't mean you give the orders and we carry them out," Jimmy said.

My feelings exactly! I thought.

Sheila didn't answer Jimmy. She picked up her things, got her coat, and left.

"I hope she never comes back," Jimmy said.

"She'll be back," I told him. "We're her committee."

Jimmy laughed. "Yeah . . . we're all one happy committee!"

I put our poster under the bed, said good-bye to Jimmy, then washed up for supper.

My mother was being pretty nice about our committee meetings. She arranged to have Fudge play at Ralph's apartment on Tuesdays and at Jennie's on Thursdays. Sam has the chicken pox, so he can't play at all.

I was glad that next week would be our last committee meeting after school. I was sick of Sheila and I was getting sick of Transportation. Besides, now that I knew a monorail system was the only way to save our city I was getting upset that the mayor and all the other guys that run things at City Hall weren't doing anything about installing one. If *I* know that's the best method of city transportation how come *they* don't know it?

The next day when I came home from school I went into my bedroom to see Dribble like I always do. Fudge was in there, sitting on my bed.

"Why are you in my room?" I asked him.

He smiled.

"You know you're not supposed to be in here. This is *my* room."

"Want to see?" Fudge said.

"See what?"

"Want to see?"

"What? What are you talking about?" I asked.

He jumped off my bed and crawled underneath it. He came out with our poster. He held it up. "See," he said. "Pretty!"

"What did you do?" I yelled. "What did you do to our poster?" It was covered all over with scribbles in every color Magic Marker. It was ruined! *It was a mess and it was ruined.* I was ready to kill Fudge. I grabbed my poster and ran into the kitchen to show it to my mother. I could hardly speak. "Look," I said, feeling a lump in my throat. "Just look at what he did to my poster." I felt tears come to

my eyes but I didn't care. "How could you let him?" I asked my
mother. "How? Don't you care about me?"

I threw the poster down and ran into my room. I slammed the
door, took off my shoe, and flung it at the wall. It made a black mark
where it hit. Well, so what!

Soon I heard my mother hollering — and then, Fudge crying.
After a while my mother knocked on my bedroom door and called,
"Peter, may I come in?"

I didn't answer.

She opened the door and walked over to my bed. She sat down
next to me. "I'm very sorry," she said.

I still didn't say anything.

"Peter," she began.

I didn't look at her.

She touched my arm. "Peter . . . please listen . . . ."

"Don't you see, Mom? I can't even do my homework without him messing it up. It just isn't fair! I wish he was never born. Never! I hate him!"

"You don't hate him," my mother said. "You just think you do."

"Don't tell me," I said. "I mean it. I really can't stand that kid!"

"You're angry," my mother told me. "I know that and I don't blame you. Fudge had no right to touch your poster. I spanked him."

"You did?" I asked. Fudge never gets spanked. My parents don't believe in spanking. "You really spanked him?" I asked again.

"Yes," my mother said.

"Hard?" I asked.

"On his backside," she told me.

I thought that over.

"Peter . . . ." My mother put her arm around me. "I'll buy you a new posterboard tomorrow. It was really my fault. I should never have let him into your room."

"That's why I need a lock on my door," I said.

"I don't like locks on doors. We're a family. We don't have to lock each other out."

"If I had a lock Fudge wouldn't have gotten my poster!"

"It won't happen again," my mother promised.

I wanted to believe her, but really I didn't. Unless she tied him up I knew my brother would get into my room again.

The next day, while I was at school, my mother bought a new yellow posterboard. The hard part was explaining to Jimmy that we had to start all over again. He was a good sport about it. He said this time he'd make sure his truck didn't look like a flying train. And I said, this time I'd make pencil marks first so my letters didn't go uphill.

Our committee met that afternoon. Sheila didn't mention the last time. Neither did we. Me and Jimmy worked on the poster while Sheila copied our written work into the booklet. We'd be ready to give our oral report to the class on Monday. Not like some committees who hadn't even started yet!

By five o'clock we had finished our poster and Sheila was almost done with the cover for our booklet. Jimmy walked over and stood behind her, watching her work.

After a minute he yelled, "What do you think you're doing, Sheila?"

I got up from the floor and joined them at my desk. I took a look at the cover. It was pretty nice. It said:

TRANSPORTATION IN THE CITY

Under that it said:

BY SHEILA TUBMAN, PETER HATCHER,
AND JAMES FARGO

And under that in small letters it said:

handwritten by miss sheila tubman

Now I knew why Jimmy was mad. "Oh no!" I said, holding my hand to my head. "How could you!"

Sheila didn't say anything.

"It's not fair," I told her. "We didn't put our names on the poster!"

"But the cover's all done," Sheila said. "Can't you see that? I'll never get the letters so straight again. It looks perfect!"

"Oh no!" Jimmy shouted. "We're not handing the booklet in like that. I'll rip it up before I let you!" He grabbed the booklet and threatened to tear it in half.

Sheila screamed. "You wouldn't! I'll kill you! Give it back to me, Jimmy Fargo!" She was ready to cry.

I knew Jimmy wouldn't tear it up but I didn't say so.

"Peter . . . make him give it back!"

"Will you take off that line about your handwriting?" I asked.

"I can't. It'll ruin the booklet."

"Then I think he should rip it up," I said.

Sheila stamped her foot. "Ooooh! I hate you both!"

"You don't really," I told her. "You just think you do."

"I know I do!" Sheila cried.

"That's because you're angry right now," I said. I couldn't help smiling.

Sheila jumped up and tried to get the booklet but Jimmy held it over his head and he's much taller than Sheila. She had no chance at all.

Finally she sat down and whispered, "I give up. You win. I'll take my name off."

"You promise?" Jimmy asked.

"I promise," Sheila said.

Jimmy set the booklet down on my desk in front of Sheila. "Okay," he said. "Start."

"I'm not going to make a whole new cover," Sheila said. "What I'll do is turn this bottom line into a decoration." She picked up a Magic Marker and made little flowers out of the words. Soon, *handwritten by miss sheila tubman* turned into sixteen small flowers. "There," Sheila said. "It's done."

"It looks pretty good," I told her.

"It would have looked better without those flowers," Jimmy said. "But at least it's fair now."

That night I showed my mother and father our new poster. They thought it was great. Especially our silver-sparkle airplane. My mother put the poster on top of the refrigerator so it would be safe until the next day, when I would take it to school.

Now I had nothing to worry about. Sheila had the booklet, the poster was safe, and our committee was finished before schedule. I went into my room to relax. Fudge was sitting on the floor, near my bed. My shoebox of supplies was in front of him. His face was a mess of Magic Marker colors and he was using my extra sharp scissors to snip away at his hair. And the hair he snipped was dropping into Dribble's bowl — which he had in front of him on the floor!

"See," he said. "See Fudge. Fudgie's a barber!"

That night I found out hair doesn't hurt my turtle. I picked off every strand from his shell. I cleaned out his bowl and washed off his rocks. He seemed happy.

Two things happened the next day. One was my mother had to take Fudge to the real barber to do something about his hair. He had plenty left in the back, but just about nothing in front and on top. The barber said there wasn't much he could do until the hair grew back. Between his fangs and his hair he was getting funnier looking every day.

The second was my father came home with a chain latch for my bedroom door. I could reach it when I stood on tip-toe, but that brother of mine couldn't reach it at all — no matter what!

Our committee was the first to give its report. Mrs. Haver said we did a super job. She liked our poster a lot. She thought the silver-sparkle airplane was the best. The only thing she asked us was, how come we included a picture of a flying train?

The City
Do you kno
your city
TRANSPORTATION IN THE CITY
BY SHEILA TUBMAN PETER HATCHER AND JAMES PARDO

More Super Ideas

Write a Description

What a Day!

Have you ever worked on a project on which everything seemed to go wrong? Maybe writing about your experience will help you recover from the disaster! First, explain what happened — you can be funny or serious. Then compare how you felt about your project with the way that Peter felt.

How to Live with Fudge . . .

It looks like living with a little brother — or sister — can be hazardous. Use Peter's experience to help you come up with a list of helpful hints for dealing with a younger sibling. Share your list with a partner. Then work together to turn your lists into a magazine advice article for older brothers and sisters.

Discuss Teamwork

All Together Now

With your partner or group, discuss how well you think Peter, Jimmy, and Sheila worked together. The teacher liked their project. Does that mean they were successful as a team? What advice about teamwork would you give them?

Draw a Comic Strip

Picture This!

Turn the story you have just read into a comic strip, and share it with classmates or your family. Draw and color the most important scenes and put the dialogue in speech balloons.

I'm in Another Dimension

by Kalli Dakos

I'm in another dimension
Where it's easy to pay attention,
Where Ms. Digby is my teacher.

I know I could read and write
And study whole days and nights,
With Ms. Digby as my teacher.

Spelling, grammar, writing, and math
All lead me down a wondrous path
When Ms. Digby is my teacher.

The days go as fast as a flash of light,
That beams to the stars in the dark of night,
Because Ms. Digby is my teacher.

I would stay here in grade four,
All my life forevermore,

To have Ms. Digby for my teacher!

For Ms. Digby

Ten
Minutes
Till
the Bus

by David L. Harrison

Ten whole minutes
Till the bus,
Scads of time,
What's the fuss?
Two to dress,
One to flush,
Two to eat,
One to brush,
That leaves four
To catch the bus,
Scads of time,
What's the fuss?

Last Night

by David L. Harrison

Last night I knew the answers.
Last night I had them pat.
Last night I could have told you
Every answer, just like that!
Last night my brain was cooking.
Last night I got them right.
Last night I was a genius.
So where were you last night!

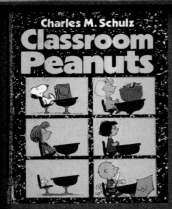

CLASSROOM Peanuts

by Charles M. Schulz

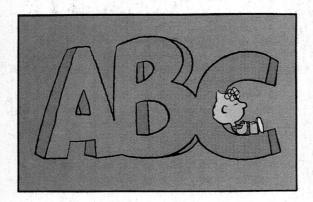

I'm New Here

BUD HOWLETT

I was so afraid. It was my first day of school in the United States and I didn't speak English.

My name is Jazmin Escalante (Haz-meen Es-ka-lan-teh). I came to America from El Salvador. I'm new here.

The day before school started I said to my mother, "Mami, I'm scared! I won't know what to do at school. I won't know where to go."

"Don't worry, Jazmin," answered my mother. "It will be all right. We'll walk to school together today so you'll know where everything is. No one will know we went ahead of time. It will be our secret."

I thought it was a great idea to go to school before all the other kids arrived. But I was still worried about speaking only Spanish in an American school.

"But Mami, I don't even speak English. I won't know what to do. I won't know what they're talking about."

Mami didn't speak very much English either. She always spoke Spanish to my father, my brother, Juanito, and me.

"We'll all learn together, won't we, Jazmin? Get Juanito and we'll go. Remember, your little brother will start school as soon as he gets all of his shots. You can help him when he starts school next week."

It was almost two miles to Elmwood School from our apartment. We walked up to the front of the school and between two buildings. The school was more modern than the school in El Salvador where I went to third grade. I never went to fourth grade. Because of the fighting it wasn't safe on the streets. I stayed home and took care of my brother. Mami said we would be safe going to school here in the United States.

She pointed to a sign. "That says 'Office.' That's where we'll go tomorrow to register, Jazmin. I'll be with you."

Together, Mami, Juanito, and I walked past the office. All the classrooms opened onto an outside covered walk. There were no children, no teachers, only us. It was very quiet. As we went down the walk our feet echoed loudly on the hard concrete. I wanted to look in a classroom, but the window in the door was too high.

"Let's walk around to the other side of the building," Mami said. "Maybe we can see in a window there."

The other windows were lower. Juanito and I ran up to the first one. I could see but Juanito couldn't, so I held him up while we looked in. The classroom was very large. It was clean and neat and the chairs and desks were all in rows. I counted. There were twenty-eight chairs. A teacher's desk with books on top of it was at the front of the room.

On the chalkboard were some neatly written words. I didn't know what they said; I only knew Spanish. I wanted so much to learn English! Butterflies danced in my stomach. What would my first day of school be like? How would I feel when those empty desks had kids in them?

Juanito was getting heavy so I put him down. We walked over to the playground.

"In the corner of the room by the door I saw some balls," said Juanito. "Do you think they play soccer here?"

"Oh, I hope so," I said. "I can play soccer well even if I can't speak English."

I wondered if they played the same games we had played in El Salvador.

Mami didn't need to get me up the next morning. I was already awake when she came into my room. I wanted to go to school but I was afraid. My throat was dry and I swallowed hard lots of times while I was getting dressed.

I wanted to look my best. I decided to wear the flowered dress I had worn to church when we first came here to San Rafael.

Usually I had breakfast, but today I couldn't eat anything and Mami didn't make me. She took my hand. "Come, Jazmin," she said. "This will be a new and wonderful adventure."

The walk didn't take long, but now the school looked different. There were buses and cars in the parking lot. The flag was up and there were people everywhere. We walked to the office. I felt better because I knew where it was. We went inside and lots of people were in line at the counter. They were all speaking English. Mami said they were filling out their papers. I hoped we had all of ours. Once, at customs, we hadn't had all the right papers and they made us go back home. Mami was holding my hand and I could feel her shaking a little. I thought it was all right for me to be scared if Mami was.

When it was our turn, the lady behind the counter spoke to us in English. I could tell Mami didn't understand. The lady called to someone in the next room and another lady came out. "*Ay, buenos días, Señora.* I am Sofia Rodriguez," she said. She spoke to Mami in Spanish and told her she would help us fill out the

papers. She was a parent who helped other Spanish-speaking families.

She took us outside and told me a little about the school. She showed me the papers we had to fill out. She seemed to know that I was afraid. She put a large, warm hand on my shoulder. It was very steady and strong. "Don't worry, Jazmin," she said. "I will see that you get to your classroom. They will like you here, *niña*, and you will like them."

Mami finished with my papers and I knew it was time to go to my classroom. I was so afraid that I was afraid to say I was afraid!

"Jazmin," said Señora Rodriguez, "they are putting you in fourth grade since you didn't attend fourth grade in El Salvador."

"Fourth grade," I thought. "I should be in fifth grade. I didn't know they would do that." Now I was afraid I would be bigger than the other children. Things were not starting out well for me.

Mami put her arm around me as we started toward my new classroom. We went the same way we had gone the day before. We passed the room I had looked into and stopped at a door that had the number 7 on it. Mami kissed me and gave me a very strong hug. "Good-bye, *bella* (bay-ya)," she said. She called me *bella* when she wanted me to know that I was special. In Spanish it means "pretty one." As she walked away, I felt very empty inside.

Señora Rodriguez took me over to the teacher. "This is Jazmin Escalante," she said. "She is new here. She's from El Salvador." I recognized my name and the words "El Salvador." "This is your teacher, Jazmin," she said to me in Spanish. "Her name is Mrs. Edwards." Señora Rodriguez left and I was alone with my new teacher and my new class.

Mrs. Edwards walked me to the front of the class. She turned me to face the boys and girls. Looking at my registration card, she said, "This is 'Jazz-min' Escalante. She has come from El Salvador. She's new here."

"Oh, no! Not 'Jazz-min'!" I thought. "Can't the teacher say my name right? Now all the other children will say it wrong, too." First I was mad at my teacher. Then I was mad at my name. "Why couldn't I have a name that was easy to say, like Maria?"

I didn't have much time to worry because Mrs. Edwards took me to a seat on one side of the room. I sat down and looked around. All of the children were looking at me. I wanted to smile but I couldn't, so I pretended to read a book I found on my desk.

Mrs. Edwards brought me some papers. She put them on my desk with a box of crayons.

"Color?" she asked. She opened the crayons and showed me that she wanted me to color the pictures. I began to color very carefully. If this was all I could do, I was going to do it well.

As I was coloring, I listened to the rest of the class. I didn't understand what they were saying, but I knew they were doing math. I could do some of the problems on the board, but no one asked me to do anything but color.

I had never felt so alone. I didn't know anyone and no one knew me. I didn't even know how to say hello. When I looked around the room I saw two other children whose skin was almost as dark as mine. Did they speak Spanish? I wondered how long it

would be before I found out if there was anyone for me to talk to.

The children soon finished doing their math and took out other books, which looked like readers. They moved into small groups but I stayed in my seat. The teacher brought me more papers to color. I picked up the reading book on my desk. At least I could look at the pictures. The reading period seemed very long.

Finally a bell rang and everyone lined up at the door to go outside. I didn't know whether to line up or stay in my seat, so I stayed.

"Jazz-min," said the teacher as she motioned to me with her hand. She took my hand and we walked outside. She called to another girl, who came over to us. I heard Mrs. Edwards say "Jazz-min" and "El Salvador" and "Spanish" to her. The two of us stood together during the recess and watched the other kids playing. The girl pointed to them and said something in English but I didn't understand what she said.

At lunchtime the teacher brought the same girl over to me. Mrs. Edwards pointed at her and said "Emily."

I repeated "Emily." Emily pointed to where the cafeteria was and showed me how to get lunch. We sat together on a bench. Several children from my class walked by and said "Hi, Jazz-min."

Then one boy shouted, "Hey, Taco!" Several others did, too. "Taco, Taco, Taco!" they yelled. They were pointing at me. Why were they being so mean?

A lady in the cafeteria made them stop, but when I looked for Emily, she was gone. I was alone. I didn't have anyone to sit with. I walked outside and sat on a bench by myself.

When the first day was over, I ran all the way home. Mami was waiting at the door and I hugged her and cried. I told her that no one at school cared about me and I didn't have any friends. "I don't want to go back to school, Mami. They made fun of me because I don't speak English and I look different. They called me 'Taco'!"

"Change out of your good dress, *bella*, and dry your eyes," said Mami.

"Let's talk with your father." Mami and Papi and Juanito all sat down with me.

"You will learn English, Jazmin, before you know it. So that will change. Where you were born, you can't change," said Mami.

"Be proud of where you come from, *bella*," said my father. He swelled out his chest. "Blood flows in your veins from the great Mayan civilization. You are a special person."

Juanito squeezed in between my father and me. He took my hand. "You are special to me, too, Jazmin," he said.

On the second day of school, I was watching the other students do their math, but I didn't have a book.

While I was wondering how to get one, the classroom door opened and a lady spoke to my teacher. "Haz-meen Es-ka-lan-teh, please," she said.

The new lady was Señora Diaz. She said my name the right way and spoke to me in Spanish. She was a teacher who would help me learn English in a special class. She was called an ESL teacher. She walked me down the hall to her room and I met several other kids who spoke Spanish. I was going to come to Señora Diaz every day for an hour and a half.

The next day, Señora Diaz gave me books in Spanish to read. She said I would get a math book and could start using it with the other students.

On Thursday, Mrs. Edwards's class went outside to play soccer. They picked teams and I was the last one chosen. I didn't know that our class played soccer on Thursdays and I had worn a dress. But when the soccer game started, I felt good for the first time since I started school, because I could play. For once I could do what everyone else did.

When the ball came to me, I dribbled it down the field and kicked it past the goalie. My team cheered, "Yeah, Jazz-min! Yeah, Jazz-min!" A few kids patted me on the back. Before the game was over, I scored another goal. We won 2 to 1 and I scored both goals. Kids talked to me all the way back to the classroom. I didn't know what they were saying, but I was happy.

At the end of my first week, Señora Diaz and El Director (the principal) called me into the library. They said that I read very well in Spanish, and my math was excellent, so they had decided to move me into fifth grade. I knew I would have to work very hard but it would be better to be with kids my age. I knew I would have to meet all new kids, but I thought I could do it.

My new class was not bad. The teacher, Mrs. Robertson, was very nice and knew a few Spanish words. When she spoke to me, she laughed because she knew her Spanish wasn't very good. The kids were very nice. They showed me where things were and helped me with the work.

A blond girl from my class went out to recess with me on my first day in fifth grade. She took my hand and we walked around the playground. She pointed at things and gave their names in English. "Tree," she said. I said it, too. "Playground," she said, pointing at the ground.

I said, "Playground."

She named more words than I could ever remember in one day. I said them all back to her. When the bell rang, she looked at me and said slowly, "My name is Allison."

I understood what she said. "My name is Haz-meen." She gave my hand a squeeze and we ran into class.

Allison walked up to Mrs. Robertson and said, "The new girl's name is 'Haz-meen,' not 'Jazz-min.' "

At lunchtime, Allison was waiting for me. When she took my hand I saw how light her skin was. We must have looked funny together. As we walked toward the cafeteria a boy who was walking behind us yelled, "Salt and pepper! Salt and pepper!" Allison dropped my hand and turned around. She grabbed the boy by the shoulders and shook him. She was yelling something at him. He turned and ran down the hall and didn't say anything.

I don't know what Allison said but she had to be the best kind of friend you could ever have. When she took my hand again I said, *"Mi amiga"* (my friend).

"Mi amiga," repeated Allison.

I had made a friend. A real friend.

I didn't feel like I was new here anymore.

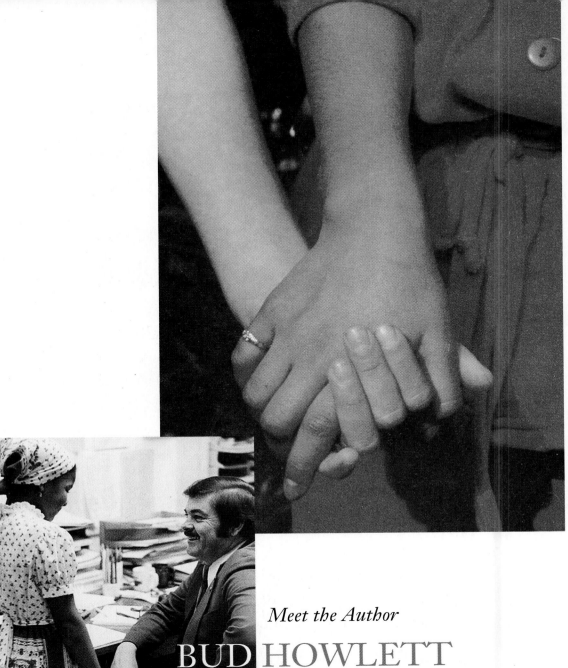

Meet the Author

BUD HOWLETT

Bud Howlett, seen here talking to a student from Haiti, is a California native who spent a lot of time in school. He started as a student, became a teacher, and ended up as an elementary school principal, a job he held for nearly twenty-four years. In between, he worked as a custodian, coached, refereed, supervised the playground, and even drove the schoolbus! When Howlett worked at the San Rafael City Schools, he knew many children like Jazmin Escalante. In his job he helped children from other countries learn English and become more comfortable in American schools. He saw close-up what it's like to be the "new kid" in class. Now Bud Howlett is a writer and a photographer. He took the photographs in *I'm New Here* to go with Jazmin's story.

New Ideas Welcome!

Write a Letter

Dear Jazmin . . .

Write a letter to Jazmin and tell her how you felt about her first day at school. You could offer her encouragement, support, or advice. Let her know whether her experience was similar to any of your experiences at school.

Draw a Picture

Classy Art . . .

Draw a picture of your classroom. Then study the pictures and reread the descriptions of Jazmin's classroom. Use your drawing to explain to a friend or family member how your classroom is similar to or different from Jazmin's.

Nuevas ideas ¡Adelante!

Comparing School Stories

Problems, Problems, Problems . . .

In *I'm New Here* and in *Tales of a Fourth Grade Nothing*, the main characters have to solve problems in school situations. Jazmin wants to fit in at a new school. Peter wants to get a project done in a new work group. Discuss with a partner how they each solve their problems.

Write a Diary Entry

New in Town?

It sure can be tough being new in town. Think of a time when you were new at school, or in your neighborhood, or in some other situation. Did any difficult, funny, or unusual things happen to you? Pick one of those episodes and write an entry in your diary telling what happened.

81

This is School? Cool!

If you think all schools are alike, think again.

THE GREATEST SHOW ON EARTH

Circus School

For some people, school is a circus. The Children of the Rainbow spin, twirl, leap, and go to school as they tour with the famous Ringling Brothers and Barnum & Bailey Circus.

82

Ballet School

At the New Ballet School in New York City, students dance their way through school. Talented children from all over the city study dance as well as regular school subjects.

School by Satellite

This fifth grader in Washington, D.C., is talking to a diver on a coral reef in Belize, in Central America. How does she do it? The Jason Project allows students at participating schools to go on field trips via satellite TV.

School on the Water

At the Alternative Elementary School Number 1, in Seattle, Washington, students use their math skills to build sailboats. They even have their own boat club!

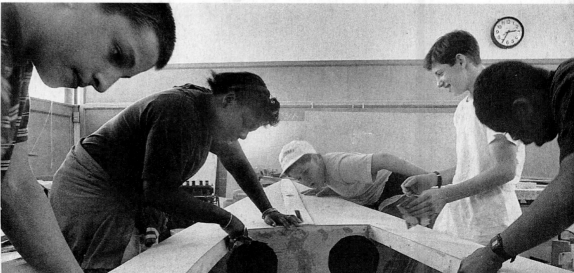

LUCAS COTT
Does Raisin Bread Arithmetic

by JOHANNA HURWITZ

Paper airplane figure 1

Lucas Cott was in Mrs. Hockaday's class. He was one of the smartest kids in the class. But because Lucas fooled around so much, most people, including Lucas himself, weren't aware how much he knew and understood during lessons.

Today Mrs. Hockaday was out ill. It was the first time all year that the teacher was absent. In fact, according to her former students, Mrs. Hockaday was never absent. Yet somehow, the impossible had come to pass and there was a substitute teacher in front of the room. Her name was Mrs. Lindenbaum.

For a boy like Lucas Cott, a substitute teacher was a real challenge. It was someone new to play a few of his tricks on. Someone who wasn't yet aware of how good he was at being bad.

During arithmetic, Mrs. Lindenbaum surprised everyone. Instead of telling them to take out their arithmetic workbooks, she handed out sheets of blank paper.

"Mrs. Lindenbaum, Mrs. Lindenbaum," called out Cricket Kaufman as she waved her hand in the air. "For arithmetic we never use these pieces of paper. We write in our workbooks."

"Thank you for that information," said the substitute. "Nevertheless, as Mrs. Hockaday didn't leave any lesson plans for me today, I have a special assignment for you to do."

Lucas looked over at Cricket. She seemed miserable. He knew she loved writing answers into her arithmetic workbook. Unlike Lucas's workbook or the workbook of most of the other students, there was no crossing out and very little erasing or smudging in Cricket's book. She worked very hard at perfection and sometimes she almost achieved it.

Mrs. Lindenbaum pulled a brown paper grocery bag out from under Mrs. Hockaday's desk. From it she removed what looked very much like a large loaf of bread. Lucas looked with amazement. It was bread!

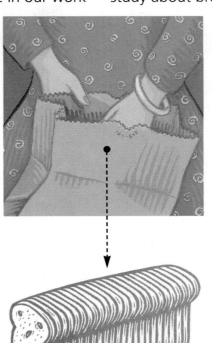

Large loaf of bread
figure 2

Mrs. Lindenbaum walked up and down the aisles and gave a slice of bread to each of the surprised students. When she was finished, every one of the 24 students in Lucas's class had a slice and the bag was empty.

"It's raisin bread," said Julio Sanchez aloud. "I love raisin bread. Why don't we study about bread every day?"

"Are you sure this is arithmetic?" asked Cricket, looking very puzzled. Usually Cricket knew everything. She certainly knew a slice of raisin bread when she saw it. It did not look at all like arithmetic.

Lucas didn't stop to worry about whether their substitute was confused about subjects. He just picked up his slice of bread and took a large bite. It tasted great.

"Do you have any cream cheese in that bag?" he called out with his mouth full.

"Stop eating that bread," Mrs. Lindenbaum instructed. "First we have to do our lesson. The raisin bread can teach us about fractions. We will also practice the scientific method of observation."

Mrs. Lindenbaum told the students to trace the slice of bread onto the sheet of paper. Then they had to mark the location

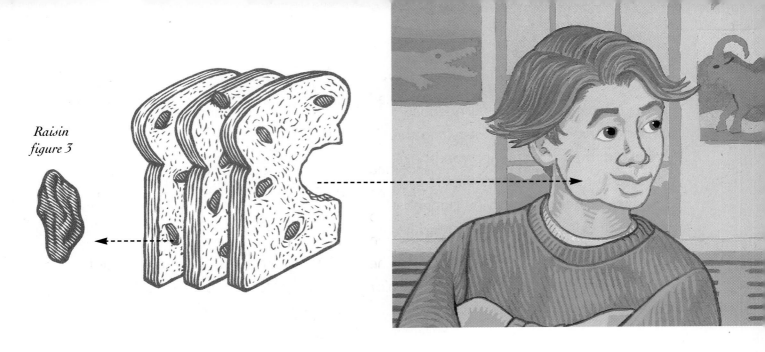

Raisin figure 3

of the raisins. Two of Lucas's raisins were moving through his digestive system so he didn't know how to mark that on his paper.

Mrs. Lindenbaum wrote some questions on the chalkboard:

1. How many slices of bread are in the loaf?
2. What fraction of the loaf is your slice?
3. How many raisins are in your slice?
4. How many raisins in the whole loaf?
5. What fraction of raisins are in your slice?
6. How much does your slice of bread weigh?
7. Look at your slice of bread with a magnifying glass. Describe what you see, smell, feel, and taste!

Mrs. Lindenbaum removed a small scale from the brown paper bag. Lucas wondered what else was in the bag. Maybe there was something else to eat. The one bite of raisin bread had whetted his appetite. Lunch time wasn't for another hour and a half.

The students took turns weighing their bread. Lucas's slice weighed the least because part was missing. But it was interesting to see that none of the slices were exactly the same. Some weighed a bit more than others. And although there were still four raisins in his remaining portion of bread plus two in his stomach, Lucas could see that some students only had a total of four or five raisins in their full slice. Julio had eight raisins.

"Hey, neat-o," said Julio when he realized he hit the raisin jackpot. When all the raisins were added together, there were 128!

"Can I eat the bread now?" Julio asked.

"Not yet," said Mrs. Lindenbaum. "Continue studying your bread and answer question number five." From her brown paper bag she removed half a dozen magnifying glasses.

Lucas picked off another tiny bit of his bread and stuck it in his mouth when no one was looking. He couldn't help it. But it wasn't fun to nibble at bread like a mouse. He wanted to chew down on a real big piece of bread.

When it was his turn with the magnifying glass, Lucas pretended he was a detective.

He'd seen an old Sherlock Holmes movie once. Sherlock Holmes would have looked for fingerprints and teeth marks and things like that. Lucas was surprised to discover the tiny ridges in the bread. Never in his life had he thought about the texture of bread. If he were an ant, he thought, it would be hard to walk across the surface of the bread. Then he rested his head on the desk, next to the bread, and inhaled deeply. There was a nice bready smell.

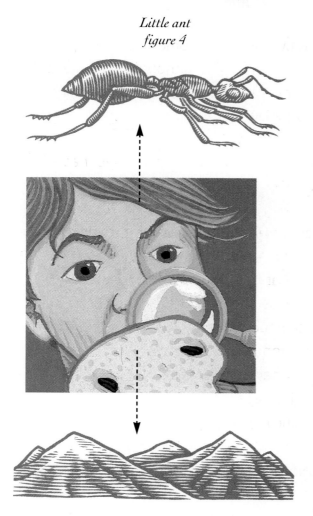

Little ant
figure 4

Really-hard-to-climb mountain
figure 5

Lucas couldn't bear it any longer. He grabbed the slice of bread and folded it in half. In two bites, it was all in his mouth: chewy and delicious.

"What are we going to study tomorrow?" he asked the substitute after he swallowed the bread. "How about pepperoni pizza?"

"I second the motion," said Julio Sanchez. He looked forward to eating $\frac{8}{128}$ or $\frac{1}{16}$ of the total pieces of pepperoni on a pizza.

"Don't worry about tomorrow. There is plenty to learn today," said Mrs. Lindenbaum. She looked into the brown paper bag again.

Lucas hoped Mrs. Hockaday wasn't too sick. Maybe just a mild case of yellow fever or smallpox. (Those were diseases he had read about in a library book. He was, after all, a pretty smart kid and knew all sorts of things one wouldn't have suspected.) He liked eating $\frac{1}{24}$ of a loaf of bread. If Mrs. Lindenbaum and her brown paper bag were around, there would be a lot of other things Lucas might learn from the sub and her unusual teaching methods.

"School is like a slice of raisin bread," pointed out Mrs. Lindenbaum. "Some of it may seem plain and a bit dull. You can't expect raisins all the time. But when you least expect it there can be a surprise, like a raisin in the midst of a piece of boring white bread."

Lucas laughed to himself. Mrs. Lindenbaum didn't know that inside his lunch bag, his mother had put a whole box of raisins.

CHILDTIMES

by Eloise Greenfield

A Play

When I was in the fifth grade, I was famous for a whole day, and all because of a play. The teacher had given me a big part, and I didn't want it. I liked to be in plays where I could be part of a group, like being one of the talking trees, or dancing, or singing in the glee club. But having to talk by myself — *uh uh!*

I used to slide down in my chair and stare at my desk while the teacher was giving out the parts, so she wouldn't pay any attention to me, but this time it didn't work. She called on me anyway. I told her I didn't want to do it, but she said I had to. I guess she thought it would be good for me.

On the day of the play, I didn't make any mistakes. I remembered all of my lines. Only — nobody in the audience heard me. I couldn't make my voice come out loud.

For the rest of the day, I was famous. Children passing by my classroom door, children on the playground at lunchtime, kept pointing at me saying, "That's that girl! That's the one who didn't talk loud enough!"

I felt so bad, I wanted to go home. But one good thing came out of it all. The teacher was so angry, so upset, she told me that as long as I was in that school, I'd never have another chance to ruin one of her plays. And that was such good news, I could stand being famous for a day.

89

THE DAY I WAS A HERO

A Personal Narrative by Anthony Yengo

Anthony Yengo

Paul Ecke Central School
Encinitas, California

Anthony Yengo's favorite hobby is writing stories, especially stories that are funny and scary. The one he enjoyed writing the most was called "A Fright for My Life." He wrote a similar one titled "A Fright for My Sister's Life."

When he was in fourth grade, Anthony acted in a school musical. Then he shared that exciting experience by writing "The Day I Was a Hero." He also drew the cover for the program.

Anthony also likes boogie boarding at the beach, playing soccer, drawing make-believe monsters, and learning to play the trombone. Anthony wants to be a writer when he grows up.

The Day I Was a Hero

I jumped up and down! I was so happy! We were giving a musical called <u>Tall Tales and Heroes</u>, and our class chose who played which hero. Each kid picked a favorite hero, and then we voted on who would get the part. I chose to be a man called John Henry, but my friend wanted to be the same hero. The next day the heroes were announced, and I was chosen to be John Henry!

After that I had to practice my part. Practicing was very hard because our whole class learned many songs, and we memorized all our lines and some dances. My part was very fun because I yelled to the crowd in a deep voice, "I'm a steel-driving man. I got pride hammering in my soul!" I pretended to hold a sledgehammer and to swing at an imaginary steel spike.

I also had another part. I was Davy Crockett's son. The whole Crockett family square-danced on the stage. The song had a catchy tune and made you want to dance until the song was over.

Days went by of singing and dancing and practicing until finally our last practice was perfect. We sang like soft water floating down a stream. It was the best.

The next night was our musical for the parents. I was nervous as I entered the auditorium in my Davy Crockett coonskin hat and fringed vest over my John Henry denim shirt, blue jeans, and suspenders. I sang like never before. I danced better, and I recited all my parts better than I ever had. When the play was over, the crowd yelled and hooted in appreciation. We all took a bow and had our pictures taken. I smiled and was so happy I could cry. That play was such fun to do that all the hard work was worth it.

About the Author
Eloise Greenfield

Even though Eloise Greenfield has written over twenty books, she says, "Writing was the farthest thing from my mind when I was growing up. I loved words, but I loved to read them, not to write them."

Greenfield started writing only after her own children were born. When her first humorous rhymes and short stories weren't accepted by publishers, she "gave up writing forever." Her "forever" lasted five or six years, until her poem, "To a Violin," was published in 1963. Since then, writing has become part of her life and of her family's life. In fact, she often asks her children to read and talk to her about her stories.

About the Illustrator
Gil Ashby

Ever since he was in second grade, Gil Ashby has known that he would be an artist. He even attended a special high school, the School of Art and Design, in his hometown of New York City. Ashby says that when he illustrates a story, he does sketches first. Then he does research and takes photographs of real people doing the action of the story. He continues drawing from the photos, and "when that's done I put on music and paint." To do the illustrations on the following pages, Ashby spent a day with a double-dutch team from New York City.

92

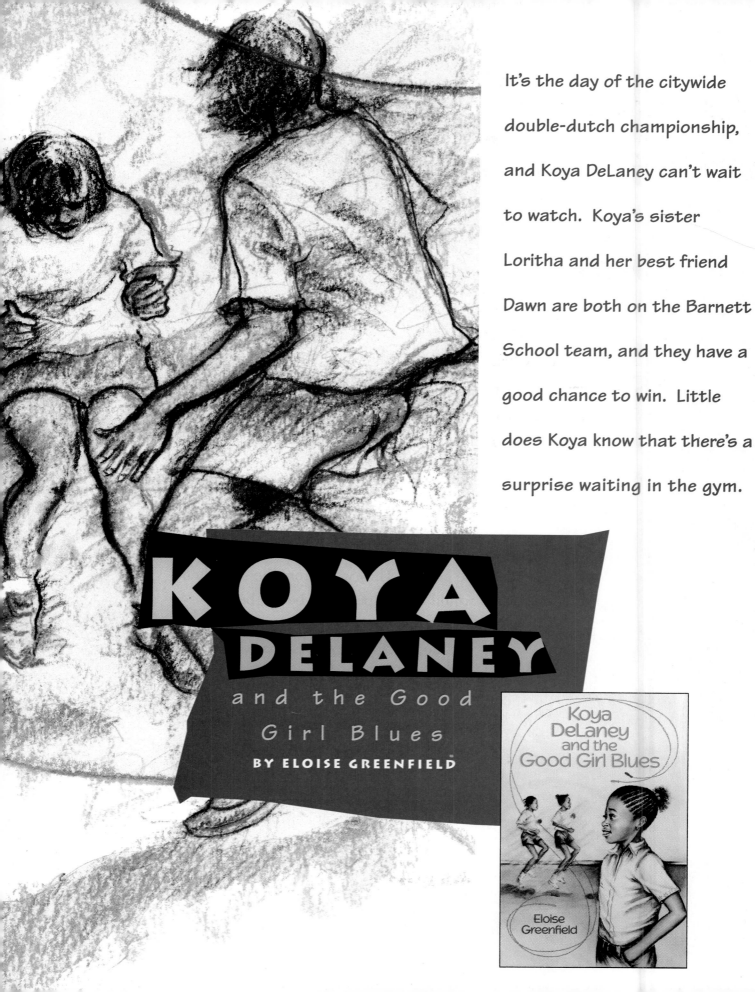

It's the day of the citywide double-dutch championship, and Koya DeLaney can't wait to watch. Koya's sister Loritha and her best friend Dawn are both on the Barnett School team, and they have a good chance to win. Little does Koya know that there's a surprise waiting in the gym.

KOYA DELANEY
and the Good Girl Blues
BY ELOISE GREENFIELD

Koya
DeLaney
and the
Good Girl Blues

Eloise
Greenfield

Koya's father found a parking space a block from the high school, and they all got out of the car and joined the other groups of people of all ages, from babies to grandparents, getting out of cars and buses, in the warm April sunshine, and moving toward the entrance of the school.

Koya loved looking at the double-dutch jumpers, in their many colors, walking throughout the crowd. They were from the six schools that would be competing to be the best in the city.

Inside, the large gym was packed and noisy. Koya had begged Ms. Harris to let her sit with the team, so while her parents headed toward the bleacher seats, she went with Loritha to look for the sign that said BARNETT. They passed the long table filled with trophies, gleaming gold and silver.

Ms. Harris saw them approaching and beckoned to them.

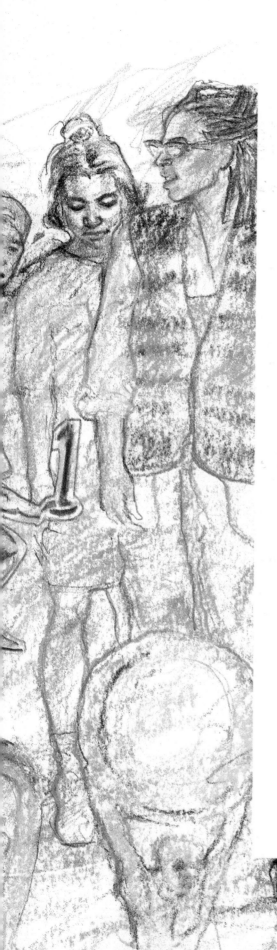

"Loritha," she said when they reached her, "we tried to get in touch with you this morning. Dawn called several times, but your line was busy."

Koya didn't like the way Ms. Harris was talking. Her tone was too gentle, as if she were feeling sorry for Loritha. Koya couldn't imagine why.

"What was she calling me for?" Loritha asked.

"Well, she had thought up a new trick for our freestyle routine," Ms. Harris said. "As a matter of fact, she dreamed it. Isn't that something? She called me early this morning to tell me about it. So we all met at school to practice. It's fantastic. I think it could really put us over."

Loritha looked confused. "You all practiced this morning?" she said.

"I'm sorry we couldn't reach you, Loritha," Ms. Harris said.

Loritha's face looked stunned. "I'm not going to be in the freestyle?"

"I'm so sorry, Loritha," Ms. Harris said, "but you want to win, don't you? Wilson's going to be tough to beat, and this trick could do it for us."

Koya looked over at Dawn, sitting with the team. Dawn was watching them, and Koya could almost see the word *guilty* stamped on her face. She knew Dawn hadn't called.

Loritha was trying to hold back her tears. "But I could learn it now," she said. "We could go to another room . . ." She looked at the clock and knew it was too late.

Ms. Harris was tired of being nice. "There's no *time* for that," she said. "You just have to *accept* this. You two take your *seats*, now."

Loritha asked one of the girls to move down one seat, so she could sit next to Dawn, and Koya took an empty seat two places away.

Loritha's disappointment had changed to anger. "You didn't call me," she said to Dawn.

"I did so," Dawn said. "I can't help it if your line was busy."

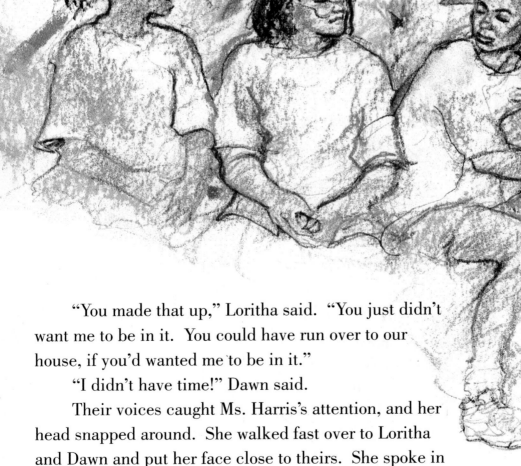

"You made that up," Loritha said. "You just didn't want me to be in it. You could have run over to our house, if you'd wanted me to be in it."

"I didn't have time!" Dawn said.

Their voices caught Ms. Harris's attention, and her head snapped around. She walked fast over to Loritha and Dawn and put her face close to theirs. She spoke in a loud whisper.

"We are a team!" she said. "I don't want you to say *another* word about this, or even *think* about it, until this competition is over. Now *concentrate* on what you came here to do, or you're going to embarrass yourselves, your families, the school, and *me*!"

As she walked away, there was a shrill whistle from the far end of the floor. The competition was about to begin.

"Take your seats, everybody." The announcer was Coach Dickinson, the high school basketball coach.

He held the microphone in his hand and let the whistle dangle from the chain around his neck. The shape of his stomach could be seen pushing against his bright-green T-shirt. "Take your seats, please."

The people in the audience who had been standing around talking walked quickly toward their seats, holding the hands of their small children to help them up the bleacher steps. When almost everybody was seated, the announcer blew the whistle again, and the room grew quiet.

Koya was sorry now that she had asked to sit with the team. She wanted to be on the other side of the room with the families and her classmates and Dr. Hanley, where she couldn't see that Loritha was hurt and angry and struggling to keep from crying. And where she couldn't see the guilt on Dawn's face.

"Okay, we're ready to start," Coach Dickinson said. "I don't know about you, but I've been really looking forward to this day. Our first citywide competition. Sixth-graders only this year, but if all goes well, next year you won't be able to take two steps without bumping into a bunch of kids jumping double-dutch, everybody from fifth grade through twelfth. Now, I want you to welcome two people who are going to help us make this happen."

He introduced two school board members who stood up to be recognized. Then he introduced the six men and women who were going to judge the competition. Each of the judges went to one of the places on the floor where ropes were laid out. The teams followed. Twenty girls and four boys. Two turners and two jumpers at each place. The turners picked up the ropes. The jumpers stood beside them, ready to jump in. They waited, poised, for the signal that would tell them to begin.

"Take your mark!" the announcer said.

There was a hush in the room.

"Get set!"

Then he blew the whistle, and the jumpers went into the ropes, not jumping fast, but trying to do all the steps they had to do, in rhythm with their partners. Koya kept

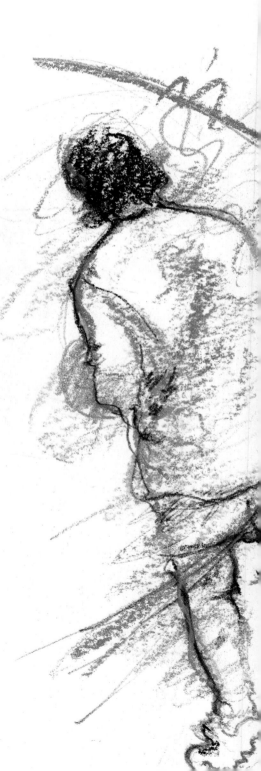

her eyes on Dawn and Loritha. As she watched, her thoughts flowed in a rhythm of their own.

They move together like twins. Like best friends. Jump on the right foot, jump on the left, turn around, jump, jump on the right foot, jump on the left. They move together. Like friends.

The judges were watching closely. Everything had to be perfect, or points would be taken off. The ropes couldn't touch. The jumpers had to go in and out of the rope correctly. Their posture had to be right.

The whistle sounded to signal the end of the first event. Ms. Harris was happy, smiling, as the audience applauded and the judges marked their score sheets.

"Freestyle, next!" the announcer said.

One minute of tricks the teams had created themselves. Loritha would have to sit down and let a substitute take her place. She left the floor and walked toward the chairs, smiling a stiff little smile, and Koya knew she was trying not to cry.

She wants to wait. Wait and cry at home. I won't look at her, I won't say anything, or she'll cry, and I'll cry, too.

Loritha took the seat beside Koya, instead of the seat she'd had before, as if she needed to sit close to someone she trusted. Koya leaned closer to her without looking at her.

"Okay, let's go!" Coach Dickinson said. "First team up is Parker!"

The girls from Parker School were nervous. They dropped the rope twice, and one girl slipped and almost fell, and finished jumping with tears rolling down her face.

Some of the other teams made small mistakes. But Wilson didn't make any. It was the team Barnett would have to beat.

Barnett performed last. Dawn and the girl who was taking Loritha's place jumped into the rope and began circling each other, exchanging places, jumping with knees high. Then they circled in the other direction. Hopped five times on one foot, then on the other. Then the turners began to stomp in rhythm with the jumpers, while still turning the rope. Koya had seen all of these tricks before. Now they were about to begin the new one.

Dawn and the other girl somersaulted out of the rope in opposite directions, jumped up and ran back in as the rope turned faster. Koya caught her breath. No other team had done anything as hard and as beautiful.

The girls somersaulted again, jumped up, and turned to run back in, but the ropes had touched and become entangled.

Koya heard Loritha gasp, and saw Ms. Harris close her eyes and give a small shake of her head. The turners quickly pulled the ropes apart, and the trick was finished, but the mistake had been made. Points would have to be taken off their score.

The last event was speed jumping. Two minutes of jumping as fast as they could. The judges would be counting the number of times the left foot hit the floor. This was Loritha's event. She would be jumping by herself.

The announcer gave the signal, and there was an explosion of movement and sound. Six ropes were whirring. Legs and sneakers flying. People in the audience cheering for their team. "Come on, you can do it! You can do it!"

Loritha jumped, left, right, left, right, left, right, speeding. She leaned forward at the waist, not moving her arms, almost not moving the top part of her body at all, as if her flying legs belonged to another person.

My sister is brave. Nobody knows she's really, really sad. Nobody but me.

"Go, Ritha!" Koya yelled.

The two minutes seemed more like two hours to Koya. She wondered if the whistle would *ever* blow. Loritha's eyes were narrowed, staring at a spot just above the floor. She was breathing through her open mouth, but once, for a moment, she pressed her lips together so tightly that deep lines dented her chin. The lost points had to be made up. Her legs kept churning.

One of the boys on another team was jumping fast, too, but only one person was keeping up with Loritha. The girl from Wilson. It looked like a tie.

The whistle finally blew.

"Yeaaaa, Barnett!" somebody yelled through the applause.

Koya watched in suspense as the judges totaled the scores and gave their decision to Coach Dickinson.

"Wooo! It was a close one!" he said. He wiped his face with an imaginary handkerchief, as if he were the one who had been jumping. It made the audience laugh. "You were great, all of you. Each one of you will receive a certificate, something you can be very proud of. And now, the winners."

He read from the card the judges had given him. "First place, Wilson! Second place, Barnett! Third place, Merritt!" He clapped loudly. "Let's hear it for Wilson! Barnett! Merritt! And all the participants!"

The teams went to the front to receive their trophies and certificates. When it was over, relatives and friends came down out of the stands, and there was hugging and kissing, hand slapping and screaming. Koya ran over to where Loritha was standing with the team and hugged her tightly. Mr. and Ms. DeLaney rushed over, too.

"Girl, you were really something!" Ms. DeLaney said.

Koya looked around and was surprised to see Ms. Harris trying to comfort the girl who had made the ropes tangle. Koya wanted to go over and say something nice, but then she saw Dawn across the room. Dawn saw her at the same time, and came running toward her, laughing, reaching out to hug her.

Koya didn't know what to do. She didn't feel like hugging someone who had been so mean to her sister. But stepping back now, with Dawn's arms so close, would be like slapping the smile off her best friend's face. She couldn't bring herself to do it. She put one arm loosely around Dawn's shoulder.

And that's when she saw Loritha's eyes, looking at her from a few feet away.

Should Koya have hugged Dawn? What is Loritha thinking? How should Koya treat Dawn and Loritha now? More than anything, Koya wants the three of them — herself, Loritha, and Dawn — to be friends just the way they have always been. She struggles to make that happen in the rest of *Koya DeLaney and the Good Girl Blues.*

Jump Right In

Sports Page

Here's your chance to be a reporter. Cover the double-dutch competition for the Barnett school newspaper. Write a newspaper story about the contest, including what happens, the way the contestants look, and how they seem to be feeling. Make your readers feel the tension and excitement.

Hold a Debate
The Right Stuff

What does it take to be a double-dutch jumper? What athletic talents or skills do you need? Do you think other school sports, such as baseball or basketball, require more or less skill and strength? Decide which sports you think are the most demanding, and jot down examples to support your choice. Then meet with a group to debate your ideas.

Write a Diary Entry
Dear Diary

Loritha probably had strong feelings about losing her place in the freestyle event. How do you think she felt about what Dawn did and about what Koya did? What about her own behavior during the competition? Write a diary entry in which Loritha expresses her thoughts and feelings.

Compare Two Teams
All for One and One for All

That sounds like a good motto for a team. Does it describe the way Loritha and her double-dutch team act? How about the way the Flying Train Committee behaves? Compare and contrast the behavior of the double-dutch team to the teamwork in *Tales of a Fourth Grade Nothing*.

**A play by Deborah Sussman,
based on the book
Alice's Adventures in Wonderland
by Lewis Carroll**

ALICE & ALEX

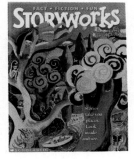

Characters

NARRATOR

ALICE } 9-year-old

ALEX } twins

MOTHER

MR. RABBIT
(a white-haired man)

CHESTER
(the hall monitor)

MARGE

MATT } 3 kids

DORA

MS. QUEEN
(a scary person)

MS. QUEEN'S GANG
(a group of two or
more people)

Scene 1 The Twins' Room

NARRATOR: Meet Alice and Alex. They're twins. They just moved to town. It's bedtime, and Alice is reading *Alice's Adventures in Wonderland* out loud to Alex. Their mother comes in.

ALICE (reading): "The Cat only grinned when it saw Alice. It looked good-natured, she thought. Still it had very long claws and a great many teeth —"

MOTHER: Not too much longer, you two. Tomorrow is your first day at a new school. I want you to be bright-eyed and bushy-tailed!

ALEX: C'mon, just one more page.

ALICE: No! One more chapter!

MOTHER: Five more minutes, then lights out.

ALICE (reading as Mother leaves): "Still it had very long claws and a great many teeth . . ."

Scene 2 At School

NARRATOR: The next thing Alice and Alex know, it's Monday morning and they're at their new school.

ALEX: Alice, there's no one else here.

ALICE (calling out): HELLO! Is anyone here?

NARRATOR: Suddenly, a small, white-haired man with a pink nose rushes by.

MR. RABBIT: Oh, dear! Oh, dear! I shall be too late!

NARRATOR: The small man pulls a watch from his pocket and checks it. He hurries on.

ALICE: Quick! Let's follow that guy.

NARRATOR: The twins chase the man down the hall.

ALICE: Mister! Hey, Mister!

ALEX: Yo! Dude!

ALICE: Excuse me —

MR. RABBIT: Oh, there you are. Listen, Susan, and you, too, George. I need four gallons of lemonade right away.

ALICE: Um, I think you have us confused with some other children.

MR. RABBIT: Don't be silly. Now hurry up.

ALEX: No, really. We're new here. Who are you?

MR. RABBIT: Mr. Rabbit, of course. Now, let's see. New students. Well, you'll have to go to the main office.

ALEX: How do we get there?

MR. RABBIT: Follow the signs.

NARRATOR: Mr. Rabbit leaves.

ALICE: This school is weird.

ALEX: Yeah. Weirder than weird.

CHESTER: Says you.

ALICE: Who said that?

CHESTER: I did. Up here.

NARRATOR: Alice and Alex look up and see a boy standing on a tall chair, grinning.

CHESTER: I'm Chester Cat, the hall monitor.

ALICE: Do you know which way we're supposed to go?

CHESTER: That depends on where you're trying to get to.

ALEX: The main office.

CHESTER: You can go left. Or you can go right.

ALICE: What's the difference?

CHESTER: One's left, and one's right.

ALEX: You mean both ways lead to the office?

CHESTER: Sure, if you walk far enough.

ALEX: Are you trying to confuse us?

CHESTER: Not at all. I'm trying to help.

NARRATOR: The twins look around, trying to decide which way to go. When they look back at Chester, he has disappeared. There's a big grin on the wall where he once stood.

ALICE: Alex! That grin was in the book I was reading last night! The Cheshire Cat disappears, except for its grin.

ALEX: Yeah, yeah. But now what?

NARRATOR: Alice walks over to a little door. A sign on the doorknob says, "OPEN ME."

ALICE: Hey, check it out! A sign.

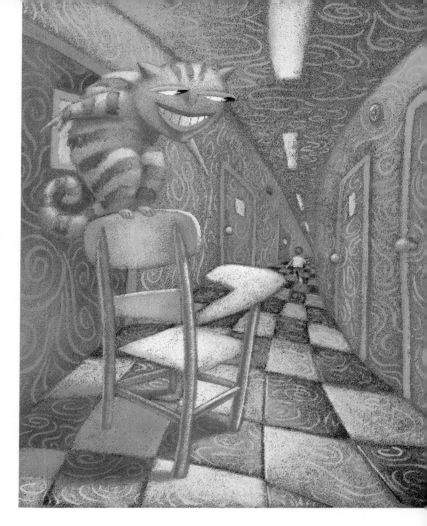

NARRATOR: Alice opens the door.

ALEX: Whoa! It's dark in there.

ALICE: Yeah, but I'm going in.

NARRATOR: Alice steps through the doorway and Alex hears —

ALICE: YIKES! I'm falling.

ALEX: Alice, are you okay?

ALICE: I'm still falling.

ALEX: You sound pretty calm about it.

ALICE: Still falling. Whooops! Hey! I just landed in a pile of humongous marshmallows.

ALEX: Really?

ALICE: Would I lie to you?

ALEX: Maybe.

ALICE: Come on down.

ALEX: Okay — if you say so.

Scene 3 The Lunchroom

NARRATOR: Alex lands next to Alice on a pile of huge marshmallows, in the corner of a large lunchroom.

ALICE: Look, we're not the only people here!

ALEX: You call those people?

ALICE: The one with the stack of hats. That's a boy . . . I think. That's a girl next to him — the one with the rabbity face and pointy ears.

ALEX: Oh. What's that sleeping on the table between them?

ALICE: It looks like a giant mouse.

NARRATOR: Alice and Alex walk over to the table.

ALICE: Hi. I'm Alice and this is my twin brother, Alex. What's with the mouse?

MARGE: This isn't any mouse. This is Dora Mouse. She's in third grade. Wake up, Dora! I'm Marge Hare and this is Matt Hatter. Now go away. There's no room here.

ALICE: What do you mean?

ALEX: There's plenty of room.

NARRATOR: The twins sit down at the table. Matt turns to Alice and looks at her hair.

MATT: You need a haircut.

ALICE: And you're rude!

MATT: Well, then, why is a raven like a writing desk?

ALEX: Is that a riddle?

ALICE: I bet I can guess that.

MARGE: You mean you think you can figure out the answer?

ALICE: Definitely.

MARGE: Then you should always say what you mean.

ALICE (confused): I do. At least, I mean what I say. That's the same thing.

MATT: Not at all. Why, you might just as well say that "I see what I eat" is the same thing as "I eat what I see."

MARGE: Oh, dear. Dora is asleep again.

MATT: So, have you guessed the riddle yet?

ALEX: No, we give up. What's the answer?

MATT: I have no idea.

ALICE: Don't you have anything better to do than ask riddles that have no answers? What a waste of time!

MATT: If you knew Time as well as I do, you wouldn't talk about wasting it. It's him.

ALEX: I don't get it.

MATT: Of course you don't. You've probably never even talked to Time!

ALICE: And you have?

MATT: Oh, yes. We were very good friends, until . . .

MARGE: They quarreled.

MATT: It was last March, at the school recital. Since then, Time won't do anything I ask. It's always noon now.

ALEX: Is that why the table is set for lunch?

MARGE: Yes, that's it. It's always lunchtime, and there's no time to clear the table.

ALICE: Then you keep moving around the table, right?

MATT: Exactly, as things get used up.

ALEX: But what happens when you get to the beginning again?

ALICE: It must get disgusting!

MATT: Now who's the rude one?

MARGE: Let's change the subject. I vote that Dora tells us a story. Wake up, Dora!

DORA: I wasn't sleeping. I heard every word you said.

MATT: Tell us a story.

DORA: Once upon a time there were two twins, a boy and a girl.

MARGE: Twins! Yeah! Let's all have some more milk.

ALEX: We haven't had any yet. So we can't have more.

MATT: You mean you can't have less. It's very easy to have more than nothing.

DORA: If you two can't behave, I won't finish the story.

ALICE: Sorry. Go ahead.

DORA: So these two twins lived at the bottom of a well —

ALEX: What did they eat?

DORA: Honey.

MATT: I want a new carton of milk. Let's change places.

NARRATOR: Everyone stands up and moves one seat to the left.

ALICE: I don't understand. Where did they get the honey?

DORA: It was a honey well!

ALEX: Ha ha ha. That's so funny I forgot to laugh!

NARRATOR: Suddenly, Ms. Queen bursts into the lunchroom. She's wearing a dress with red hearts all over it. A noisy gang follows her.

MS. QUEEN: There they are! Grab them!

ALICE: Wait! Is she talking about us?

MS. QUEEN: Someone has stolen the bologna sandwiches! You are all under arrest! Off with your heads!

MS. QUEEN'S GANG (*together*): We'll get them!

ALEX: But we didn't do it!

MS. QUEEN: Do you like bologna sandwiches?

ALEX: Well, sure, but —

MS. QUEEN: Just as I thought. Guilty guilty guilty! Grab them!

NARRATOR: A big guy in a football helmet grabs Alex. A guy in a catcher's mask chases Alice.

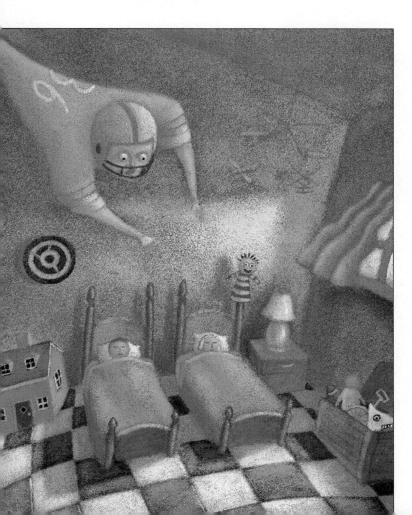

MS. QUEEN'S GANG (*together*): Grrrr! Your heads are our heads now!

ALICE: No! Help!

ALEX: Get this creep off me!

MS. QUEEN: Off with their heads! Off with their heads!

Scene 4 The Twins' Room

NARRATOR: It's morning in the twins' bedroom.

MOTHER: Wake up, sleepyheads! Wake up!

NARRATOR: Alice and Alex open their eyes. They are safe at home. The book *Alice's Adventures in Wonderland* lies open on the floor.

MOTHER: You'll be late for school if you don't hurry.

ALICE: I had the weirdest dream.

ALEX: I bet mine was weirder.

ALICE: Oh, yeah? Did yours have a talking mouse in it?

ALEX: Yes, as a matter of fact.

ALICE: Really?

ALEX: And a disappearing —

ALICE: — hall monitor?

ALEX (*surprised*): Yeah. How did you know?

ALICE: Let's just say I read the book.

The End

EARTH PATROL
PRESERVE AND PROTECT

CONTENTS

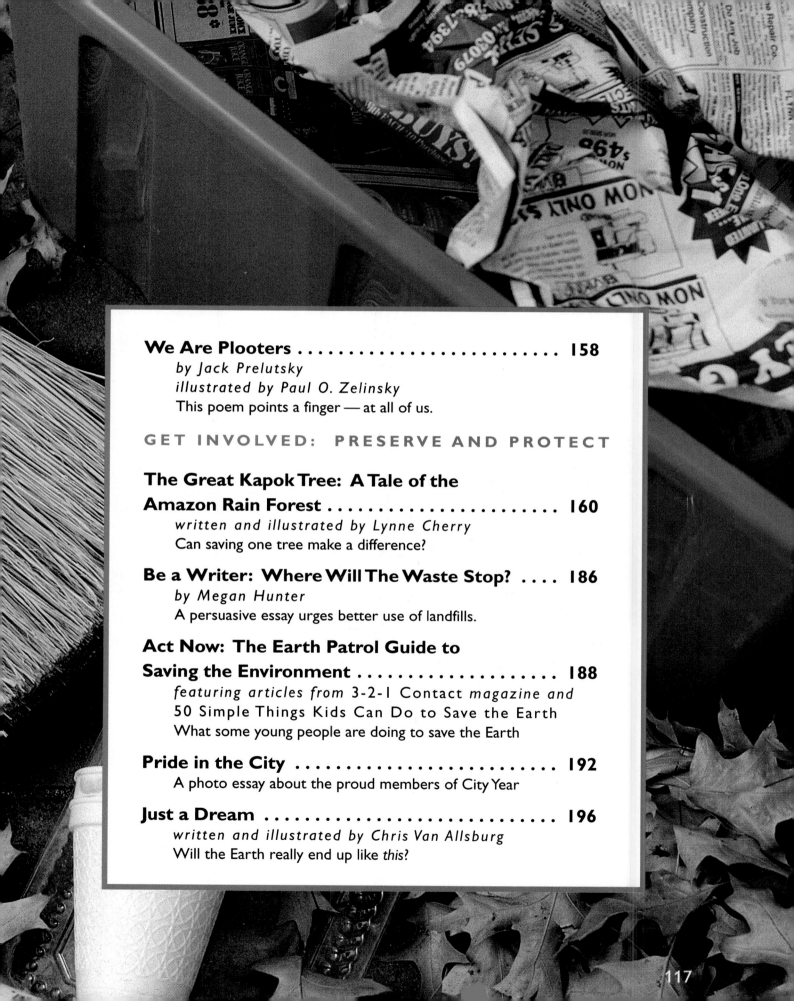

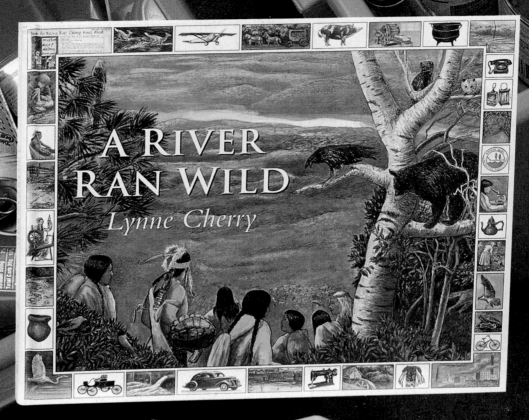

A River Ran Wild

by Lynne Cherry

How did a dead river in Massachusetts come back to life?

In the same book . . .

More about how pollution can ruin a river and how concerned people can help save it.

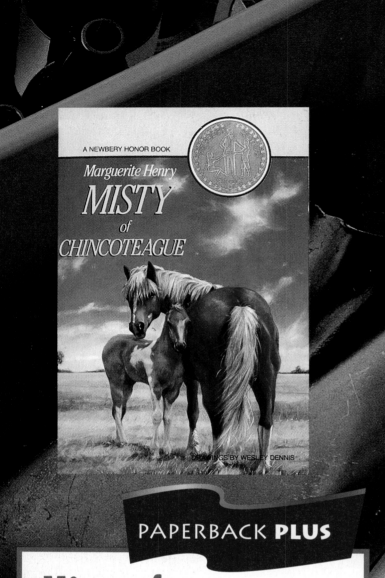

A NEWBERY HONOR BOOK

Marguerite Henry

MISTY of CHINCOTEAGUE

DRAWINGS BY WESLEY DENNIS

PAPERBACK **PLUS**

Misty of Chincoteague

by Marguerite Henry

Can two children tame the wild mare and her young filly Misty?

In the same book . . .

A lot more about the real Misty, where she lived, and other fun facts about horses.

More Earth Books

Someday a Tree
by Eve Bunting
After someone dumps chemicals that poison her favorite oak tree, Alice plants an acorn nearby, hoping that another tree will start to grow.

Sato and the Elephants
by Juanita Havill
A Japanese ivory carver becomes a stone carver instead, when he finds out that elephants are killed to supply him with ivory.

Earth Keepers
by Joan Anderson and George Ancona
This three-part photo essay describes a community garden in New York, Lynn Rogers's work with black bears, and the environmental studies done by the crew of the *Clearwater*.

Alligators: A Success Story
by Patricia Lauber
Once an endangered species, the alligator is making a comeback, thanks to caring citizens and new laws.

Listening to Crickets: A Story About Rachel Carson
by Candice F. Ransom
A biography of the writer and biologist whose work helped make people aware of threats to the environment.

A SIERRA CLUB BOOK

THE GREAT YELLOWSTONE FIRE

CAROLE G. VOGEL AND KATHRYN A. GOLDNER

IN YELLOWSTONE NATIONAL PARK, heat and water escape from the earth into a land of mystery. Where volcanoes once erupted, strange creations of nature now bubble and hiss. Colorful, steaming pools dot fields of bunchgrass and sagebrush. Geysers gurgle and shoot columns of superheated water high into the air.

Around these simmering landforms rise the rugged Rocky Mountains of Wyoming, Montana, and Idaho. Sharp gray peaks capped with snow tower above green forests. Streams and rivers tumble through deep gorges.

Lodgepole pine trees blanket much of Yellowstone. These trees grow tall and thin with few branches. In the dense forests, their tops mesh together, and little sunlight filters through. Open meadows and groves of spruce, fir, and aspen trees interrupt the pines.

A dramatic fountain of steam and hot water shoots skyward from Castle Geyser, just one of about 10,000 geysers, hot springs, and other thermal features in Yellowstone.

Yellowstone's patchwork of habitats provides homes for many kinds of animals. Near steaming geysers and hot springs, bison graze in open meadows. Moose and deer browse on tender shoots of cottonwood and willow. On steep mountainsides, golden eagles build nests on rocky ledges, and bighorn sheep traverse the jagged rocks. The rivers and lakes of the park provide food and nesting sites for trumpeter swans, white pelicans, and other water birds.

In 1872, the vast area known as Yellowstone was declared a national park to preserve its special landforms, wildlife, and wilderness for future generations to enjoy. The rules of the national park protect the animals from hunters and the trees from loggers. But no one can protect the forests from the forces of nature. As in ages past, summertime brings wildfire to Yellowstone.

In 1886, fourteen years after the formation of the park, Yellowstone officials declared fire the enemy. Although fire had been part of the wilderness for thousands of years, firefighters armed with axes and

An elk and her young calf share a quiet moment by a stream. Seven large herds of elk roam the meadows and forests of Yellowstone.

The variety of animal life in the park is remarkable, ranging from black bears like this little cub (top) to flocks of waterbirds such as the American white pelican (bottom).

shovels were now sent to stamp out blazes. For many years, there was no effective way to combat flames in areas far from roads. After World War II, lookouts were stationed on mountaintops to watch for smoke, and smoke jumpers parachuted from airplanes into hard-to-reach places. Wildfires were extinguished as soon as possible.

Fallen trees, dead pine needles, and other natural litter continued to pile up on the forest floor. As the lodgepole forests aged, pine bark beetles attacked the trees, until thousands of dead and dying pines filled the forests. No major fires cleared away this buildup of fuel.

Over the years, as scientists learned more about forests, they discovered that fire is not the enemy. By clearing the land and releasing the minerals locked in dead wood, fire creates and maintains a variety of habitats. Like sunshine and rain, fire is necessary to the health of the wilderness.

In 1972, scientists convinced park officials to allow fire to play its role in nature once again. Under the new policy, firefighters battled only blazes started by humans and those natural fires that threatened people or buildings. Precipitation in all seasons kept much of Yellowstone moist, so most natural fires died quickly.

In 1988, park officials expected another normal fire season. After a dry winter, spring precipitation was high. Fires ignited by lightning all fizzled out.

Then, in June, conditions changed. The air turned hot and dry, and practically no rain fell. Day after day, the sun beat down on Yellowstone. Lakes and streams shrank. In the meadows, grasses shriveled. In the forests, dead lodgepole pines and fallen branches became parched. Slowly, the landscape changed from lush green to withered brown.

Thunderstorms rumbled across the park but brought no rain. Lightning ignited many small fires. Some died quickly, while others sprang to life. The fires burned unevenly, scorching here, singeing there. They

In the summer of 1988, lightning started more than forty-five fires in Yellowstone — twice the usual number for one summer.

leapfrogged through the forests, leaving patches of trees and ground cover untouched. Pushed along by dry summer winds, the fires grew.

Just over the park boundary in Targhee National Forest, woodcutters accidentally started another fire. The flames quickly spread into Yellowstone. Firefighters battled this blaze and several others that threatened buildings, but they could not stop the fires.

By midsummer, almost 9,000 acres of Yellowstone's 2.2 million acres had burned. Fires raged through forests that had taken hundreds of years to grow. No rain was expected for weeks, and officials were worried. On July 15, they decided to fight all new natural blazes. Within a week, they began to battle all existing ones, as well. Yet the fires continued to spread.

Wildfires usually burn more slowly at night, then rev up with the heat of day. But in the summer of 1988, dry night winds blew down from high ridges, fanning the blazes. Day and night, ground fires crackled through dead pine needles, branches, and logs,

The landscape became a patchwork of colors that reflected the pattern of burn. Scorched brown trees separated the areas blackened by the hottest flames from the green areas left untouched (above). Hot flames leapt up tinder-dry tree trunks (left).

blackening the forest floor. In some places, they scorched the bases of trees but left the tops green. In other areas, the ground fires burned hotter and toasted needles in the crowns of the trees a dusty rust color.

The hottest flames clawed up the trunks of large trees. Treetops ignited in seconds, and smoke poured into the sky. Lodgepole pines burst apart, hurling bits of glowing wood through the air. These tiny blazing embers landed on dry branches or grass and kindled spot fires far ahead of the fire fronts.

Advancing as much as five to ten miles a day, the fires hopscotched through the wilderness. Among the burned forests and meadows, they left unburned areas of green trees and brown grass.

From sunup to sunset and into the night, nearly 9,500 firefighters from all parts of the country battled the blazes. Many of these men and women prepared firebreaks. They cleared strips of ground of everything that could burn. Sometimes they scraped the land with hand tools; at other times, they detonated explosives or set small backfires. They sprayed trees and buildings with water or fire-retardant foam and snuffed out spot fires.

To fight remote blazes, firefighters hiked into the backcountry. Smoke

Firefighters tried every known technique to control the blazes. On the roads, fire engines often shared the smoky landscape with animals trying to keep out of the fire's way (above). In the roadless wilderness, planes dropped pink fire retardant to smother the flames (left).

jumpers parachuted in. Sometimes fire crews dropped water or fire retardant onto the blazes from helicopters and airplanes.

Yet the fires defied everyone's best efforts. Blazes subdued by water or retardant leapt back to life. Small fires grew and joined with bigger fires. Flames skipped over prepared firebreaks, roads, and rivers. One blaze even jumped the Grand Canyon of the Yellowstone River. By mid-August, experts agreed that only a change in weather could stop the fires.

But the forecast for hot, dry weather remained

unchanged. On August 20, the day that would be called Black Saturday, gale-force winds fanned every blaze in the park. Flames rampaged through forests and meadows. Smoke billowed high into the sky, and gray ash rained down.

Powerless, firefighters could only stand and watch while fire consumed another 160,000 acres. More of Yellowstone was blackened on this one day than in the previous 116 years. The amount of burned area in the park had doubled.

In late summer, fires inside and outside Yellowstone whipped toward several towns neighboring the park. Flames threatened many buildings inside Yellowstone, as well. Weary firefighters battled the blazes for twelve to fourteen hours a day.

Despite the raging fires, many people refused to cancel their vacations. They came to see the smoke, the wildlife, and the world's most famous geyser, Old Faithful.

Close to Old Faithful stands the rustic Old Faithful Inn, built in stagecoach days from logs, shingles, and stone. When it was completed in 1904, the inn and a cluster of buildings stood alone amid the geysers. Today, the inn is but one of many buildings—stores, gas stations, other lodges—that make up Old Faithful Village.

During the dry days of early September 1988, fire burned toward the famous geyser and the wooden structures of the nearby village. On the morning of September 7, officials began to evacuate tourists and workers from the area. Most people cooperated, but a few refused to leave.

At 2:00 P.M., the wind gathered speed. Beyond a nearby ridge, flames danced in the treetops. Lodgepole pines pitched and swayed, and the smell of burning trees filled the air. As the blaze swept up the far side of the ridge, fire-engine crews drenched buildings with water or fire-retardant foam. Other firefighters turned on a sprinkler system at the edge of the village complex.

At 3:30, Old Faithful erupted. Minutes later, a wall of flames whipped over the ridge. Roaring like jets in takeoff, the fire rolled down

Fire roared over a ridge in Upper Lamar Valley;

a similar blaze approached Old Faithful.

130

On September 7, fire whipped down the hillside behind Old Faithful Village. The wind shifted, and suddenly flames headed toward the buildings.

the forested hillside. Trees ignited like torches. Clouds of smoke turned the sky orange . . . then bronze . . . then gray. . . .

Within minutes, fire engulfed a pine grove on the edge of the village. Cabins burst into flames. A truck burned and then exploded.

Park employees, reporters, and the few remaining visitors fled toward the relative safety of the parking lot around Old Faithful Inn. Smoke stung their eyes and throats. Hot coals pelted their backs and flew past their heads.

Fire crews sprayed the buildings as pumper trucks raced through the smoky village to extinguish spot fires. A rooftop sprinkler system flooded the shingles of the inn.

Minutes later, the fire reached the edge of the village. Engulfed in thick smoke and threatened by blazing embers, historic Old Faithful Inn was saved by a rooftop sprinkler system.

For more than an hour, the fire roared and crackled around the village. It jumped a barren stretch of land and continued to burn on the other side. Bypassed by the flames, Old Faithful geyser erupted right on schedule. Its spray mixed with the ash-laden air and drained away, a gray slurry.

When the smoke finally cleared, twenty structures on the outskirts of the village—mostly cabins and storage buildings—lay in smoldering ruins. But Old Faithful Inn and the other major buildings survived unharmed.

For three more days, fires roared through Yellowstone. Then, on September 11, a light snow fell. In the following days, moist fall weather slowed the flames, and the thick smoke began to break up and drift away. Though fires smoldered for many weeks, the major battle was over.

All through the summer, while the forests and meadows were burning, the animals followed their instincts, and most survived. Small meadow animals, such as squirrels and mice, hid from flames in underground burrows. Large mammals, such as bears and elk, seemed to sense the movement of the fires and wandered away.

Once the flames had passed, wildlife quickly returned to the burned sites. Insects fed on charred trees, and birds snapped up the insects. Squirrels and chipmunks scrounged for seeds. Hawks and owls hunted the small animals that had lost their hiding places.

In recently burned areas, elk licked the ash for minerals (left); squirrels and owls searched for food in the charred forest (right). During the summer of 1988, nearly one-half of Yellowstone was touched by flames.

In moist sites, new plant growth soon poked through the blackened earth, but the nourishing green shoots grew too sparsely to feed all the animals. Already lean from grazing on drought-stricken land, deer, bison, and elk could not build up thick fat reserves. They faced a difficult winter.

By late November, heavy snows chilled Yellowstone. The seven previous winters had been mild, and few large mammals had died. Now, bigger-than-normal herds of elk, deer, and bison competed for a smaller-than-normal food supply. Many of these grazing animals began to starve. During storms and cold snaps, hundreds of the very young and the very old died. Their frozen bodies provided food for bears, coyotes, and bald eagles.

Coyotes and other scavenging animals feasted on elk and deer that perished during the harsh winter after the fire.

More animals than usual migrated into neighboring forests and towns in search of food. Outside Yellowstone, park rules did not protect the animals. Hunters killed far more elk and bison than in previous years.

In the spring, melting snow moistened the parched ground of Yellowstone. Unharmed roots of blackened grasses and shrubs absorbed the water. Countless seeds that had survived in the soil swelled with moisture. Many other seeds drifted into the burned areas from nearby patches of healthy vegetation. Together with sunlight and the nutrients from burned wood and underbrush, the water triggered an ancient cycle of regrowth.

Grasses sprouted and wildflowers bloomed. Aspens grew new branches and leaves. Berry bushes blossomed and thrived. Freed from their cones by the fires, lodgepole pine seeds germinated. Among the new flowers and grasses, tiny green pine trees dotted the ash.

The elk and bison that survived the harsh winter fattened up on the rich new growth. Bears feasted on berries, and porcupines nibbled fresh, green grass. Squirrels and mice flourished on the abundance of new seeds. Woodpeckers in search of insects pounded holes in dead trees, creating nesting sites for songbirds.

Within a few growing seasons, a carpet of grasses, flowers, shrubs, and tiny tree seedlings will transform most of Yellowstone's burned areas into lush meadows. These new meadows will provide a bounty of food for the animals.

As the bushes and shrubs continue to grow, they will shade the sun-loving plants beneath them. Gradually the grasses and flowers will die. The lodgepole pine seedlings will poke above the other plants; in a decade, they will be three to four feet high.

Eventually wind will knock down most of the blackened trees. Along streams and rivers, the toppled trunks will support the

A bison grazed on tender new grasses, her calf at her side, as springtime brought renewal to the park.

banks. They will break up the current and improve the habitat for trout and other fish.

The young pines will grow taller and taller, and within forty years new lodgepole forests will replace the forests that burned. The high branches of the pines will grow together and prevent sunlight from reaching the forest floor. In the dim understory, the bushes and shrubs will die; they will no longer provide berries and shoots for hungry animals. The new dense stand of trees will contain little variety of food. Most animals will move on to new meadows created by more recent fires.

Summer wildfires have been changing the landscape of Yellowstone for at least 12,000 years. Most of the time, fires burn relatively small areas and alter the landscape only slightly. But every 250 to 400 years, a combination of drought, strong winds, and fuel buildup produces colossal wildfires that sweep through the aging lodgepole forests and change the landscape more significantly.

Below the surface of Yellowstone, forces far more powerful than wildfire have been shaping the land for millions of years — the forces of volcanism. Long ago, violent volcanic eruptions helped sculpt the mountains and plateaus of this region. Today, volcanic fires still simmer in the form of hot, melted rock two miles underground. The heat from this rock fuels the park's geysers, fumaroles, mudpots, and hot springs.

Someday far in the future, volcanoes will again erupt at Yellowstone. As in the distant past, these underground fires will alter the pattern of mountains and plateaus.

Much sooner, massive wildfires will again roar through Yellowstone. As in the summer of 1988, these surface fires will spark the renewal of meadows and forests.

Geologic wonders such as Minerva Terrace at Mammoth Hot Springs are the work of volcanic forces even more powerful than wildfire.

138

Meet the Authors

Kathryn A. Goldner

Carole G. Vogel

In 1981, Carole Vogel and Kathryn Goldner wrote *Why Mount St. Helens Blew Its Top,* and they have been writing together ever since. They have written books for children, science activity books, and magazine articles. What is it like to write a book with another person? Vogel and Goldner say that when they work together, they learn from each other. They also help each other over the rough places.

One of the hard things about working together, however, is being honest with each other. That is especially true when something written by the other person needs more work. Another problem is deciding whose name comes first on the cover. Vogel and Goldner say that they take turns. So — how will their names appear on their next book?

Hot Ideas

Write a Postcard

Before Your Very Eyes

You are one of the tourists at Old Faithful Inn during the Yellowstone fire. How do you feel? Terrified? Excited? Write a postcard describing your feelings and what you see, smell, and hear. Illustrate your message if you wish.

Write a Want Ad

Smokey the Bear Needs Help!

He needs you to write a want ad for a job fighting forest fires in Yellowstone National Park. In the ad, tell what qualities you are looking for in a firefighter, what skills are needed, and what kind of experience would be helpful. Explain why the job is important so that lots of people will apply.

In Tonight's News

Give a series of progress reports about the Yellowstone fire as if you were a television reporter on the evening news. Try to create a sense of danger and suspense so your audience knows what it feels like to be at the scene of the disaster. You might also perform with a partner and be "co-anchors."

Camping Tips

People camping in the wilderness during hot and dry weather might need some tips. Make a pamphlet or poster explaining what conditions are right for a forest fire and how fires get started by nature and by people. List things that campers can do to avoid starting a forest fire accidentally.

Smoke Jumpers

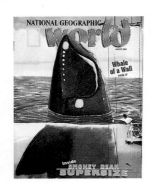

Wherever fires erupt and roads don't go — that's where you'll find smoke jumpers. They parachute into remote mountain wilderness throughout the western United States, including Alaska. Their mission: to prevent small wildfires from growing into large ones. Employed by the Forest Service and the Bureau of Land Management, smoke jumpers have been fighting fires since 1940.

Smoke jumpers land close to a forest fire. They work to prevent the fire from spreading. They rely on obstacles such as rivers, creeks, lakes, and logging roads to help contain the fire. Sometimes they dig a fire line — a dirt path several feet wide through the surrounding vegetation. Their goal is to let the fire burn out while keeping it from reaching the treetops. If it does reach the treetops, there is no way to put out the fire from the ground. A plane carrying fire retardant might be called in to help.

Once the fire is out, smoke jumpers watch for smoke and feel chunks of timber. They must make sure that no areas are still hot. They call this part of their job mopping up.

Smoke jumpers spend sleepless nights listening to a forest fire roaring in the distance. They breathe thick smoke, work up a terrible sweat, and get covered by dirt and ash. At the end of a mission, smoke jumpers have aching bodies. They may face a 20-mile hike to get home. Smoke jumpers have a dangerous but vital job — they save millions of acres of forestland every year.

BY JANICE KOCH

Rocky Touchdown A mountain slope presents a challenge to a smoke jumper. This one landed face down. Knowing how to land on different kinds of terrain — thick forests, steep hills, lakes — is an essential smoke jumper skill.

All Geared Up and Ready to Go

Smoke jumper Margarita Phillips is well suited to fight a fire. Smoke jumpers put together and repair their own gear — except for their boots and helmets. The equipment Phillips jumps with weighs 85 pounds.

MAIN PARACHUTE

Within five seconds of leaving the plane, a smoke jumper's parachute opens. It is carried inside a backpack.

HELMET

A motorcycle helmet has a protective metal face guard.

RESERVE CHUTE

If the main parachute does not open, the reserve chute gets pulled into service.

JUMPSUIT

The heavily padded jumpsuit is made of the same material as bulletproof vests worn by police officers. Smoke jumpers wear fire-resistant clothing underneath.

LEG POCKETS

Inside go candy bars, long johns, and the "bird's nest" — looped nylon strap (shown on top of the pack-out bag) that smoke jumpers use to descend if they land in a tree.

PACK-OUT BAG

Tucked away in a jumpsuit, this bag is empty at first. Most fire fighting equipment is dropped to the ground in a separate container. Once a fire is out, a smoke jumper puts the equipment in the bag so it can be carried out.

From August 1994 issue of *National Geographic World*. Copyright © 1994 by *National Geographic World*. *World* is the official magazine for Junior Members of the National Geographic Society. Reprinted by permission.

Native American

Keepers of the Earth

The native people of North America speak of their relationship to the Earth in terms of family. The Earth is not something to be bought and sold, something to be used and mistreated. It is, quite simply, the source of our lives — our Mother. And the rest of Creation, all around us, shares in that family relationship. The Okanagan people of the Pacific Northwest speak of the Earth as Mother, the Sun as Father and the animals as our brothers and sisters. This view of the world was held by the Navajo and the Abenaki, the Sioux and the Anishinabe and most of the aboriginal people of this continent. They saw their role on this Earth not as rulers of creation, but as beings entrusted with a very special mission — to maintain the natural balance, to take care of our Mother, to be Keepers of the Earth.

Stories

told by Joseph Bruchac

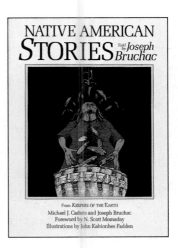

NATIVE AMERICAN
STORIES *Told by Joseph Bruchac*

From KEEPERS OF THE EARTH
Michael J. Caduto and Joseph Bruchac
Foreword by N. Scott Momaday
Illustrations by John Kahionhes Fadden

Birdfoot's Grampa

The old man
must have stopped our car
two dozen times to climb out
and gather into his hands
the small toads blinded
by our lights and leaping,
live drops of rain.

The rain was falling,
a mist about his white hair
and I kept saying
you can't save them all,
accept it, get back in
we've got places to go.

But, leathery hands full
of wet brown life,
knee deep in the summer
roadside grass,
he just smiled and said
*they have places to go to
too.*

Gluscabi and the Wind

an Abenaki legend

Long ago, Gluscabi lived with his grandmother, Woodchuck,
in a small lodge beside the big water.

One day Gluscabi was walking around when he looked out
and saw some ducks in the bay.

"I think it is time to go hunt some ducks," he said. So he took
his bow and arrows and got into his canoe. He began to paddle
out into the bay and as he paddled he sang:

> Ki yo wah ji neh
> yo ho hey ho
> Ki yo wah ji neh
> Ki yo wah ji neh.

But a wind came up and it turned his canoe
and blew him back to shore. Once again
Gluscabi began to paddle out and this
time he sang his song a little harder:

Eagle

KI YO WAH JI NEH
YO HO HEY HO
KI YO WAH JI NEH
KI YO WAH JI NEH.

But again the wind came and blew him back to shore. Four times he tried to paddle out into the bay and four times he failed. He was not happy. He went back to the lodge of his grandmother and walked right in, even though there was a stick leaning across the door, which meant that the person inside was doing some work and did not want to be disturbed.

"Grandmother," Gluscabi said, "what makes the wind blow?"

Grandmother Woodchuck looked up from her work. "Gluscabi," she said, "why do you want to know?"

Then Gluscabi answered her just as every child in the world does when they are asked such a question.

"Because," he said.

Grandmother Woodchuck looked at him. "Ah, Gluscabi," she said. "Whenever you ask such questions I feel there is going to be trouble. And perhaps I should not tell you. But I know that you are so stubborn you will never stop asking until I answer you. So I shall tell you. Far from here, on top of the tallest mountain, a great bird stands. This bird is named Wuchowsen, and when he flaps his wings he makes the wind blow."

"Eh-hey, Grandmother," said Gluscabi, "I see. Now how would one find that place where the Wind Eagle stands?"

Again Grandmother Woodchuck looked at Gluscabi. "Ah, Gluscabi," she said, "once again I feel that perhaps I should not tell you. But I know that you are very stubborn and would never stop asking. So, I shall tell you. If you walk always facing the wind you will come to the place where Wuchowsen stands."

"Thank you, Grandmother," said Gluscabi. He stepped out of the lodge and faced into the wind and began to walk.

He walked across the fields and through the woods and the wind blew hard. He walked through the valleys and into the hills and the wind blew harder still. He came to the foothills and began to climb and the wind still blew harder. Now the foothills were becoming mountains and the wind was very strong. Soon there were no longer any trees and the wind was very, very strong. The wind was so strong that it blew off Gluscabi's moccasins. But he was very stubborn and he kept on walking, leaning into the wind. Now the wind was so strong that it blew off his shirt, but he kept on walking. Now the wind was so strong that it blew off all his clothes and he was naked, but he still kept walking. Now the wind was so strong that it blew off his hair, but Gluscabi still kept walking, facing into the wind. The wind was so strong that it blew off his eyebrows, but still he continued to walk. Now the wind was so strong that he could hardly

stand. He had to pull himself along by grabbing hold of the boulders. But there, on the peak ahead of him, he could see a great bird slowly flapping its wings. It was Wuchowsen, the Wind Eagle.

Gluscabi took a deep breath. "GRAND-FATHER!" he shouted.

The Wind Eagle stopped flapping his wings and looked around. "Who calls me Grandfather?" he said.

Gluscabi stood up. "It's me, Grandfather. I just came up here to tell you that you do a very good job making the wind blow."

The Wind Eagle puffed out his chest with pride. "You mean like this?" he said and flapped his wings even harder. The wind which he made was so strong that it lifted Gluscabi right off his feet, and he would have been blown right off the mountain had he not reached out and grabbed a boulder again.

"GRANDFATHER!!!" Gluscabi shouted again.

The Wind Eagle stopped flapping his wings. "Yesss?" he said.

Gluscabi stood up and came closer to Wuchowsen.

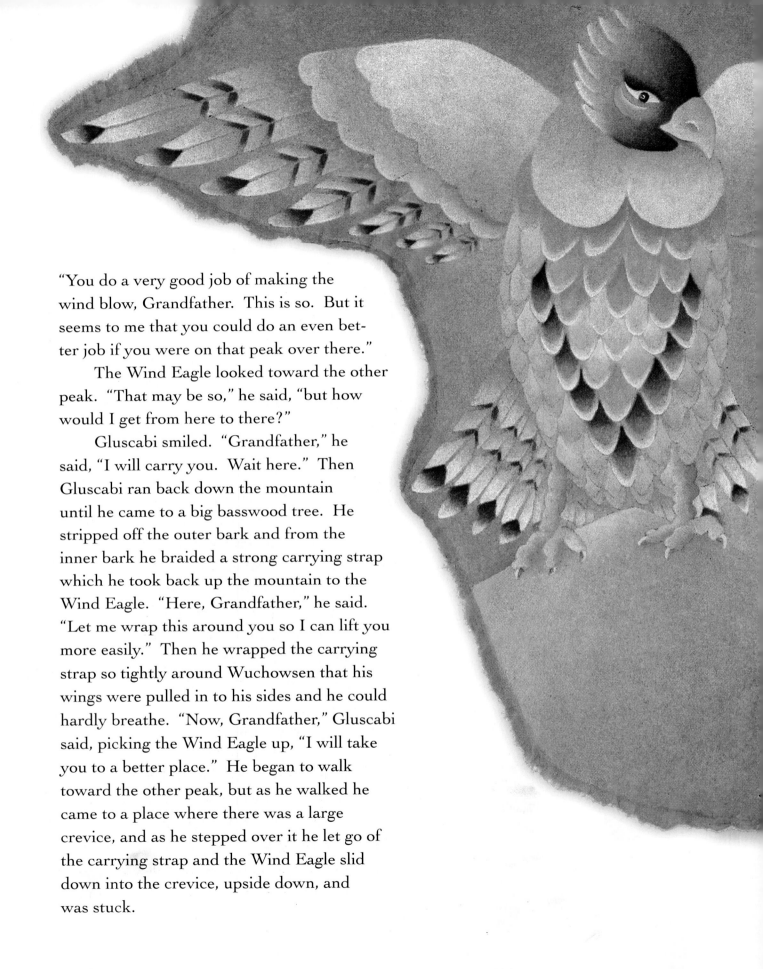

"You do a very good job of making the wind blow, Grandfather. This is so. But it seems to me that you could do an even better job if you were on that peak over there."

The Wind Eagle looked toward the other peak. "That may be so," he said, "but how would I get from here to there?"

Gluscabi smiled. "Grandfather," he said, "I will carry you. Wait here." Then Gluscabi ran back down the mountain until he came to a big basswood tree. He stripped off the outer bark and from the inner bark he braided a strong carrying strap which he took back up the mountain to the Wind Eagle. "Here, Grandfather," he said. "Let me wrap this around you so I can lift you more easily." Then he wrapped the carrying strap so tightly around Wuchowsen that his wings were pulled in to his sides and he could hardly breathe. "Now, Grandfather," Gluscabi said, picking the Wind Eagle up, "I will take you to a better place." He began to walk toward the other peak, but as he walked he came to a place where there was a large crevice, and as he stepped over it he let go of the carrying strap and the Wind Eagle slid down into the crevice, upside down, and was stuck.

"Now," Gluscabi said, "it is time to hunt some ducks."

He walked back down the mountain and there was no wind at all. He walked till he came to the treeline and still no wind blew. He walked down to the foothills and down to the hills and the valleys and still there was no wind. He walked through the forests and through the fields, and the wind did not blow at all. He walked and walked until he came back to the lodge by the water, and by now all his hair had grown back. He put on some fine new clothing and a new pair of moccasins and took his bow and arrows and went down to the bay and climbed into his boat to hunt ducks. He paddled out into the water and sang his canoeing song:

> Ki yo wah ji neh
> yo ho hey ho
> Ki yo wah ji neh
> Ki yo wah ji neh.

But the air was very hot and still and he began to sweat. The air was so still and hot that it was hard to breathe. Soon the water began to grow dirty and smell bad and there was so much foam on the water he could hardly paddle. He was not pleased at all and he returned to the shore and went straight to his grandmother's lodge and walked in.

"Grandmother," he said, "what is wrong? The air is hot and still and it is making me sweat and it is hard to breathe. The water is dirty and covered with foam. I cannot hunt ducks at all like this."

Grandmother Woodchuck looked up at Gluscabi. "Gluscabi," she said, "what have you done now?"

And Gluscabi answered just as every child in the world answers when asked that question. "Oh, nothing," he said.

"Gluscabi," said Grandmother Woodchuck again, "tell me what you have done."

Then Gluscabi told her about going to visit the Wind Eagle and what he had done to stop the wind.

"Oh, Gluscabi," said Grandmother Woodchuck, "will you never learn? Tabaldak, The Owner, set the Wind Eagle on that mountain to make the wind because we need the wind. The wind keeps the air cool and clean. The wind brings the clouds which give us rain to wash the Earth. The wind moves the waters and keeps them fresh and sweet. Without the wind, life

will not be good for us, for our children or our children's children."

Gluscabi nodded his head. "Kaamoji, Grandmother," he said. "I understand."

Then he went outside. He faced in the direction from which the wind had once come and began to walk. He walked through the fields and through the forests and the wind did not blow and he felt very hot. He walked through the valleys and up the hills and there was no wind and it was hard for him to breathe. He came to the foothills and began to climb and he was very hot and sweaty indeed. At last he came to the mountain where the Wind Eagle once stood and he went and looked down into the crevice. There was Wuchowsen, the Wind Eagle, wedged upside down.

"Uncle?" Gluscabi called.

The Wind Eagle looked up as best he could. "Who calls me Uncle?" he said.

"It is Gluscabi, Uncle. I'm up here. But what are you doing down there?"

"Oh, Gluscabi," said the Wind Eagle, "a very ugly naked man with no hair told me that he would take me to the other peak so that I could do a better job of making the wind blow. He tied my wings and picked me up, but as he stepped over this crevice he dropped me in and I am stuck. And I am not comfortable here at all."

"Ah, Grandfath . . . er, Uncle, I will get you out."

Then Gluscabi climbed down into the crevice. He pulled the Wind Eagle free and placed him back on his mountain and untied his wings.

"Uncle," Gluscabi said, "it is good that the wind should blow sometimes and other times it is good that it should be still."

The Wind Eagle looked at Gluscabi and then nodded his head. "Grandson," he said, "I hear what you say."

So it is that sometimes there is wind and sometimes it is still to this very day. And so the story goes.

People throw away . . .

MUCH TOO MUCH

In one year, people in the United States throw away enough trash to fill a bumper-to-bumper line of garbage trucks reaching halfway to the moon.

Every year, forty million acres of tropical rain forest are destroyed worldwide. That's an area larger than the state of California.

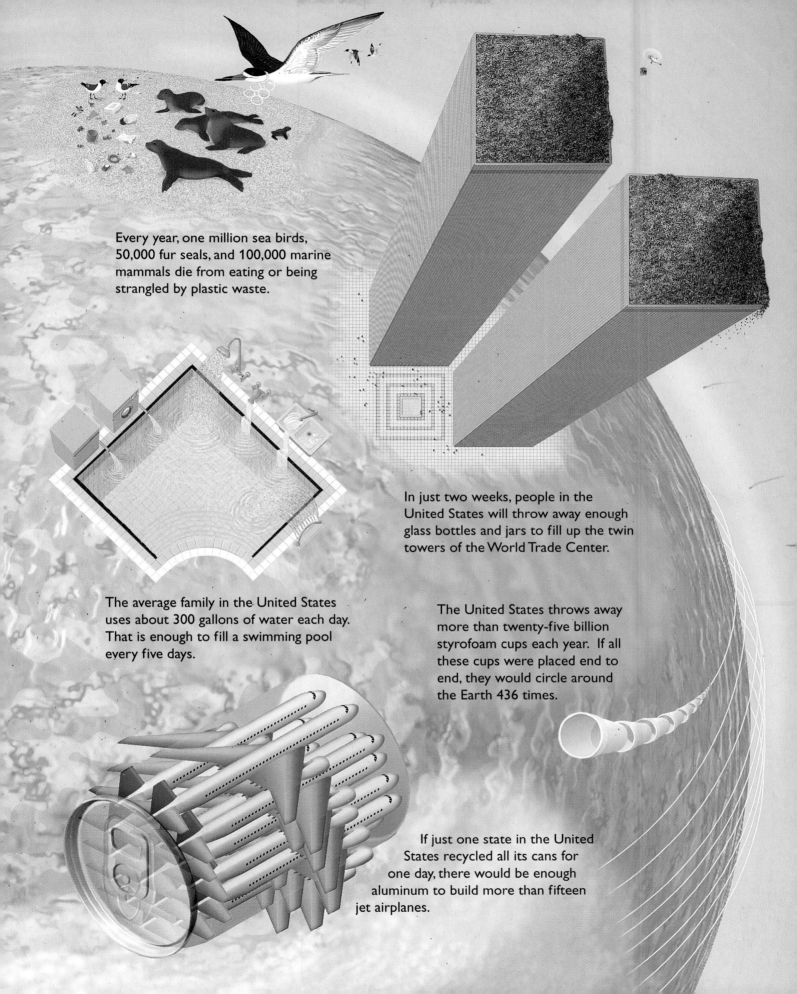

Every year, one million sea birds, 50,000 fur seals, and 100,000 marine mammals die from eating or being strangled by plastic waste.

In just two weeks, people in the United States will throw away enough glass bottles and jars to fill up the twin towers of the World Trade Center.

The average family in the United States uses about 300 gallons of water each day. That is enough to fill a swimming pool every five days.

The United States throws away more than twenty-five billion styrofoam cups each year. If all these cups were placed end to end, they would circle around the Earth 436 times.

If just one state in the United States recycled all its cans for one day, there would be enough aluminum to build more than fifteen jet airplanes.

We Are Plooters

by Jack Prelutsky

illustrated by Paul O. Zelinsky

We are Plooters,
We don't care,
We make messes
Everywhere,
We strip forests
Bare of trees,
We dump garbage
In the seas.

    We are Plooters,
    We enjoy
    Finding beauty
    To destroy,
    We intrude
    Where creatures thrive,
    Soon there's little
    Left alive.

        Underwater,
        Underground,
        Nothing's safe
        When we're around,
        We spew poisons
        In the air,
        We are Plooters,
        We don't care.

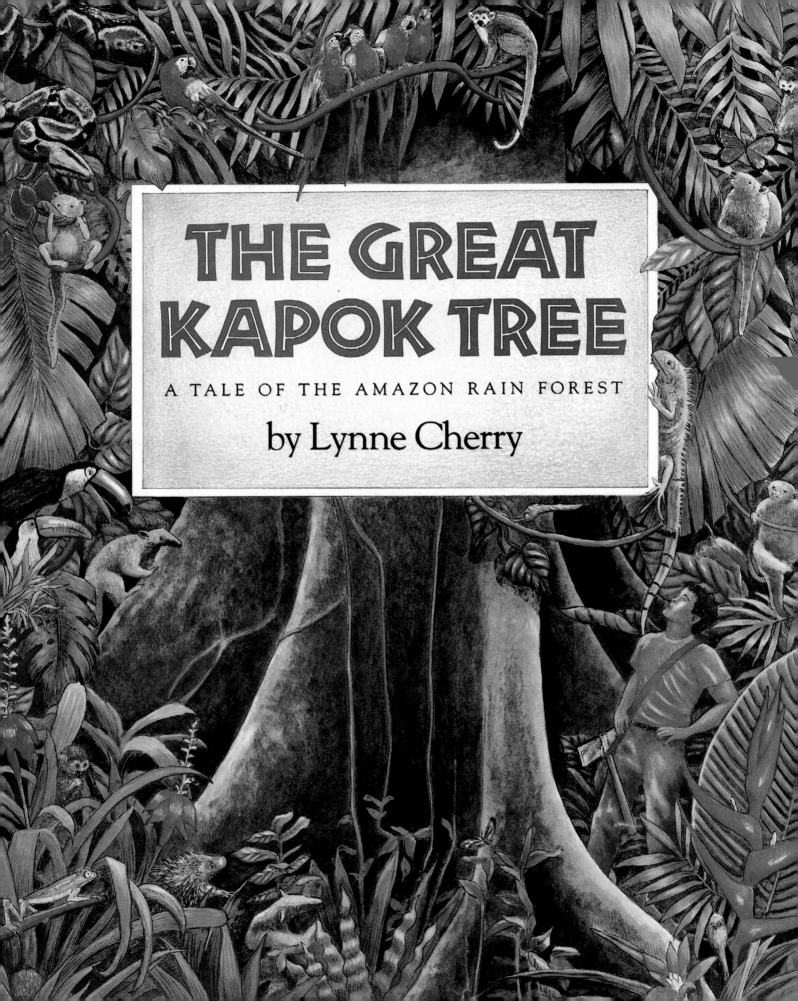

THE GREAT KAPOK TREE

A TALE OF THE AMAZON RAIN FOREST

by Lynne Cherry

In the Amazon rain forest it is always hot, and in that heat everything grows, and grows, and grows. The tops of the trees in the rain forest are called the canopy. The canopy is a sunny place that touches the sky. The animals that live there like lots of light. Colorful parrots fly from tree to tree. Monkeys leap from branch to branch. The bottom of the rain forest is called the understory. The animals that live in the understory like darkness. There, silent snakes curl around hanging vines. Graceful jaguars watch and wait.

And in this steamy environment the great Kapok tree shoots up through the forest and emerges above the canopy.

This is the story of a community of animals that live in one such tree in the rain forest.

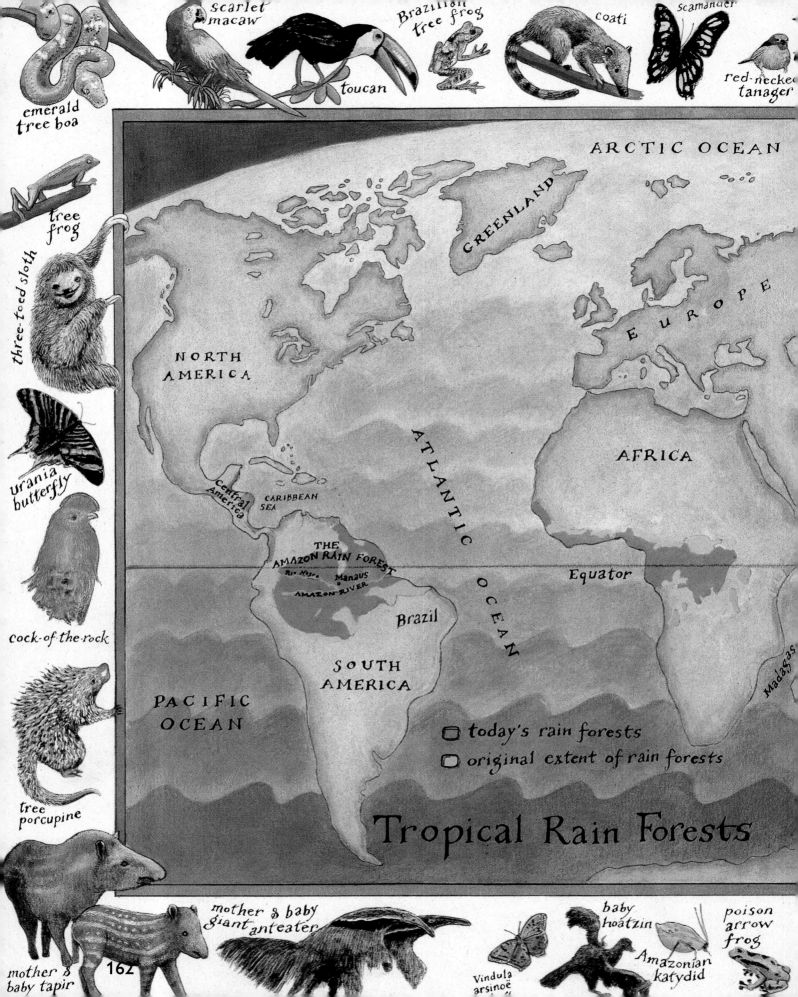

emerald
tree boa

scarlet
macaw

toucan

Brazilian
tree frog

coati

scamander

red-necked
tanager

tree
frog

three-toed sloth

urania
butterfly

cock-of-the-rock

tree
porcupine

mother &
baby tapir

162

mother & baby
giant anteater

Vindula
arsinoë

Amazonian
katydid

baby
hoatzin

poison
arrow
frog

ARCTIC OCEAN

GREENLAND

EUROPE

NORTH
AMERICA

AFRICA

Central
America

CARIBBEAN
SEA

ATLANTIC
OCEAN

THE
AMAZON RAIN FOREST

Rio Negro   Manaus
AMAZON RIVER

Equator

Brazil

SOUTH
AMERICA

PACIFIC
OCEAN

Madagascar

☐ today's rain forests
☐ original extent of rain forests

Tropical Rain Forests

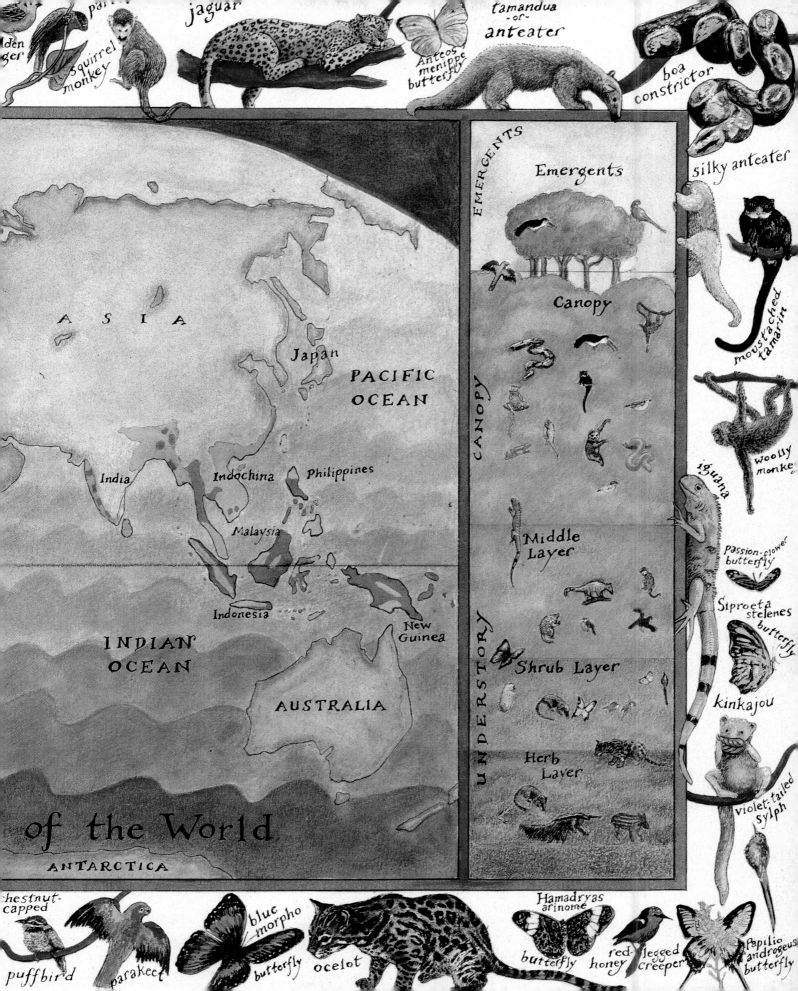

jaguar

tamandua
~or~
anteater

Anteos
menippe
butterfly

boa
constrictor

squirrel
monkey

silky anteater

EMERGENTS

Emergents

moustached
tamarin

CANOPY

Canopy

iguana

woolly
monkey

A S I A

Japan

PACIFIC
OCEAN

passion-flower
butterfly

Middle
Layer

Siproeta
stelenes
butterfly

India   Indochina   Philippines

UNDERSTORY

kinkajou

Malaysia

Shrub Layer

Indonesia

New
Guinea

INDIAN
OCEAN

Herb
Layer

AUSTRALIA

violet-tailed
Sylph

of the World

ANTARCTICA

chestnut-
capped

blue
morpho

Hamadryas
arinome

puffbird   parakeet   butterfly   ocelot   butterfly   honey creeper

red-legged

Papilio
androgeus
butterfly

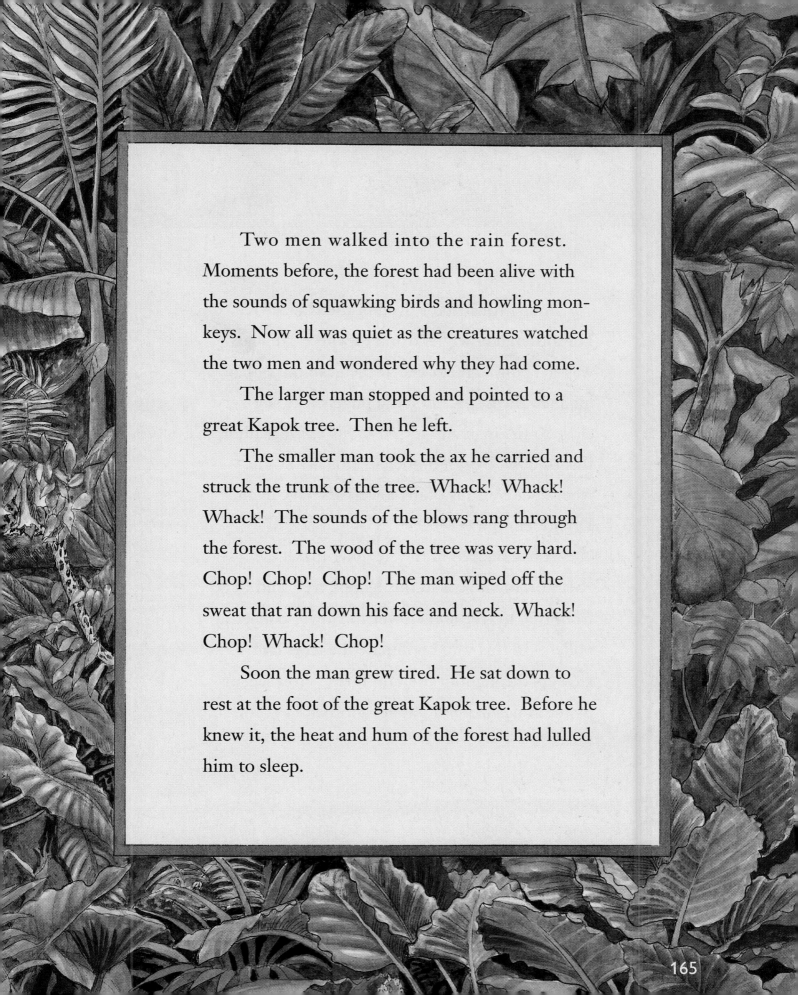

Two men walked into the rain forest. Moments before, the forest had been alive with the sounds of squawking birds and howling monkeys. Now all was quiet as the creatures watched the two men and wondered why they had come.

The larger man stopped and pointed to a great Kapok tree. Then he left.

The smaller man took the ax he carried and struck the trunk of the tree. Whack! Whack! Whack! The sounds of the blows rang through the forest. The wood of the tree was very hard. Chop! Chop! Chop! The man wiped off the sweat that ran down his face and neck. Whack! Chop! Whack! Chop!

Soon the man grew tired. He sat down to rest at the foot of the great Kapok tree. Before he knew it, the heat and hum of the forest had lulled him to sleep.

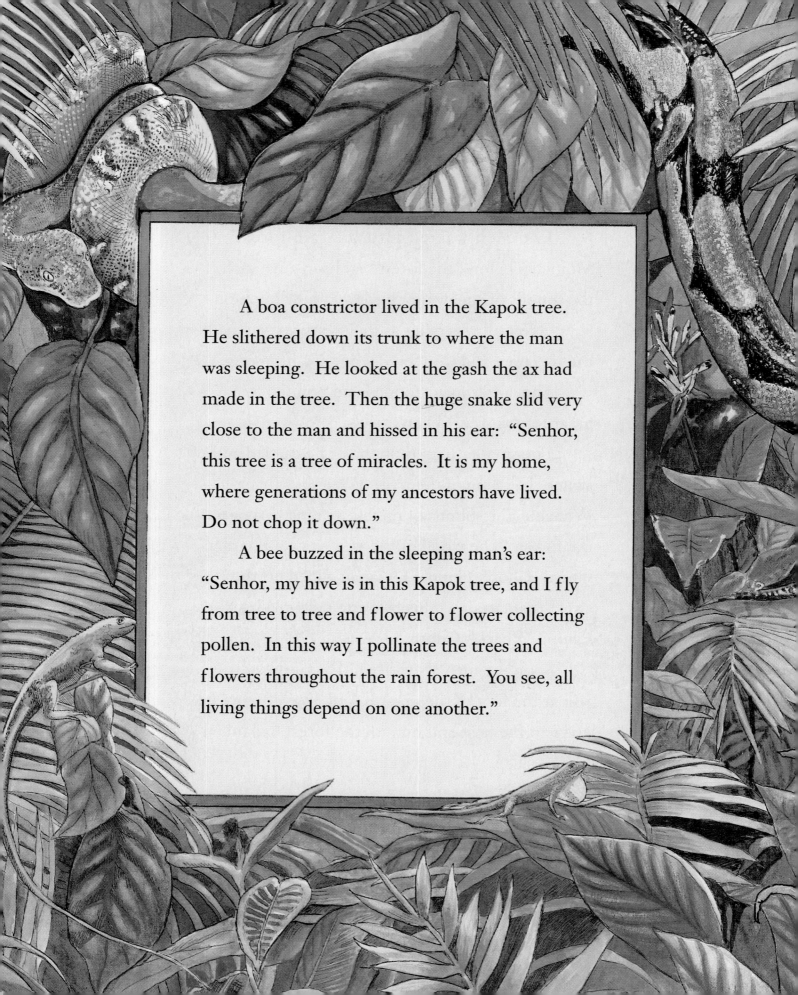

A boa constrictor lived in the Kapok tree. He slithered down its trunk to where the man was sleeping. He looked at the gash the ax had made in the tree. Then the huge snake slid very close to the man and hissed in his ear: "Senhor, this tree is a tree of miracles. It is my home, where generations of my ancestors have lived. Do not chop it down."

A bee buzzed in the sleeping man's ear: "Senhor, my hive is in this Kapok tree, and I fly from tree to tree and flower to flower collecting pollen. In this way I pollinate the trees and flowers throughout the rain forest. You see, all living things depend on one another."

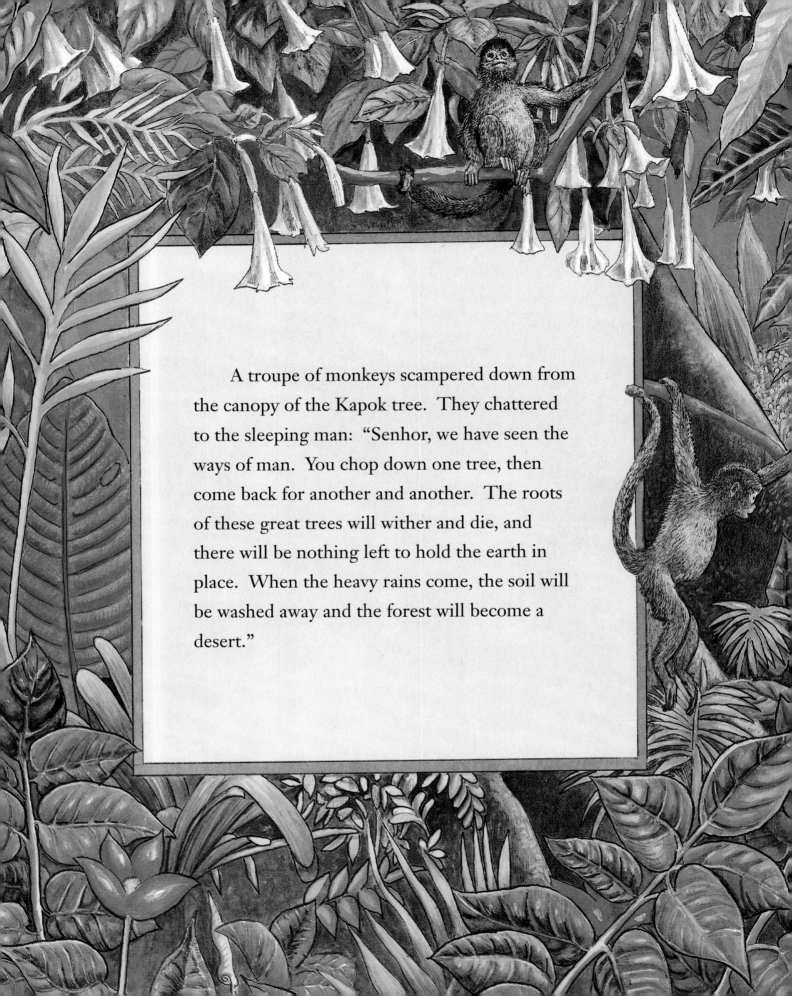

A troupe of monkeys scampered down from the canopy of the Kapok tree. They chattered to the sleeping man: "Senhor, we have seen the ways of man. You chop down one tree, then come back for another and another. The roots of these great trees will wither and die, and there will be nothing left to hold the earth in place. When the heavy rains come, the soil will be washed away and the forest will become a desert."

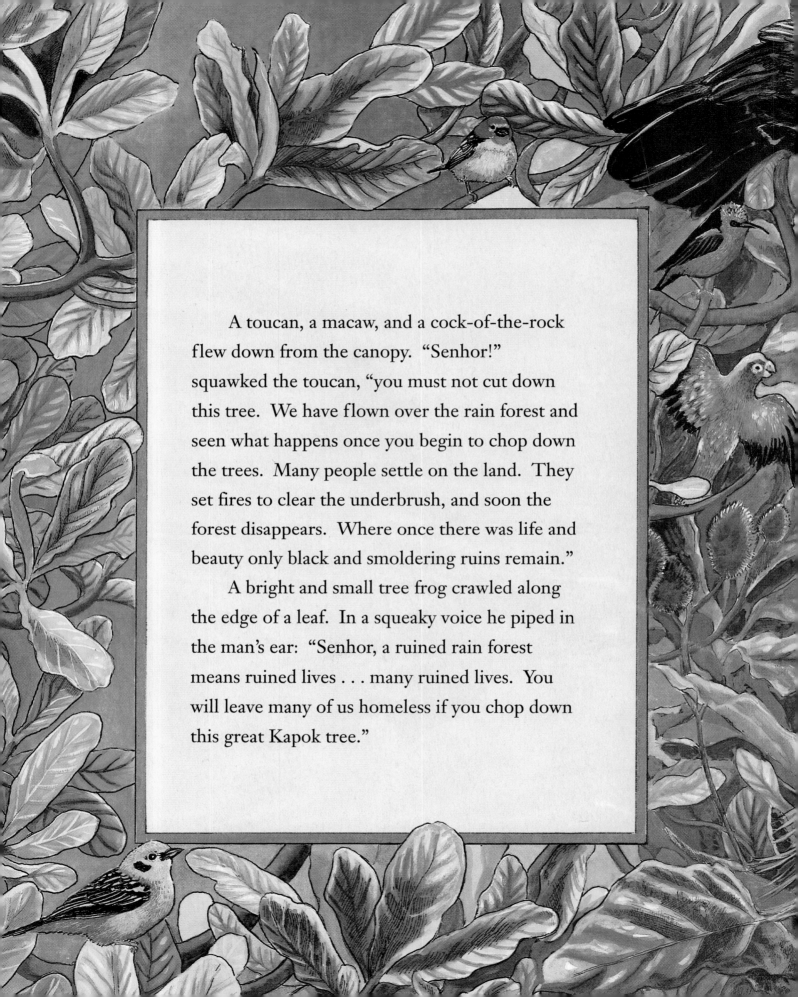

A toucan, a macaw, and a cock-of-the-rock flew down from the canopy. "Senhor!" squawked the toucan, "you must not cut down this tree. We have flown over the rain forest and seen what happens once you begin to chop down the trees. Many people settle on the land. They set fires to clear the underbrush, and soon the forest disappears. Where once there was life and beauty only black and smoldering ruins remain."

A bright and small tree frog crawled along the edge of a leaf. In a squeaky voice he piped in the man's ear: "Senhor, a ruined rain forest means ruined lives . . . many ruined lives. You will leave many of us homeless if you chop down this great Kapok tree."

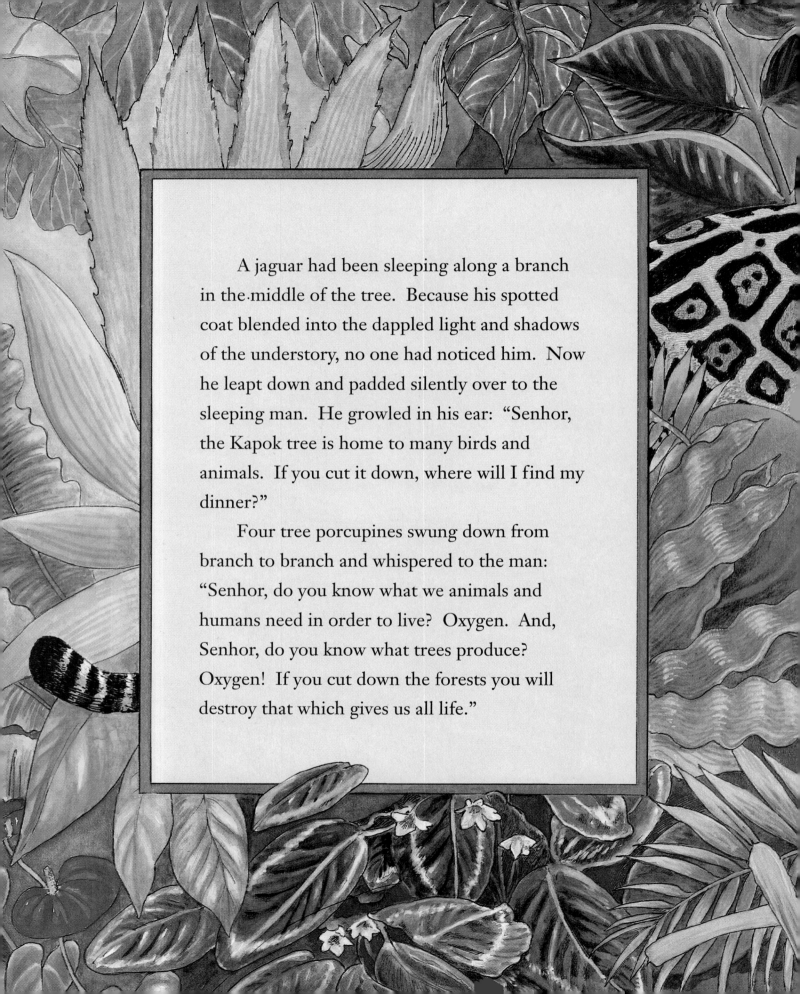

A jaguar had been sleeping along a branch in the middle of the tree. Because his spotted coat blended into the dappled light and shadows of the understory, no one had noticed him. Now he leapt down and padded silently over to the sleeping man. He growled in his ear: "Senhor, the Kapok tree is home to many birds and animals. If you cut it down, where will I find my dinner?"

Four tree porcupines swung down from branch to branch and whispered to the man: "Senhor, do you know what we animals and humans need in order to live? Oxygen. And, Senhor, do you know what trees produce? Oxygen! If you cut down the forests you will destroy that which gives us all life."

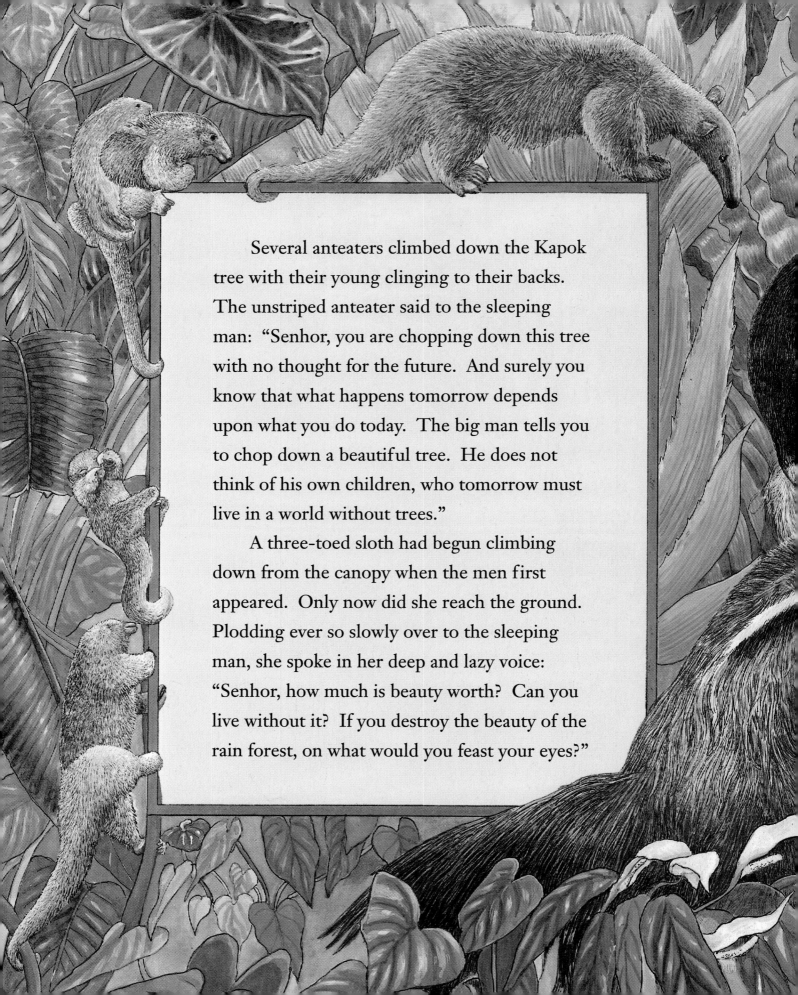

Several anteaters climbed down the Kapok tree with their young clinging to their backs. The unstriped anteater said to the sleeping man: "Senhor, you are chopping down this tree with no thought for the future. And surely you know that what happens tomorrow depends upon what you do today. The big man tells you to chop down a beautiful tree. He does not think of his own children, who tomorrow must live in a world without trees."

A three-toed sloth had begun climbing down from the canopy when the men first appeared. Only now did she reach the ground. Plodding ever so slowly over to the sleeping man, she spoke in her deep and lazy voice: "Senhor, how much is beauty worth? Can you live without it? If you destroy the beauty of the rain forest, on what would you feast your eyes?"

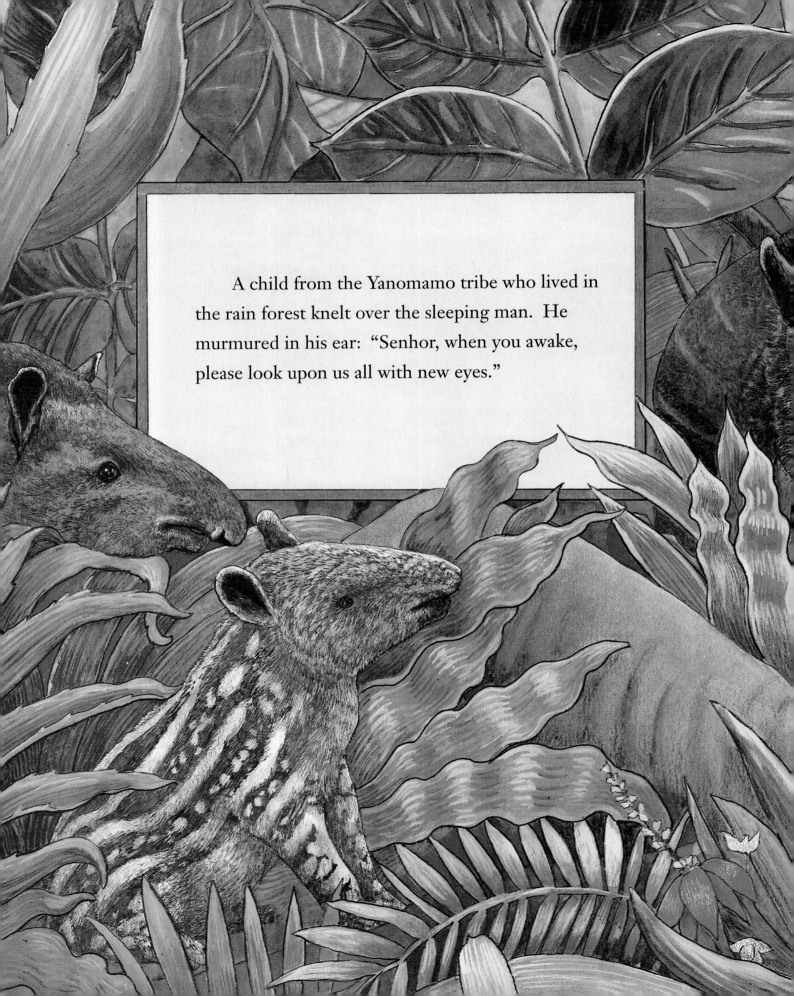

A child from the Yanomamo tribe who lived in the rain forest knelt over the sleeping man. He murmured in his ear: "Senhor, when you awake, please look upon us all with new eyes."

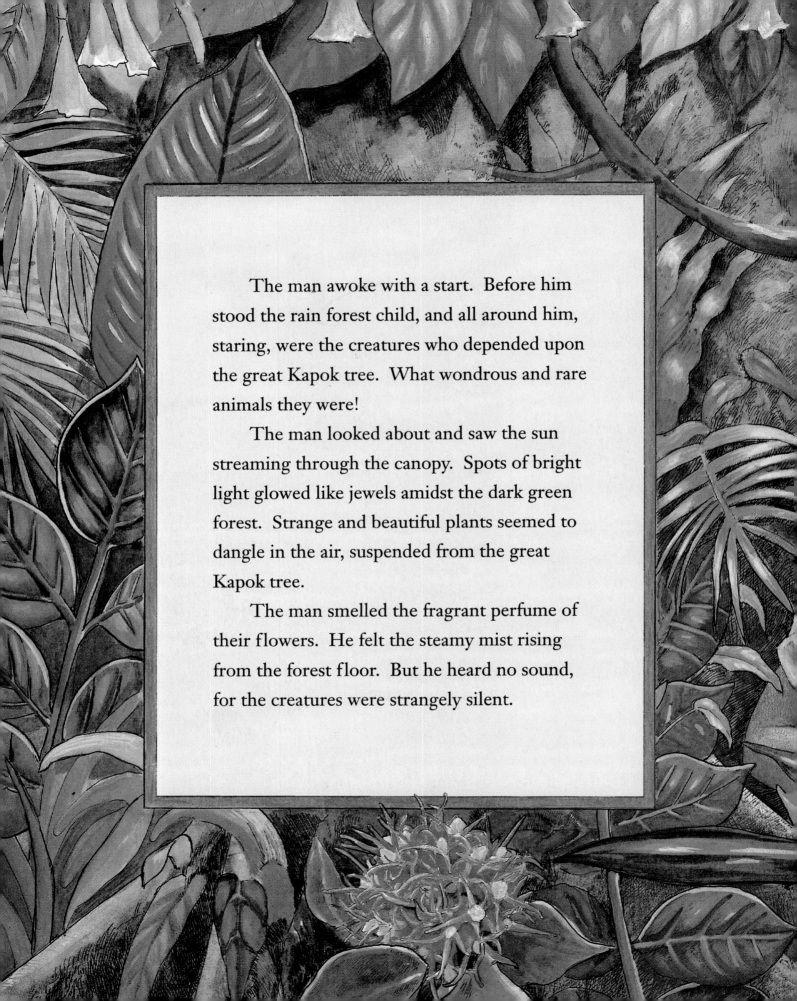

The man awoke with a start. Before him stood the rain forest child, and all around him, staring, were the creatures who depended upon the great Kapok tree. What wondrous and rare animals they were!

The man looked about and saw the sun streaming through the canopy. Spots of bright light glowed like jewels amidst the dark green forest. Strange and beautiful plants seemed to dangle in the air, suspended from the great Kapok tree.

The man smelled the fragrant perfume of their flowers. He felt the steamy mist rising from the forest floor. But he heard no sound, for the creatures were strangely silent.

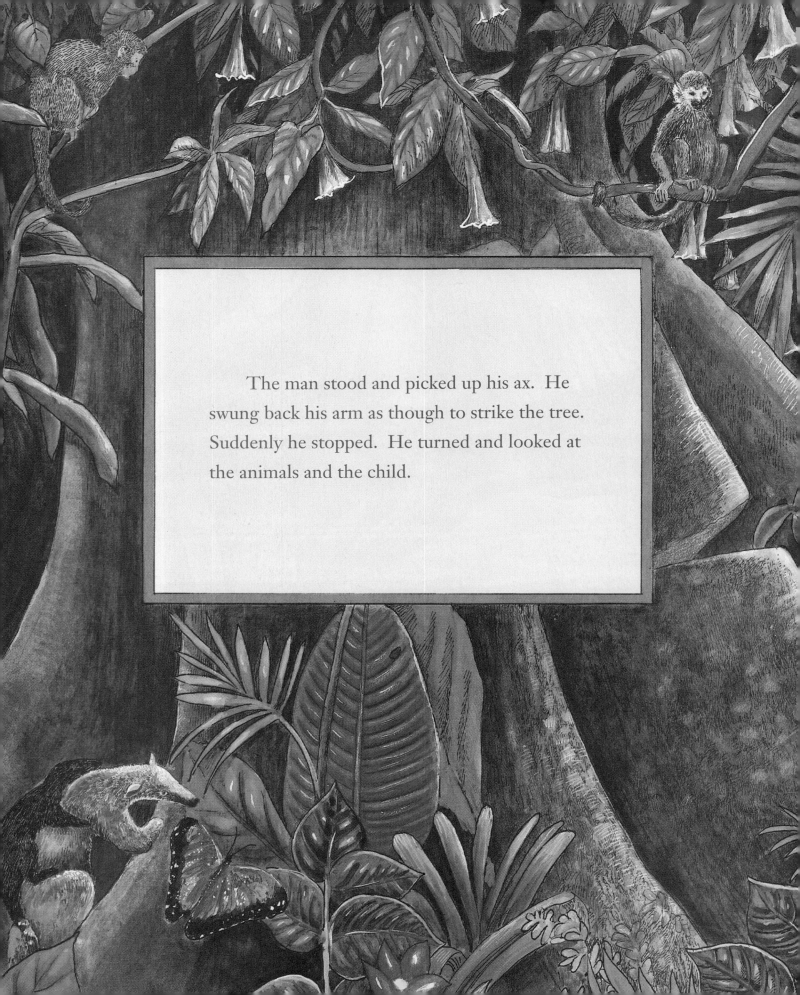

The man stood and picked up his ax. He swung back his arm as though to strike the tree. Suddenly he stopped. He turned and looked at the animals and the child.

He hesitated. Then he dropped the ax and
walked out of the rain forest.

Meet
LYNNE CHERRY

Lynne Cherry has strong feelings about preserving and protecting the environment. "Nature is the most beautiful thing in the world," she says. "That's why it kills me to see it destroyed, whether in this country or somewhere else."

She wrote *The Great Kapok Tree* to spread the alarm about the endangered Amazon rain forest. To prepare for her work on *The Great Kapok Tree,* Cherry visited the Amazon rain forest in Brazil to study the animals that live there and the plants that grow there. She wanted her drawings to be as accurate as possible.

Cherry continues to work hard to make people more aware of our fragile environment. Her book *A River Ran Wild* tells the true story of the troubled Nashua River in Massachusetts.

SPREAD

ACT OUT THE STORY

Buzz Like a Bee! Slither Like a Snake!

Perform *The Great Kapok Tree* with a group of class-mates. Each person can play a character from the story. Remember that each animal and the boy have special messages, and unique ways of delivering the messages to the man. Rehearse your play, and then perform it for the rest of your class.

MAKE A POSTER

"Preserve and Protect"

Spread the word! Pick one of the animals' messages to the man and turn it into a "Preserve and Protect" poster to help save the rain forest. Summarize the message as a slogan. Then make a poster featuring the animal and its slogan.

THE WORD

"Boy, Was I . . ."

How do you think the man felt when he woke up surrounded by all those animals? What thoughts went through his mind? Write a paragraph that describes what the man might have been thinking.

COMPARE AND CONTRAST

Two Forests

You've "visited" two forests — the rain forest in *The Great Kapok Tree* and the forest in *The Great Yellowstone Fire.* How are the forests similar? How are they different? Using the illustrations and photos to help you, write a compare-contrast paragraph or hold a discussion with your partner or a group.

Where Will the Waste Stop?

A Persuasive Essay by Megan Hunter

Megan had some ideas for solving a problem that she saw in her town. She wrote this essay to persuade other people to help.

Megan Hunter
Washington Elementary School
Fargo, North Dakota

"I like to write because it is fun, and it is a good way to express your thoughts without talking," said Megan. "I like to talk — don't get me wrong — but writing is just as great!" Megan wrote this essay when she was in the fourth grade.

In addition to writing, Megan likes to sing, act, swim, and read. She also enjoys downhill skiing, watching movies, and spending time with her family, friends, and pets.

Where Will the Waste Stop?

Landfills are a big problem. As I was riding in the car, I saw trash blowing, but not just anywhere. It was blowing outside of the landfill. It just blows out of the landfill and litters the places around it.

Even for a town like mine with 75,000 people in it, landfills are filling fast. Of the 180 acres of landfill space we have, 40 acres are being used. It is expected to be too full to hold trash in 25 to 30 years.

It makes me ashamed of my city, especially when I think that I live in a clean town. How can we attract visitors to our town when one of the borders is a dirty landfill?

I feel that something needs to be done before our city is completely bordered by trash. The things we can do to help are numerous. Here are three of them. One: Call the city government and ask about building fences around the landfill. Two: Recycle. The less trash there is, the less trash there will be blowing around, and the slower the landfill will fill up. Three: Call the city government and remind them that some people do not recycle. Ask if the workers at the landfill would recycle everything that is recyclable. Then there will be more space in the landfill, and it will last longer.

Remember — if you put your mind to something, you can accomplish it.

ACT

NOW

Kids Making

A Difference

Kids all over are

working to save the

Earth. Here are four

examples from *3-2-1*

***Contact* magazine.**

Hope for KOPE

Kids at the Hawthorne School in Salt Lake City, UT, started a club called KOPE — Kids Organized to Protect the Environment. For the last three years, they've been working to turn a polluted creek bed into a nature park.

Half hidden in trees, the creek was full of tires, cement blocks and trash. The kids named the place "Hidden Hollow" and decided to clean it up. At the first clean-up event, 300 kids showed up to volunteer!

KOPE kids turned an old creek bed into a nature park.

"We wanted a place where kids can study plants in their natural environment," 10-year-old Tami Curtis told CONTACT.

The KOPE kids then learned that land developers had plans to turn the area into a parking lot. So they organized a "Hope for Hidden Hollow Conference." They invited kids from schools all across the city to help save the Hollow.

"We made a slide show to let people know what was happening," says Tami. She gave the developers a tour of the area to get them to change their minds. That didn't work.

But the KOPE kids didn't give up hope. They signed petitions, talked to local business people and went to city council meetings. And guess what? The council agreed to turn the area into a park! This spring, the kids will help plant shrubs, trees and flowers in the three-acre nature park.

"We didn't give up because we wanted a better place to live," says Tami. "I think our work shows other kids that they can make a difference."

Dynamic Duo

Rebecca and Phillippa Herbert of West Covina, CA, have also done tons for their neighborhood.

The two sisters discovered that many of their neighbors weren't recycling their trash. People thought it was a hassle to take the garbage to a local recycling center.

"So we thought, 'What if we start a recycling center in our front yard?'" Rebecca says. "That way, it would be easy for people to recycle."

Rebecca, 11, and Phillippa, 13, handed out information flyers in their neighborhood. The flyer said "Please help us recycle and save the Earth." It told when their center would be open. And it included tips on how to separate trash.

"We got cardboard boxes and labeled them Glass, Newspapers and Metals," Phillippa explains. "Every Saturday, we sat by the boxes and

waited for people to drop off their trash."

The girls would then bring the boxes to a local recycling center. But they don't recycle trash in their front yard anymore. Their neighbors now do it on their own. Thanks to the girls, people recycle tons of stuff that otherwise would end up in landfills.

What's Up?

Kids at the Upper Bucks Vocational Technical School in Pennsylvania believe in kid power, too. They're building an 85-foot-tall windmill — right in front of their school!

The kids have high hopes for the windmill. They say it will produce enough electricity to power the electronic billboard in their school cafeteria, as well as their school radio station!

They also plan to use solar energy to help the windmill produce even more power. "We're going to put up the solar panels at the base of the windmill," says Jason Overholt. He's one of the student builders. "That way, we can also power the lights in our parking lot."

The windmill will save lots of energy, Jason told CONTACT. "Plus, windmills don't pollute the environment."

Kids in Pennsylvania have high hopes for the windmill they're building.

Melanie Essary speaks out against air pollution at a Senate hearing.

S.T.O.P. Starts

Lots of kids are pollution busters. Just ask Russell Essary, 11, of Forest Hills, NY. He and his younger sister Melanie have about 12,000 kids across the U.S. helping them solve pollution problems. They're all members of KiDS S.T.O.P.

Russell first started KiDS S.T.O.P. to battle the shrinking of the ozone layer. (The ozone layer is an invisible shield that protects Earth from the sun's harmful ultraviolet rays.)

Russell found out that the coolant in air conditioners is made of chemicals called CFCs. CFCs destroy the ozone layer. So KiDS S.T.O.P. got to work. They helped get a state law passed. Now all air conditioning fluid must be recycled. (That way, CFCs aren't released into the air.)

When Senator Al Gore (he's now Vice President) heard about the state law, he wrote to KiDS S.T.O.P. "He wanted to make it a national law," Russell says. And that's what happened. It's part of the 1990 Clean Air Act. Better still, CFCs will soon no longer be used.

There's no stopping the eco-kids. As Melanie told CONTACT, "If kids don't save the Earth, who will?"

from an article by Wendy Williams

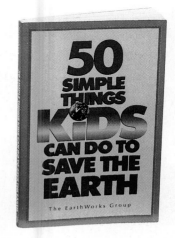

Dream a Better World

**A clean, healthy environment is possible.
It starts with a dream . . . .**

I like to imagine what it would be like if we had no environmental problems. I imagine a beautiful world. The air is clean, there is no such thing as Styrofoam. I imagine I wake up in my own house, eat my usual foods. But while I'm walking to school, I realize that the air seems clean. In school, the water I wash my hands with is clean. When I ask my teacher about pollution, she says there is no such word. I also ask her about the Alaskan oil spill. She says there were never any oil spills. I can't believe it. I ask my friend to pinch me so I can wake up. Then I do wake up. But I want the world to be like my dream.

This was written by Gideon Javna, age nine.

I'm Gideon's uncle and I'm about to be a dad for the first time. I am very excited. But I wonder what the world will be like for my child. Will he or she be able to enjoy the beautiful blue sky and the sound of the ocean at the beach? . . . Or be able to walk in the woods? . . . Or be able to listen to birds singing on a still day? I hope so. That is my dream.

Dreams are the way we decide what we want. We imagine something . . . and then we make it happen. It is an amazing part of being a human being.

So if you care about saving the Earth — and I know you do — then keep dreaming. Let your imagination show you which way to go. Dream a better world.

This was written by John Javna, age forty.

PRIDE IN THE

Many American cities suffer from overcrowding, pollution, and too much garbage. But the young people of City Year are working to change all that.

City Year members are between seventeen and twenty-three years old and are from all different backgrounds. They take pride in working to make their cities better places to live.

City Year members work at full-time jobs in community-service projects such as building houses for the homeless, teaching in schools, planting gardens, cleaning up parks and playgrounds, and helping senior citizens. It's hard work. But City Year members know at the end of each day that they have helped put a little pride back into the communities they serve.

Peggy Johnson of Boston, Massachusetts, joined City Year in 1994, after talking to friends who were already members. She was inspired. So she signed up.

"City Year helps you down the line," Peggy says. "If you want to go to college it helps you get into college. It opens a lot of doors for you."

CITY

Peggy gets up and takes the subway to Boston's City Hall Plaza to meet her City Year corps. "I leave my house at 7:30. I come here, and then I find out what we're going to do today."

"It's good because you get to meet people. For instance, there are people who have already gone to college and there are people who are taking a year off to come here."

Peggy and the corps do physical training to warm up — and wake up — before going to their projects. "We have to wear our City Year jackets, pants, sweaters, shirts, boots, and book bags," says Peggy.

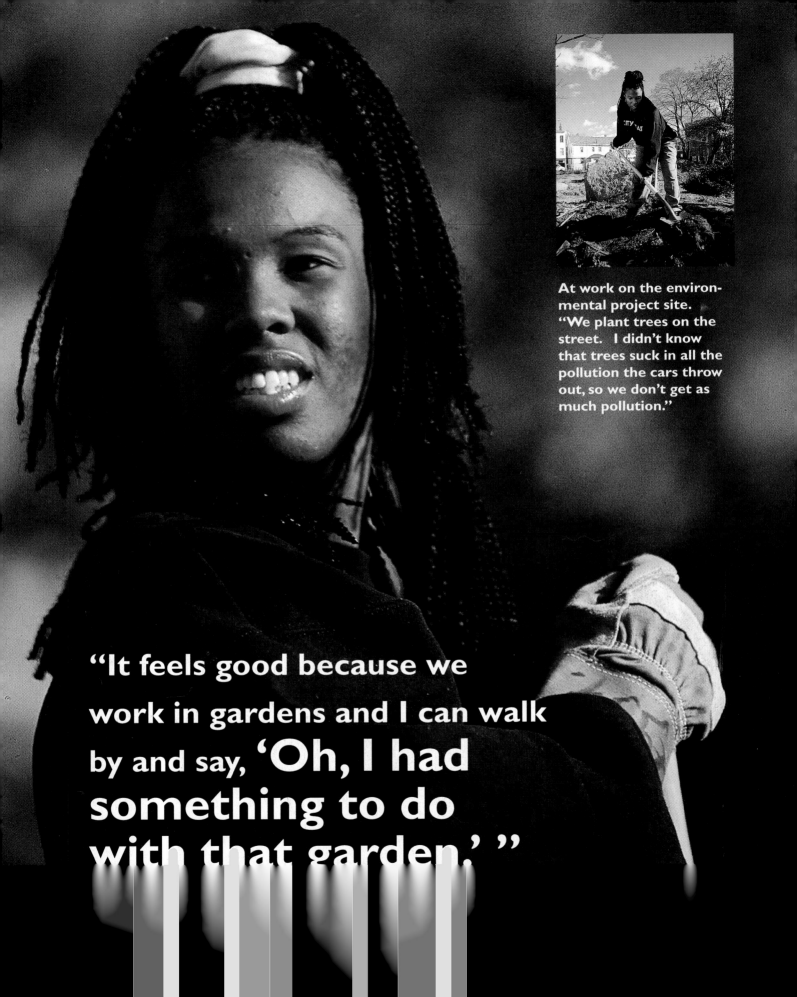

At work on the environmental project site. "We plant trees on the street. I didn't know that trees suck in all the pollution the cars throw out, so we don't get as much pollution."

"It feels good because we work in gardens and I can walk by and say, 'Oh, I had something to do with that garden.' "

Peggy on City Year: "Doing community service, that's what we do. That is what City Year's all about."

Peggy's team gets together for lunch.

City Year friends take a break. Peggy says that she has "always loved learning about other people's cultures."

At the end of a long, busy day, Peggy and her team- mates are tired but happy.

Meet
Chris
Van Allsburg

For Chris Van Allsburg, the author and illustrator of many award-winning books, words and pictures go together. But for *Just a Dream,* the words and pictures came together in an unusual way. Van Allsburg says that most of the time "A story starts with a picture in my mind . . . . If I have nothing to do, an idea comes. With *Just a Dream* it was different. I started with the idea of getting kids concerned about pollution . . . . The hard thing when you're writing about real things — like pollution — as opposed to fiction, is to write a good story."

The pictures he uses to illustrate this very good story show Van Allsburg's special way of imagining things. His pictures are full of surprises. He likes to put things where you don't expect to see them, such as a bed on top of a smokestack or in a tree. He often shows things from unusual points of view too, such as houses as they would look from the sky.

Van Allsburg says that when he reads a book, he imagines how the people and the places look. When he writes a book, he likes to leave the reader with something to imagine too. "I like turning a face away a little bit . . . . I also like leaving something out of the story. There must be something to ponder at the end."

Van Allsburg's first book, *The Garden of Abdul Gasazi,* told about a small white dog named Fritz. Since then, Fritz has become something of a trademark. If you look hard enough, you will find him somewhere in most of Van Allsburg's books. Can you find him in *Just a Dream?*

JUST A DREAM

STORY AND PICTURES BY CHRIS VAN ALLSBURG

As usual, Walter stopped at the bakery on his way home from school. He bought one large jelly-filled doughnut. He took the pastry from its bag, eating quickly as he walked along. He licked the red jelly from his fingers. Then he crumpled up the empty bag and threw it at a fire hydrant.

At home Walter saw Rose, the little girl next door, watering a tree that had just been planted. "It's my birthday present," she said proudly. Walter couldn't understand why anyone would want a tree for a present. His own birthday was just a few days away, "And I'm not getting some dumb plant," he told Rose.

After dinner Walter took out the trash. Three cans stood next to the garage. One was for bottles, one for cans, and one for everything else. As usual, Walter dumped everything into one can. He was too busy to sort through garbage, especially when there was something good on television.

The show that Walter was so eager to watch was about a boy who lived in the future. The boy flew around in a tiny airplane that he parked on the roof of his house. He had a robot and a

small machine that could make any kind of food with the push of a button.

Walter went to bed wishing he lived in the future. He couldn't wait to have his own tiny plane, a robot to take out the trash, and a machine that could make jelly doughnuts by the thousands. When he fell asleep, his wish came true. That night Walter's bed traveled to . . . the future.

Walter woke up in the middle of a huge dump. A bulldozer was pushing a heap of bulging trash bags toward him. "Stop!" he yelled.

The man driving the bulldozer put his machine in neutral. "Oh, sorry," he said. "Didn't see you."

Walter looked at the distant mountains of trash and saw half-buried houses. "Do people live here?" he asked.

"Not anymore," answered the man.

A few feet from the bed was a rusty old street sign that read FLORAL AVENUE. "Oh no," gasped Walter. He lived on Floral Avenue.

The driver revved up his bulldozer. "Well," he shouted, "back to work!"

Walter pulled the covers over his head. This can't be the future, he thought. I'm sure it's just a dream. He went back to sleep.

But not for long . . .

Walter peered over the edge of his bed, which was caught in the branches of a tall tree. Down below, he could see two men carrying a large saw. "Hello!" Walter yelled out.

"Hello to you!" they shouted back.

"You aren't going to cut down this tree, are you?" Walter asked.

But the woodcutters didn't answer. They took off their jackets, rolled up their sleeves, and got to work. Back and forth they pushed the saw, slicing through the trunk of Walter's tree. "You must need this tree for something important," Walter called down.

"Oh yes," they said, "very important." Then Walter noticed lettering on the woodcutters' jackets. He could just make out the words: QUALITY TOOTHPICK COMPANY. Walter sighed and slid back under the blankets.

Until . . .

Walter couldn't stop coughing. His bed was balanced on the rim of a giant smokestack. The air was filled with smoke that burned his throat and made his eyes itch. All around him, dozens of smokestacks belched thick clouds of hot, foul smoke. A workman climbed one of the stacks.

"What is this place?" Walter called out.

"This is the Maximum Strength Medicine Factory," the man answered.

"Gosh," said Walter, looking at all the smoke, "what kind of medicine do they make here?"

"Wonderful medicine," the workman replied, "for burning throats and itchy eyes."

Walter started coughing again.

"I can get you some," the man offered.

"No thanks," said Walter. He buried his head in his pillow and, when his coughing stopped, fell asleep.

But then . . .

Snowflakes fell on Walter. He was high in the mountains. A group of people wearing snow-shoes and long fur coats hiked past his bed.

"Where are you going?" Walter asked.

"To the hotel," one of them replied.

Walter turned around and saw an enormous building. A sign on it read HOTEL EVEREST. "Is that hotel," asked Walter, "on the top of Mount Everest?"

"Yes," said one of the hikers. "Isn't it beautiful?"

"Well," Walter began. But the group didn't wait for his answer. They waved goodbye and marched away. Walter stared at the flashing yellow sign, then crawled back beneath his sheets.

But there was more to see . . .

Walter's hand was wet and cold. When he opened his eyes, he found himself floating on the open sea, drifting toward a fishing boat. The men on the boat were laughing and dancing.

"Ship ahoy!" Walter shouted.

The fishermen waved to him.

"What's the celebration for?" he asked.

"We've just caught a fish," one of them yelled back. "Our second one this week!" They held up their small fish for Walter to see.

"Aren't you supposed to throw the little ones back?" Walter asked.

But the fishermen didn't hear him. They were busy singing and dancing.

Walter turned away. Soon the rocking of the bed put him to sleep.

But only for a moment . . .

A loud, shrieking horn
nearly lifted Walter off his mat-
tress. He jumped up. There were
cars and trucks all around him,
horns honking loudly, creeping
along inch by inch. Every driver
had a car phone in one hand and a
big cup of coffee in the other.
When the traffic stopped completely, the honking grew even
louder. Walter could not get back
to sleep.

Hours passed, and he won-
dered if he'd be stuck on this
highway forever. He pulled his
pillow tightly around his head.
This can't be the future, he
thought. Where are the tiny airplanes, the robots? The honking
continued into the night, until
finally, one by one, the cars became quiet as their drivers, and
Walter, went to sleep.

But his bed traveled on . . .

Walter looked up. A horse stood right over his bed, staring directly at him. In the saddle was a woman wearing cowboy clothes. "My horse likes you," she said.

"Good," replied Walter, who wondered where he'd ended up this time. All he could see was a dull yellow haze.

"Son," the woman told him, spreading her arms in front of her, "this is the mighty Grand Canyon."

Walter gazed into the foggy distance.

"Of course," she went on, "with all this smog, nobody's gotten a good look at it for years." The woman offered to sell Walter some postcards that showed the canyon in the old days. "They're real pretty," she said.

But he couldn't look. It's just a dream, he told himself. I know I'll wake up soon, back in my room.

But he didn't . . .

Walter looked out from under his sheets. His bed was flying through the night sky. A flock of ducks passed overhead. One of them landed on the bed, and to Walter's surprise, he began to speak. "I hope you don't mind," the bird said, "if I take a short rest here." The ducks had been flying for days, looking for the pond where they had always stopped to eat.

"I'm sure it's down there somewhere," Walter said, though he suspected something awful might have happened. After a while the duck waddled to the edge of the bed, took a deep breath, and flew off. "Good luck," Walter called to him. Then he pulled the blanket over his head. "It's just a dream," he whispered, and wondered if it would ever end.

Then finally . . .

Walter's bed returned to the present. He was safe in his room again, but he felt terrible. The future he'd seen was not what he'd expected. Robots and little airplanes didn't seem very important now. He looked out his window at the trees and lawns in the early morning light, then jumped out of bed.

He ran outside and down the block, still in his pajamas. He found the empty jelly doughnut bag he'd thrown at the fire hydrant the day before. Then Walter went back home and, before the sun came up, sorted all the trash by the garage.

A few days later, on Walter's birthday, all his friends came
over for cake and ice cream. They loved his new toys: the
laser gun set, electric yo-yo, and inflatable dinosaurs. "My best
present," Walter told them, "is outside." Then he showed them
the gift that he'd picked out that morning — a tree.

After the party, Walter and his dad planted the birthday present. When he went to bed, Walter looked out his window. He could see his tree and the tree Rose had planted on her birthday. He liked the way they looked, side by side. Then he went to sleep, but not for long, because that night Walter's bed took him away again.

When Walter woke up, his bed was standing in the shade of two tall trees. The sky was blue. Laundry hanging from a clothesline flapped in the breeze. A man pushed an old motorless lawn mower. This isn't the future, Walter thought. It's the past.

"Good morning," the man said. "You've found a nice place to sleep."

"Yes, I have," Walter agreed. There was something very peaceful about the huge trees next to his bed.

The man looked up at the rustling leaves. "My great-grandmother planted one of these trees," he said, "when she was a little girl."

Walter looked up at the leaves too, and realized where his bed had taken him. This was the future, after all, a different kind of future. There were still no robots or tiny airplanes. There weren't even any clothes dryers or gas-powered lawn mowers. Walter lay back and smiled. "I like it here," he told the man, then drifted off to sleep in the shade of the two giant trees — the trees he and Rose had planted so many years ago.

Dream On

Write a Letter

Best of All

"So, Walter, your favorite birthday present is . . . a tree?" How do you think Walter would explain that? Write a letter from Walter to a friend or relative. Include Walter's feelings about all the birthday presents he got in *Just a Dream* and why he likes the tree best.

Perform a Scene

On Stage

Bring one of Walter's dreams to life. Work with one or two classmates to choose a dream scene and to decide who will play each part. Add some action and dialogue to the scene, and then present it to your class.

224

Take Your Pick: Poem, Story, or Drawing

What a Chore!

Think about Walter's household chores and how he felt about them. Do you feel about your chores the way Walter felt at the beginning of the story or more like what he felt at the end? What would happen if you didn't do your chores? What if no one in the world did those particular chores? Respond with a poem, story, or drawing.

Compare Two Stories

Wake-up Call

Walter sure learns a lot in his sleep! After thinking about how Walter changes in *Just a Dream*, look back at *The Great Kapok Tree*. How are the two stories similar? How are they different? Write about your ideas or discuss them with a classmate or your group.

SUPER SLEUTHS

Contents

FINGER PRINT LIFTERS

EVIDENCE

EXHIBIT A

CAM JANSEN
and the
Mystery at the Monkey House

DAVID A. ADLER
Illustrated by Susanna Natti

PAPERBACK PLUS

Cam Jansen and the Mystery at the Monkey House

by David A. Adler

Monkey see. Monkey do. Monkey disappear!

In the same book . . .

More about how monkeys — and other animals —
live in modern zoos, as well as a folktale that's
really a story for you to solve.

#24

The Boxcar Children

THE MYSTERY OF THE HIDDEN PAINTING
created by
GERTRUDE CHANDLER WARNER

PAPERBACK **PLUS**

The Mystery of the Hidden Painting

a Boxcar Children Mystery by Gertrude Chandler Warner

Finding the hidden painting leads to an even bigger mystery.

In the same book . . .

More about jewel robberies in history and fiction, as well as fun facts about minerals and gems.

More Marvelous Mysteries

Susannah and the Purple Mongoose Mystery
by Patricia Elmore

Susannah and her pals, Lucy and Knievel, turn their detective skills to finding out who wants to destroy Miss Quigley's house.

The Mystery of the Hidden Beach
by Gertrude Chandler Warner

The Boxcar Children and their new cousin, Soo Lee, solve an ecological mystery.

Encyclopedia Brown: Boy Detective
by Donald J. Sobol

Meet Leroy "Encyclopedia" Brown in this first book in the series.

Sebastian (Super Sleuth) and the Copycat Crime
by Mary Blount Christian

Detective John Quincy Jones needs the help of his canine partner Sebastian (Super Sleuth) to find the missing manuscripts.

The Fourth Floor Twins and the Fish Snitch Mystery
by David A. Adler

The Fourth Floor Twins, Donna and Diane and Gary and Kevin, think something is very fishy about one of their neighbors. This calls for an investigation.

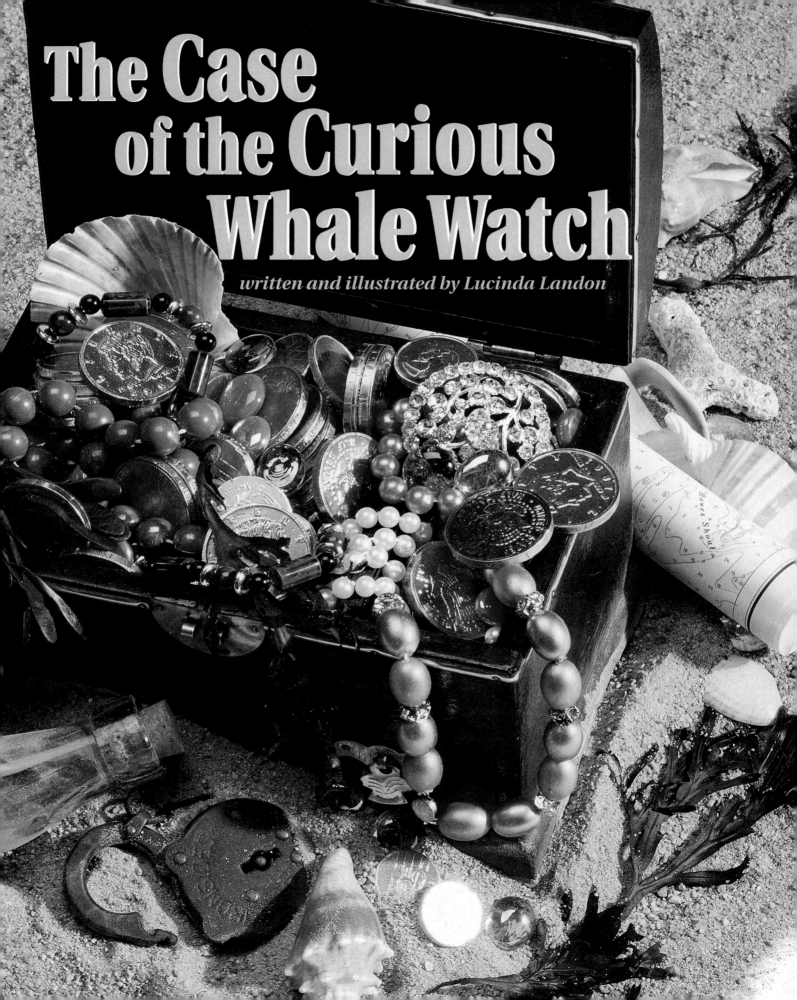

The Case of the Curious Whale Watch

written and illustrated by Lucinda Landon

Meg Mackintosh
and
The Case of the Curious Whale Watch

Search the pictures for key clues

2 A Solve-It-Yourself Mystery

Lucinda Landon

"Sharks!

Hammerhead sharks," said Peter. "That's what I want to see."

"It figures you'd be more interested in sharks than whales," Meg Mackintosh said to her brother, as they walked down the pier.

"This whale watch expedition is a grand idea," said Gramps. "What do whales watch, anyway?"

"*We* are going to watch *them*," said Meg, checking her binoculars. She had also brought her camera, notebook, and detective kit — just in case.

"The captain of the boat is quite famous," Gramps went on. "When he's not running whale watches, he's searching for a long-lost treasure that was buried by pirates in the 1800s, or so the story goes."

"Pirates?" said Peter.

"Lost treasure?" said Meg. "Sounds like a mystery!"

Meg, Peter, Gramps, and Skip boarded the *Albatross*.

"Welcome aboard!" boomed a hearty voice.
"I'm Captain Caleb Quinn.

"That's my mate, Jasper,
helping the other passengers.

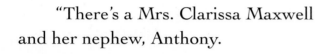

"There's a Mrs. Clarissa Maxwell
and her nephew, Anthony.

"And a nice old gentleman,
Mr. Oliver Morley,

and a young student named
Carlos de Christopher.

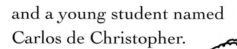

"That's Dr. Peck, Dr. Susan
Peck, a marine biologist. I guess
we're all here. OK, Jasper, cast off."

"Are you really searching for a lost treasure?" Meg asked the captain, as they headed out to sea.

"I have an old treasure map. I'll show it to you," the captain offered. He went up to the pilothouse and returned with the map. The other passengers gathered around.

"My great-great-uncle got it from a sailor in New Zealand many years ago; he sent it to his brother, and it was passed down through the family until it got to me. Here it is, still in the original envelope. He sent this scrimshaw, too. It's a carving of a whale on a whale's tooth."

"Did you ever find the treasure?" Meg asked.

"Never did. In all these years, no one has figured out where it is. Well, on with the whale watch. I'll lock this back up. Come on, Peter, you can help me steer."

"The treasure must be worth a lot of money," said Peter, as he followed the captain up to the pilothouse.

"I'll bet it's worth millions!" said Carlos.

"I could *use* millions," said Anthony. "Don't tell Auntie, but I'm broke if my horse doesn't win at the track today."

"That map should be destroyed," Dr. Peck said to Mr. Morley. "Those treasure hunters are always digging up the environment."

"The map looked quite authentic," replied Mr. Morley. "But I doubt the captain will ever find the treasure."

"Just think," Mrs. Maxwell said wistfully, "all those gems just sitting there."

"I wish I could solve the mystery for Captain Quinn," said Meg. She noticed Mr. Morley's magnifying glass. "Are you a detective?" she asked.

"Oh, no. Not me," said Mr. Morley.

"Thar she blows!" yelled Gramps.

Gramps was right. In the distance, a whale spouted water. Then more whales came to the surface for air.

"Whales travel in groups called pods. In the spring they migrate north to cooler waters," explained the captain. He had turned off the engines and come down from the pilothouse to point out the different whales.

Meg took photographs with her instant camera and jotted in her notebook. "We're studying whales in school," she said to Anthony.

"They're just a bunch of big fish. I only came along for the ride," he replied and stretched out to sunbathe.

"Whales aren't big fish," Meg corrected him. "They're mammals."

"And they'll be extinct if we don't protect them," Dr. Peck added. "I'm researching their migratory patterns. I was just awarded a grant."

"*My* grant money might be cut," grumbled Carlos. "Then I wouldn't be able to return to college."

Mrs. Maxwell was busier filing her fingernails than watching the whales. "May I put my purse up in the pilothouse for safekeeping?" she asked the captain.

"If you like," Captain Quinn answered. "But hurry, so you don't miss anything."

In a few minutes Mrs. Maxwell returned, and seconds later the captain let out a shout. "Look! There's a finback whale!" he exclaimed. "It's one of the largest and fastest whales. They can grow to be seventy feet long and weigh as much as sixty-five tons."

Dr. Peck ran up to the pilothouse to take photos.

Peter had a telephoto lens, too. "I should get some great shots," he said to Meg. "Much better than that little instant camera of yours."

Meg ignored Peter and went over to Gramps and Mr. Morley.

"I'm hoping to retire soon," Meg overheard Mr. Morley say. "A few investments would help."

"I hate to cut this short," said Gramps, "but I'm feeling a bit seasick. I think I'll go in the cabin and lie down."

Meanwhile, Meg noticed Jasper slipping into a lifeboat with one of Peter's comic books. "Do you help the captain hunt for the treasure?" she asked.

"Never have," Jasper answered. "But I wouldn't mind finding that treasure myself. I'd never have to get on a boat again."

Suddenly, Mrs. Maxwell shrieked, "Look how they jump in the air!"

"That's called breaching," said Captain Quinn. "Some say the whales leap out of the water like that to try to scratch the barnacles off their skin."

Dr. Peck came down from the pilothouse, and Carlos went up to use the telescope. Then he returned to the deck to see some whales that had come quite close to the boat.

"I've already shot three rolls of film," said Peter, as he reloaded his camera. "What time is it, anyway?"

"It's exactly eleven-forty," answered Mr. Morley, flicking his pocket watch open and shut.

Albatross

"Quick! On the other side!" yelled Peter, aiming his camera. "SHARK FINS!"

Everyone raced through the passenger cabin to the port side of the boat.

"It's not a shark," said Dr. Peck. "It's a humpback whale and her calf. The calf stays with the mother, feeding and learning, for about a year, during which the mother is quite protective of the calf."

"Watch! She's fluking her tail!" exclaimed Meg. "Everyone over here. Let me take your picture with the whales in the background."

"You're blocking my sun," complained Anthony, as Meg was snapping the picture.

Albatross

"No, it's a storm — and it's moving in fast," said Captain Quinn, observing the clouds. "Looks like a doozy of a nor'easter. Everybody inside, it's going to get rough. And where's that mate of mine?"

Inside the cabin, Gramps was still asleep on the bench. Captain Quinn went to the pilothouse to start up the engines. They could hear the rain begin.

"Dr. Peck is missing," worried Mrs. Maxwell. "Where is she?"

"That's not all that's missing!" said the captain, bursting back into the cabin. "My treasure map is gone! Somebody broke into the strongbox in the pilothouse and stole it. It's got to be one of you!"

The passengers looked at each other in silence. Then the cabin door blew open and in came Dr. Peck. She was drenched.

"Where were you?" said Anthony.

"*She* was in the pilothouse earlier," said Peter. "I saw her."

"I've been on the deck observing the whales," snapped Dr. Peck. "Not that it's any of your business."

"What's all the noise about?" grumbled Gramps, rubbing his eyes.

While Captain Quinn told Gramps and Dr. Peck what had happened, Meg grabbed her knapsack and darted up to the pilothouse to inspect the scene of the crime.

The padlock on the strongbox had been broken. A handkerchief and some broken pieces of metal lay nearby. Meg got out her magnifying glass to examine the clues. Then she took a photograph.

WHAT CAN YOU DEDUCE
FROM THE SCENE OF THE CRIME?

"That's Mrs. Maxwell's handkerchief," said Peter. "It's got 'CM' on it, and the captain said that her first name is Clarissa. And those are pieces of a nail file. I saw her filing her nails, too."

"Sure it's my hankie and my nail file!" cried Mrs. Maxwell. "Someone must have taken them from my purse."

"Or maybe you just wanted it to look that way," said Carlos.

"I didn't steal that old map," she answered defiantly.

"Let me examine the padlock," said Peter. "I might be able to tell if it was broken by a left-handed or right-handed person."

"Is anything else missing, Captain Quinn?" Meg asked.

"No . . . that's it," replied the captain.

"Don't worry, Captain," Peter said confidently. "I'll find that map if I have to search everywhere and everyone. I *am* the president of my Detective Club. By the way, is there any reward?"

Meg rolled her eyes. But she knew Peter was serious about solving the mystery. If I'm going to solve this, she thought to herself, I'd better do it fast — before Peter does and before we get back to shore.

"What time is it?" Meg asked Mr. Morley.

"Sorry, I don't know. My watch is jammed shut," he answered.

Meg took out her notebook and began to make a list of all the suspects and their possible motives. Before long, she realized it wouldn't be easy to spot the thief.

WHY NOT?

Just about everybody aboard the *Albatross* had a motive!

Meg was still looking over her list of suspects when Peter burst into the pilothouse. "That mate Jasper has been sneaking around all morning," he said to Meg. "I bet he had something to do with the theft."

"Jasper's had a million chances to steal the map," replied Meg. "Why would he pick today?"

"Then what about Carlos?" Peter pointed his finger accusingly. "Weren't you in the pilothouse using the captain's telescope?"

"Everything was fine when I left there," Carlos protested.

"Well, someone definitely stole my hankie and nail file from my purse," said Mrs. Maxwell, who was still clutching Anthony's hand.

"But nothing else was missing?" asked Meg. "Your wallet and all of your money are still there?"

"Yes . . . it's all there," she answered, somewhat flustered.

"What about you, Anthony?" Peter looked at him. "It's no secret that you need some cash . . . or is it?"

"Oh, no, not my little Anthony," said Mrs. Maxwell. "He'd never steal a thing."

"Just like that humpback protecting her calf," said Meg quietly.

"Humpback? What are you talking about?" said Mr. Morley.

"What about *you*, Meg?" Mrs. Maxwell interrupted. "You've been snooping around about that treasure map all day!"

"Meg wouldn't steal the map," Peter defended her. "She'd rather solve mysteries than cause them."

"Well, I'd be careful if I were you," warned Anthony. "Playing detective could get you into trouble."

Now I *have* to solve the case, Meg thought to herself, before I become a suspect! She thought hard. It's the timing that's important. The thief must have struck after the captain left the pilothouse and came down to point out the whales. Where was everyone after that?

Meg thought back to what had happened. She decided to draw a picture of the boat and, with the help of her photos, map out where everyone had been.

Meanwhile, the storm was getting rough. All of the passengers were huddled in the cabin, except Peter, who was timing how long it would take to run up the steps to the pilothouse, break into the strongbox, and then run back down. Captain Quinn and Jasper were busy guiding the *Albatross* through the dense fog.

"How's it going?" Gramps asked Meg, peering over her shoulder. He still looked a bit green.

"Well, it's hard to say," said Meg. "Peter thinks the nail file and handkerchief point to Mrs. Maxwell. But I doubt she would leave her tools at the scene of the crime.

I think Carlos was in the pilothouse last, but it's possible someone slipped up after him. I'm still trying to figure out everyone's alibi. I also have some instant photos I took. They might show something," she confided in him.

"Let's see," said Gramps. "Nice shot of me and Skip."

Mr. Morley was sitting nearby. "I'd check out that Dr. Peck if I were you," he whispered. "She's been acting very suspiciously."

Peter overheard them and decided to get to Dr. Peck first. A wave pitched the *Albatross* sharply; Peter knocked into her and was able to dump her camera bag on the floor. The top of a lens case came off and out fell . . .

THE TREASURE MAP!

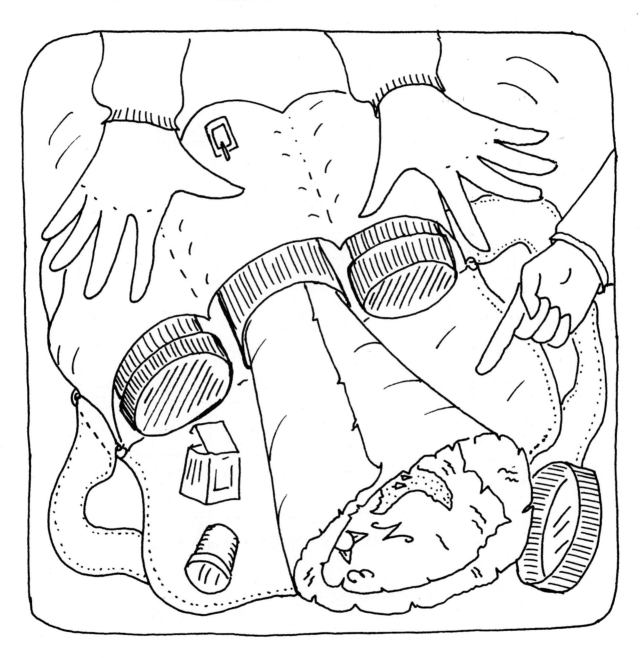

"What have we here?" said Peter triumphantly. "Looks like I've found our crook. You can forget all about your little deductions, Meg-O. The case of the missing treasure map is *closed.*"

"What? How did that get there?" exclaimed Dr. Peck. "I didn't take that map. I never touched it!"

"Wait until the Detective Club hears about this," boasted Peter, as he handed the map over to Captain Quinn.

"I knew she did it," said Anthony. "Scientists are creepy."

"She said she thought treasure maps should be destroyed," said Mr. Morley. "I guess she really meant it."

"Is it the same map?" asked Carlos. "She could have copied it."

"That's my map, all right," said the captain. "I'm going to have to tell the police about this, but first we have to get through this storm."

"You're all wrong!" cried Dr. Peck. "I didn't steal the map!"

I believe her, Meg thought to herself. Something doesn't make sense. Meg looked over her drawings and photos to try to figure out what.

After a moment, Meg knew she was right. The case
was *not* closed. Dr. Peck couldn't have stolen the map.

WHY NOT?

"Dr. Peck did go up to the pilothouse to take photographs," Meg explained to Gramps. She had pulled him
out on deck, out of earshot of the others. "But Carlos
went up there to use the telescope *after* she did, and he

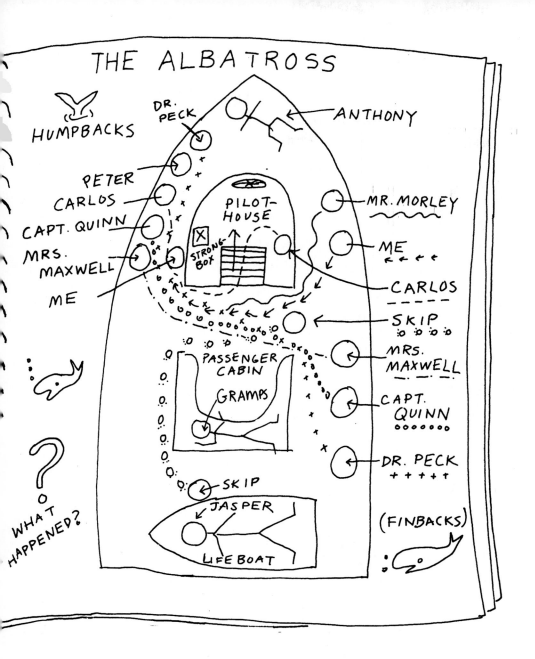

THE ALBATROSS

said everything was fine. Dr. Peck was on the deck with the rest of us until the storm. I remember talking to her then, and she's in the group photo I took."

"But if Dr. Peck didn't do it," said Gramps, "how did the map get in her camera bag?"

"Maybe somebody else — I don't know who — took the map and then planted it on Dr. Peck. You know, like a red herring, to throw us off the track," Meg replied.

"You mean they figured out where the treasure was and then ditched the map on Dr. Peck?" Gramps scratched his head.

"That would be pretty fast thinking," said Meg. "Four generations of Quinns haven't been able to find the treasure. But why would someone steal the map only to return it?" Meg decided to have another look at the map. She headed up to the pilothouse to talk to Captain Quinn.

"This whole thing is as foggy to me as that weather out there," said Captain Quinn, as he leaned over the steering wheel and gazed out to sea. "I don't understand why a professor of ocean life would want to steal my old map. I suspect the gold and gems are worth a tidy sum, but I've logged a lot of hours looking for that treasure — it won't come easy."

"I don't think Dr. Peck *did* steal the map," Meg said, and explained why. "Could I see the map again?"

"Help yourself," said the captain. "It's back in the strongbox."

Meg took out the map, then noticed the scrimshaw and took it out, too. "At least the thief didn't bother with this," she said.

Meg studied the map and scrimshaw with her magnifying glass, and went over her notes and photographs again. After a while she realized that, although Peter had found the treasure map, something else was missing.

WHAT?

The envelope. They'd found the map, but not the envelope it came in. Where was it? And what difference could an old envelope make? Meg wondered.

Suddenly there was a loud CLUNK. The lights in the cabin blinked and went out. The engine was dead; the *Albatross* drifted in the storm.

"Jumping jellyfish!" yelled the captain. "Don't worry, Meg. I'll go down below and help Jasper get her going again. You stay here."

Meg could hear the other passengers scurrying about in the cabin below.

"What's happened to the power?" asked Carlos nervously.

"We're not going to sink, are we?" said Anthony.

"Are we stranded with a dangerous criminal aboard?" exclaimed Mrs. Maxwell.

"I'm not dangerous . . . and I'm not a criminal," insisted Dr. Peck. "This is absurd!"

"I found the treasure map on you," said Peter. "That's pretty strong proof."

"Where *is* the map?" asked Mr. Morley. "Someone may try to steal it again while the lights are out."

Meg clutched the map tightly, but what she was really thinking about was the envelope. In a moment, she figured out what had happened to it — and suddenly the whole case fell into place. She ran down to the cabin.

"Listen, everybody. Dr. Peck *didn't* steal the map. I know who did!"

WHO?

"Mr. Morley!" Meg announced. "He stole the treasure map!"

"What? Not I! What would I want with a worthless old map?" asked Mr. Morley.

"Nothing," Meg agreed. "But you did want the stamp on the envelope the map was sent in. You noticed that it was very old and valuable — you even had your magnifying glass and stamp-collecting book to verify it. You waited until Captain Quinn was out of the pilothouse and everyone else was busy watching the whales, and then you snuck in and stole it. You took the treasure map to throw us off the track, and you planted it on Dr. Peck to make her look guilty. You figured that no one would ever miss the envelope or stamp."

Mr. Morley turned red as a lobster. "You have no proof. You're just playing detective," he protested. "Why, I've had no opportunity to take the map, even if I wanted to!"

"That's not true," said Meg. "You did have an opportunity."

WHEN?

"When we all ran to the port side of the boat to see the whales, you weren't there," Meg explained. "My photos prove it — you're not in the group shot. And when I mentioned that Mrs. Maxwell and Anthony were acting like a humpback whale and her calf, you didn't know what I was talking about — because you weren't there when we saw them. You were in the pilothouse stealing the map and the envelope. Anthony was sunbathing. Jasper was reading Peter's comic books in the lifeboat. Gramps was asleep in the cabin and didn't see you. The rest of us were on deck. You took Mrs. Maxwell's nail file to break the padlock and used her handkerchief to wipe off your fingerprints. Then you rolled up the map and stuffed it into Dr. Peck's camera-lens case, which she had left on the bench in the cabin. I think you ripped the stamp off the envelope and threw the envelope overboard to be rid of it. And I think I know where you put the stamp, too."

WHERE?

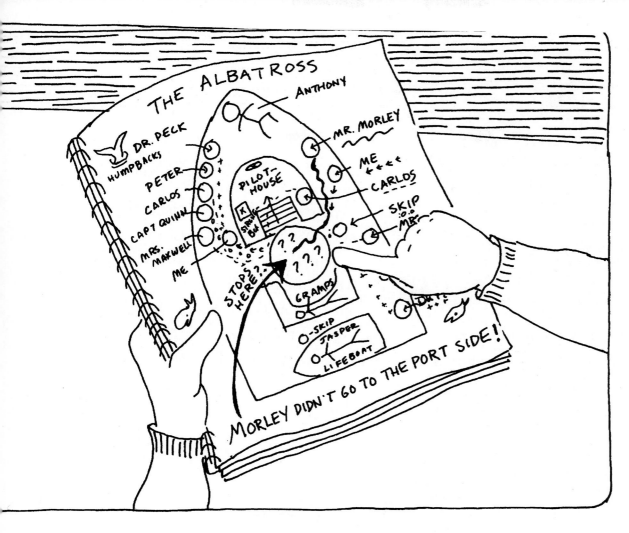

"I bet it's in your pocket watch," Meg continued. "At eleven-forty, you snapped it open and told Peter what time it was. That was before the theft. But afterward, when I asked you the time, you said your watch was jammed shut. Ten-to-one you quickly hid the stamp inside to keep it safe and dry."

"This is absolutely ridiculous," Mr. Morley insisted. "I refuse to listen to any more of these wild accusations. This amateur sleuth has clearly invented this story for her own amusement."

Captain Quinn stepped forward. "I think we'd better see your watch," he said. "If Meg's theory is as farfetched as you say, surely you won't mind if we have a look."

Peter added, "If you didn't do it, you have nothing to hide!" The others agreed. They stared at Mr. Morley as he fumbled for his pocket watch. Meg held her breath.

Mr. Morley scowled as he handed the pocket watch over to the captain.

Sure enough, the stamp was there. Just as Meg had suspected.

"I never thought you'd miss one little stamp," groaned Mr. Morley. "But such a valuable little stamp . . . an 1855 New Zealand. I can't believe I let it slip through my fingers."

"He was going to let me be arrested!" cried Dr. Peck.

There was another clunk and the engine started up. The lights flickered back on.

"I got her going again, Cap!" shouted Jasper.

"The police will take care of Mr. Morley when we get back to shore," said Captain Quinn. "It's nice to have a valuable stamp, but I'm really just happy to have my old treasure map back — even though I still don't know where the treasure is."

"But that's not all!" exclaimed Meg. "I think I can help you with that, too."

HOW?

Meg got out her magnifying glass and the scrimshaw. "If you look at the scrimshaw carefully, the whale looks like the island on the treasure map. And if you turn the map this way, it resembles a whale. I noticed it when I was examining

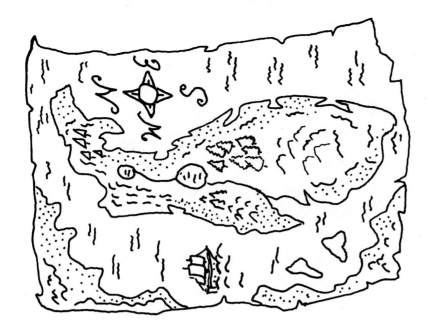

the clues. I think the sailor gave your great-great-uncle both the map and the scrimshaw so that they would complement each other in telling the location of the treasure. So, if someone stole the map, they still couldn't figure out where the treasure was. You need *both* of them to find it.

"See," Meg continued. "The eye on the scrimshaw whale looks like an 'X.' I bet that 'X' marks the spot on the island where you should look for the treasure."

The captain's jaw dropped in surprise.

"Now that I see it, it makes perfect sense," he said. "As simple as putting one plus one together. In fact, I think I recognize the spot . . . it's at . . . wait a minute. I want to be the one to find it first. Thanks, Meg!"

"I guess you really solved two mysteries at once,"
Gramps said to Meg a few weeks later. "The Case of the
Missing Treasure Map and the Case of the Missing Treasure."

"You amazed even me," Peter admitted. "But I did get
some great photos of the whales."

"And look what Captain Quinn gave me for solving the
mystery," said Meg. "A whale watch!"

Meet the Author and Illustrator

Lucinda Landon

Clues are everywhere in a Meg Mackintosh mystery! They are in the drawings and in the words, and that's the way Lucinda Landon wants it. She wrote *and* illustrated *Meg Mackintosh and The Case of the Curious Whale Watch*. Landon says, "Writing the Meg Mackintosh series gives me the opportunity to combine a love of drawing with my love of mysteries. It's fun to design books with clues hidden in both the text and the black and white illustrations."

When Landon was working as a children's librarian at her local library, children were always asking her for mysteries. Those requests inspired her to write a word-and-picture mystery that became the first of the Meg Mackintosh books. In all the mysteries, Landon says, you are "invited to match wits with Meg, to try to solve the case by answering the questions posed throughout."

Detective at Work!

How Good a Detective Are You?

How and when did you figure out who did it? Was it before Meg solved the case? Whom did you suspect first? Write a "detective report" to file with the chief of detectives explaining how you reacted to this "solve-it-yourself" mystery.

Role-play

Who . . . Me?

When looking for a criminal, detectives focus on motive, means, and opportunity — the *why*, *how*, and *when* of a crime. With a partner, role-play a scene in which a detective, such as Meg, questions one of the suspects in the whale watch case. The detective should try to find out why, how, and when the suspect might have committed the crime.

Draw a Diagram

Pin Them Down

Meg uses a picture to pin down where everyone is when the crime takes place. Make your own picture pinning down the time and location of all the members of a group you know. You might show where in your house your family is at 7:15 A.M., who sits where on the bus, or you and your friends at a favorite activity.

Write a Want Ad

Wanted: Super Sleuths

What does it take to be a good detective? Work with several classmates to come up with a list of characteristics. For clues, look at how Meg Mackintosh solves her case. Then look back at *Hurray for Ali Baba Bernstein* or discuss other detective stories you know, and add to your list. Finally, use your list to create a want ad for Super Sleuths.

Mystery Masterpieces

A Gallery of Stolen Art

Now you see them — Now you don't. All of the works of art on these pages have been stolen. Art masterpieces are very valuable; for example, *The Concert* is worth more than $50 million. But famous works of art are also easy to recognize. Who would display a well-known "hot" artwork? Who would buy it? Who would steal it? Those are questions the super sleuths of many nations are still trying to answer.

Tête, by the modern Spanish artist Pablo Picasso. Stolen from a gallery in Chicago, Illinois, in 1994. This 1928 painting of a head (*tête* means "head" in French) is small — only $21\frac{1}{2}$ by $12\frac{1}{2}$ inches — and easy to carry and to hide. Where is it hidden now? If you can find out, there's a $50,000 reward!

The Concert, by seventeenth-century Dutch painter Jan Vermeer. Stolen from the Isabella Stewart Gardner Museum in Boston, Massachusetts, in 1990. In the daring robbery of the Gardner, thieves took only a few valuable works. Had someone "placed an order" for these particular masterpieces?

The Scream, by Norwegian painter Edvard Munch. Stolen from the National Gallery in Oslo, Norway, in 1994. Copies of this very well-known 1893 painting appear on posters, mugs, and T-shirts all over the world. Who *just had to have* the original?

An ancient Chinese *Ku*, a bronze goblet that was used in ceremonies over 3,000 years ago. Stolen from the Isabella Stewart Gardner Museum in Boston, Massachusetts, in 1990. Together, the twelve works of art stolen from the Gardner are worth more than $300 million. Will the biggest art theft in history ever be solved?

GOT

SCHOLASTIC DynaMath

Fingerprints help cops get the drop on crooks!

WHORL

ARCH

I was fast asleep when the Chief called me from headquarters. "Sarah Snoop," he snapped. "Get down to the Metropolitan Museum of Math, pronto! Someone stole the painting *Whistler's Math Teacher*. I need a detective who can crack the case."

At the museum, I lucked out! The first thing I found was a fingerprint on a wall at the scene of the crime.

A measly fingerprint may not sound like much to you. But in my business, it can help crack a tough case. Why? Everyone has a different set of prints. They never change. So cops like me can use them to finger crooks.

All prints fit into one of four categories. (See above.) To catch the crook, I compared the fingerprint I found at the crime scene to fingerprints of all the known art thieves in town. Two prints matched exactly, and I had my man: Lefty LaSpoil!

What's it like to work with fingerprints? Step into my crime lab. It's time you found out!

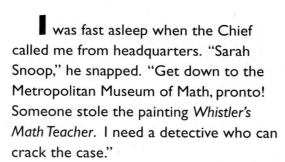

WHAT YOU NEED
Two white index cards
A piece of scratch paper
A pencil
Clear tape
A magnifying glass (optional)

CHA!

by John Shabe

LOOP

MIX

1. MAKING A PRINT

✔ Use the pencil to scribble a dark black mark (about the size of a quarter) on scratch paper.

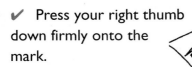

✔ Press your right thumb down firmly onto the mark.

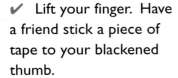

✔ Lift your finger. Have a friend stick a piece of tape to your blackened thumb.

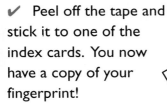

✔ Peel off the tape and stick it to one of the index cards. You now have a copy of your fingerprint!

2. IDENTIFYING YOUR PRINT

✔ Study your fingerprint closely. (Use a magnifying glass, if you have one.) Which group does your fingerprint fall into?

3. WHOSE PRINTS ARE WHOSE?

✔ Make a second copy of your thumbprint on another index card. Write your name on this one. Have some classmates do the same.

✔ Gather together your cards and the cards of three or four of your class-mates. Put the cards *without* names into one pile. Put the cards *with* names in an-other pile. Shuffle both piles.

✔ Work with your friends to match each identified fingerprint to the same fingerprint on a card that's missing the name.

DON'T STOP NOW! Make a graph showing the number of kids in your class who have different kinds of prints.

JULIAN, Secret Agent

by Ann Cameron

We Meet the Mighty One

We went over to Gloria's house and had lunch. Afterward we started patrolling, riding our bikes around.

It seemed like criminals were staying away from us. By the middle of the afternoon it was really hot, and we were tired.

Around four o'clock we decided to patrol supermarkets. We thought some criminal might go there to get food and take it back to his hideout.

Everything was normal in the first three supermarkets — kids crying, mothers or dads pushing shopping carts, kids trying to ride the carts

like scooters, people knocking over hundreds of cans of tuna fish, kids *demanding* a certain kind of candy advertised on TV.

The fourth supermarket was one I'd never been to before.

We patrolled the same way we had patrolled the others — checking the parking lot first, looking for guns in the backseats of cars, dead bodies, things like that. No luck.

We stopped and looked at a dog inside a car.

"Isn't he cute?" Gloria said. She wants a dog even more than Huey and I do.

She touched the window glass, and the dog tried to sniff her hand. Then he looked at her very hard with big brown eyes, and whined, and panted a little, and panted a little more. He put his big, shaggy paws against the window.

A woman came up behind us. "It's a crime!" she said.

"We aren't doing anything!" Huey said.

"Not you," the woman said. "The car. The dog. The windows. It's a crime!"

She pushed by us and went toward the store.

"What's the crime?" Huey said.

"We have to investigate," I said.

"Here, pooch!" Gloria called, and put her hand against the window. But the dog didn't jump up again. He just looked at Gloria, and whined, and dropped his head against the seat.

"That dog is sick," Gloria said.

"It must be really hot in the car," Huey said.

"I wonder how long he's been in there," I said.

"He needs to get out," Gloria said. "The sun has made that car like an oven. That's what the crime is — that he can't get out. We have to tell the person who owns the car!"

"Let's get the license number!" I said.

We went around to the front of the car to find the license plate. Gloria wrote it down: MIGHTY-1.

Then we went into the store and asked for the manager.

A small man came down from the high booth where the money and receipts are kept.

"I'm the manager," he said. "What can I do for you?"

"It's about a dog," I said. "A dog stuck in a car. The windows are closed, and he looks sick."

"He probably *is* sick," the manager said. "He could even die on a day like today if he's left there too long."

"Here's the license number," Gloria said. She showed him her notebook.

" 'Mighty-one'!" said the manager. "Hmm!" He climbed into his booth and used the microphone.

"Will the owner of a car with the license plate Mighty-one come to the manager's office?" he said.

Then he climbed down from the booth and stood with us, and we waited to see who would answer his call.

A man came toward us. He was the biggest man I ever saw. He must have been practically seven feet tall. He had two huge bags of groceries that he was balancing on his shoulders. He was wearing shorts, and a T-shirt that said RAMBO! He had muscles every place on his body that you could have a muscle, and he looked mean.

I pictured myself getting mashed, pictured Dad standing by my bed afterward, shaking his head sadly and saying, "Julian, you went too far."

Huey looked from the man's toes up to his head and back down again, three times, and whispered to the store manager, "When he gets here, why don't *you* talk?"

The manager smiled. "You children just speak up," he said. "You can do it."

"I'll do it," Gloria said. "I love dogs!"

Just then MIGHTY-1 came to a stop, practically on top of us and big as a skyscraper.

He looked at the manager. "So what did you call me for?" he asked.

Gloria looked up at him. "You have a dog?" she asked.

"So what?" MIGHTY-1 said.

"It's too hot to leave him in a car with the windows rolled up. He could die," Gloria said.

MIGHTY-1 glared at her. Then he glared at the manager. "You called me over here to let three little *kids* mess in my business?"

"The children are right," the manager said.

"Look," said MIGHTY-1, pointing his finger down at the manager's nose. "When I bought that dog, they told me he was a strong, healthy dog. They didn't say anything about car windows. That dog is tough. He can take it."

I hoped Gloria would say something more. But when I looked around, Gloria was gone!

MIGHTY-1 stuck his chin out. Then he stuck it back in so he could look down and see us.

"Didn't anybody ever tell you that kids should just mind their own business till they grow up? Especially your girlfriend!"

"She's not my girlfriend!" I said. "She's my friend!"

I won't let anybody say I have a girlfriend — not even a huge, mean man who's seven feet tall.

"Friend or girlfriend," MIGHTY-1 said. "Makes no difference. You tell her —"

And then we all saw that Gloria was back.

"You!" MIGHTY-1 roared.

Gloria smiled her prettiest smile. "Excuse me," she said. "I was checking your car. Your dog just fainted!"

MIGHTY-1's mouth hung open, like the door of a cave.

"Crumbles *fainted!*" he said. He dropped all his groceries
and ran for the door.

Stuff rolled out of the grocery sacks — a dozen rawhide
fake dog bones, thirty-five cans of dog food, a ball with
a bell inside, five boxes of Wheaties, Breakfast of
Champions, a book called *How to Be a He-man*, and a
magazine with an article called "79 Exercises for
Your Toes."

The manager started picking
things up, and we helped him.

Suddenly the manager got a huge grin on his face, just the kind Huey gets. He picked up a book from the magazine rack and stuck it in one of the grocery sacks, under the dog food cans.

The title was *How to Take Care of Your Dog*.

"Sometimes I have to do mischievous things," he said. "I just can't help myself. Now we need to take some water out to Crumbles," he said.

So we went to the back of the store, put water in a bucket, and took it out to the parking lot.

Crumbles was lying on the ground in the shade. MIGHTY-1 was kneeling next to him, rubbing the dog's neck.

"We brought some water," the manager said.

MIGHTY-1 looked up. "Thank you," he said.

The manager dunked Crumbles's head in the bucket of water. Then he held Crumbles's mouth open and poured some water into it.

Crumbles blinked.

"Crumbles! You're all right! You're going to be fine! Aren't you?" MIGHTY-1 said.

Crumbles made a little noise, something like a sigh.

"Oh, my sweet, adorable Crumbles!" said MIGHTY-1, and kissed him on the nose.

Meet the Author
Ann Cameron

Do you ever wonder where a fictional character comes from? Ann Cameron got the idea for Julian and his adventures from stories that her real-life friend Julian told her. One story was about a "pudding that he and his little brother Huey ate when they weren't supposed to . . . I thought it was . . . something that must have happened to nearly every single child." So, Cameron reasoned, just about every child would like that kind of story.

Cameron knew she wanted to be a writer by the time she was in the third grade, but she's had other jobs, too. She once babysat for twenty-three cats!

Meet the Illustrator
Larry Johnson

Larry Johnson's third-grade teacher admired his drawing and encouraged him to do more artwork. From then on, he says, he was drawing constantly. As a teenager, Johnson made friends with some professional basketball players by sending them portraits he had done of them. After art school, he was a messenger for the *Boston Globe* newspaper — which rejected over 100 of his sports cartoons before hiring him as a sports cartoonist! Today, in addition to illustrations like those here, Johnson's work includes paintings, cartoons, and even

275

Mighty Fine Ideas!

Write a Paragraph

Learn Your Lesson

Julian and his friends learn a lesson at the supermarket, and so does MIGHTY-1. But they are different lessons. In your group, discuss the lessons different characters learn. Then choose one lesson to write about. Write a paragraph explaining how the character learns that lesson. You might try writing your paragraph in the character's "voice."

Create a Pamphlet

Safety First

Why is it dangerous to leave a pet in a car with the windows rolled up in hot weather? Do some research to find out. Then make a protect-your-pet pamphlet. Use words and pictures to explain what happens inside the car and how these conditions can affect an animal. You might even get permission to display your pamphlet at a pet supply store.

It's in the Bag!

What can a detective learn from a bag of groceries? To find out, work with a partner to "fill" a grocery bag. List things a famous TV character or fairy tale character might buy at the supermarket. Include obvious clues. Add some false clues: other things the character might buy that will confuse the "detective." See if your classmates can figure out who your shopper is.

Clue Me In

MIGHTY-1 is not what he seemed at first, but there are some clues to the secret side of his personality. Compare and contrast the kind of clues that reveal MIGHTY-1's secret to the kind of clues that help Meg Mackintosh solve the The Case of the Curious Whale Watch.

My Dog, Sammie

A Description by Bridget Hudson

Bridget is a keen observer of her dog, as shown in her description. Could you pick out Sammie in a crowd?

Bridget Hudson
Friday Harbor Elementary School
Friday Harbor, Washington

"I wrote about Sammie because he is very, very funny, and I love him," explained Bridget when she wrote this description in the fourth grade. Bridget has seven animals: Sammie, three cats, a turtle, a guinea pig, and a goldfish. The animals don't always get along!

Bridget has thought about becoming an architect or an ice skater.

My Dog, Sammie

My dog, Sammie, is so cute and funny. He's my very special friend.

I got him at the pound. The first time I saw him he was tied between two trees, standing on his hind legs and balancing on tippy toes. He was making a racket! That's why he was tied outside. He was a big, white, fluffy Samoyed about one-and-a-half years old. We took him for a walk, and when we stopped by our car, he pulled us in and wouldn't get out. I think he knew he was going home with us.

Sammie's eyes are as brown as chocolate. At night his eyelashes glow. His ears are short and soft. He listens with them intensely. Sammie's tail sways, and when he's dreaming, his tail will dust the floor. When he walks, his fur behind his legs looks exactly like feathers.

When he goes down to the pond to get a drink, he will go for a little swim. When he's wet, he smells really musty. His hair behind his ears curls like he's had a perm. When he's dry, he feels as soft as a bunny.

When he breathes, his breath smells like dog food. When he talks to us and to other dogs, his bark is short and high.

His smile is always on.

That's my dog, Sammie!

You Be the DETECTIVE

Who Stole the Car?

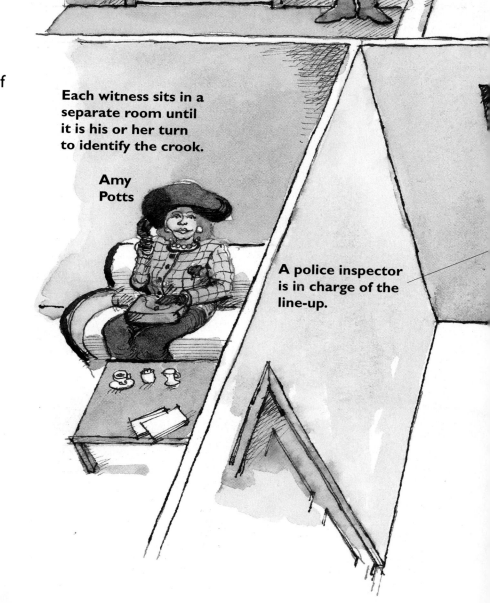

The men in the line-up look like Percy. They were all asked to take part by the police.

Police Officer

Each witness sits in a separate room until it is his or her turn to identify the crook.

Amy Potts

A police inspector is in charge of the line-up.

O ne day, Gloria Burger, wife of the American Ambassador, her mother Amy Potts, and her son Hiram Burger, Jr., see a crook driving off in the family car. All three see him clearly and give his description to Detective Dodd. They say he is short and thin, with dark, curly hair, a black beard and big, bushy eyebrows. The police, who think that the villain is Percy Pike, quickly organize an identification parade, called a line-up. The Burgers and Amy Potts come to identify the crook. But Percy, who is a cunning man, tries to fool them by changing his looks. Which of the men in the line-up is Percy Pike?

THE LINE-UP

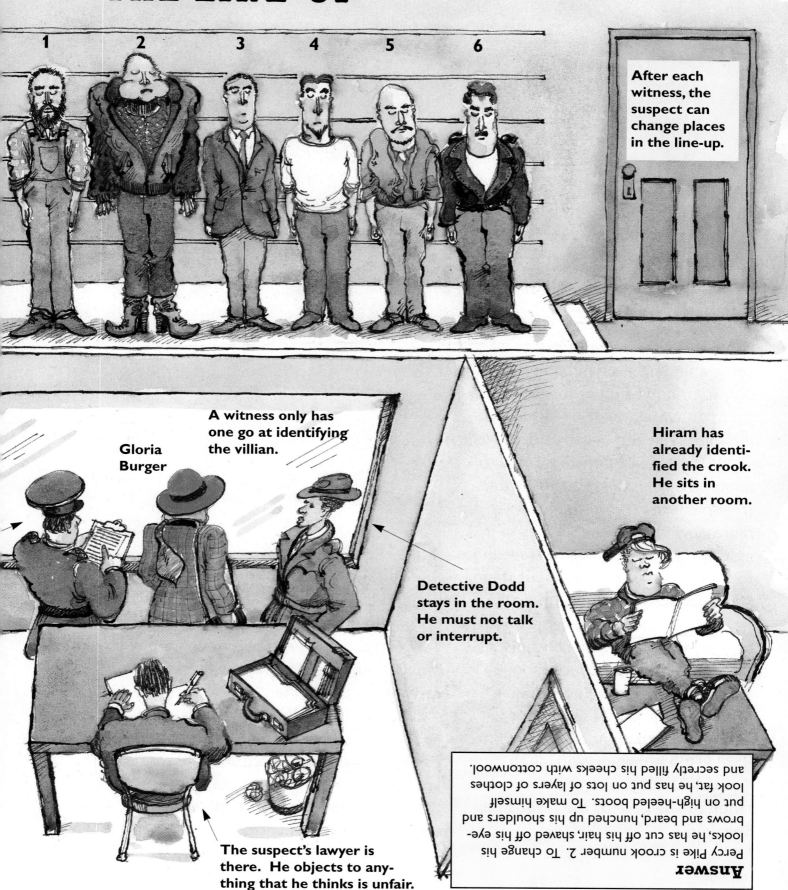

After each witness, the suspect can change places in the line-up.

Gloria Burger

A witness only has one go at identifying the villian.

Detective Dodd stays in the room. He must not talk or interrupt.

Hiram has already identified the crook. He sits in another room.

The suspect's lawyer is there. He objects to anything that he thinks is unfair.

Answer

Percy Pike is crook number 2. To change his looks, he has cut off his hair, shaved off his eyebrows and beard, hunched up his shoulders and put on high-heeled boots. To make himself look fat, he has put on lots of layers of clothes and secretly filled his cheeks with cottonwool.

Meet the
AUTHOR
Donald J. Sobol

When he was young, Donald Sobol thought he might like to become a singer or a baseball player. But he couldn't sing or hit! What he *could* do was write. He started writing in college and never stopped.

What kind of person is Donald Sobol? For one thing, he loves the freedom writing gives him to explore new ideas. He also likes to investigate foreign places by traveling to them and by reading about them. And Sobol does not give up easily. He sent his first Encyclopedia Brown mystery to twenty-six publishers before it was printed! Since then, he's written over twenty Encyclopedia Brown books. Sobol says, "Outwitting you, the reader, is hard, but harder still is making you laugh." Can he outwit you *and* make you laugh in *The Case of the Disgusting Sneakers*?

Meet the
ILLUSTRATOR
Michael Chesworth

Michael Chesworth spent his childhood in the country, where he enjoyed playing in the woods and making pictures. "My earliest memories of school are painting and drawing," he says. "Then I did cartoons as I got older." Today he's still drawing — for a living. Chesworth advises young people who want to become artists to work hard: "Draw what *you really like* and other people will like it too . . . . Draw every day." Drawing is not the *only* thing Chesworth does. He also loves computers and enjoys skiing, scuba diving, and reading.

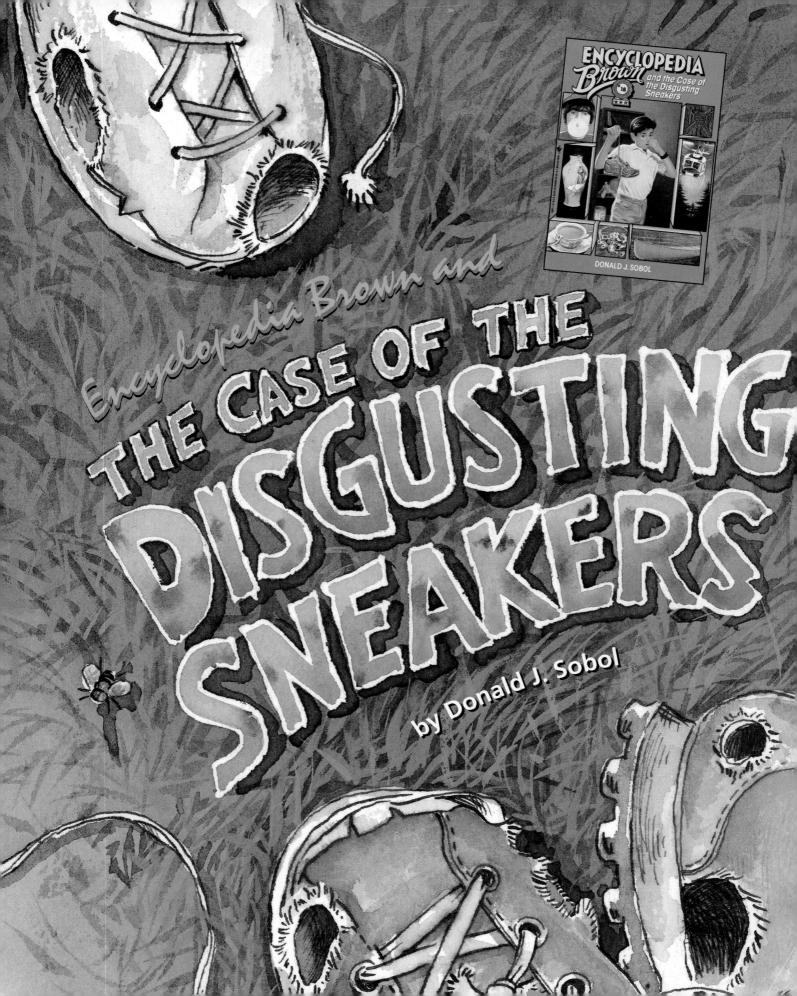

On the day of the Disgusting Sneaker Contest, Phoebe Eastwood, last year's champion, walked into the Brown Detective Agency. She had on shoes.

Encyclopedia immediately knew something was afoot.

All year Phoebe had prepared for the defense of her title by wearing the same pair of sneakers. She had them in really disgusting shape.

"I want to hire you," she said, laying twenty-five cents on the gas can beside Encyclopedia. "Some girl swiped my right sneaker."

Bad as her left sneaker was, her right sneaker was worse. It had two large holes in front. Her toes poked through like stunned tadpoles.

"I kept the sneakers outside the garage," Phoebe said. "Mom never allows them in the house. She says the smell would make an elephant faint."

All at once Encyclopedia wished he were somewhere else, like somersaulting down a ski jump.

"Go on," he said bravely.

"An hour ago I was sitting in the garage, clipping my toenails, the ones that show through the right sneaker," Phoebe said. "The door was open, and I noticed a girl running across my yard."

"Who was it?" Sally asked.

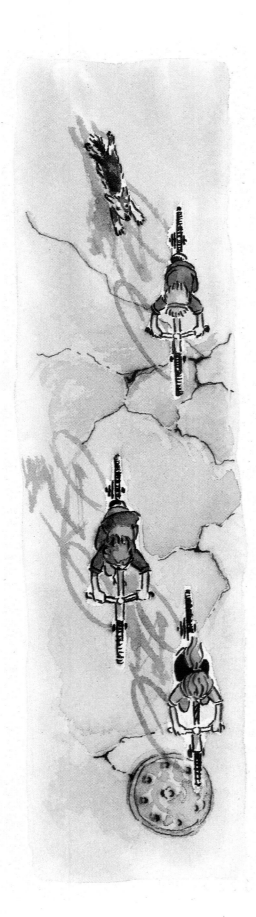

"I only saw her back," Phoebe said. "But she was carrying my sneaker."

"Whoever stole your sneaker wants to stop you from winning again," Sally said. "That means she's in the Disgusting Sneaker Contest herself."

"Then go out to South Park and watch the contest," Phoebe urged. "Maybe you can spot the thief."

Encyclopedia cared less than zero about getting up close and personal with the rottenest sneakers in Idaville.

Still . . . duty called.

As they biked to South Park, Phoebe told the detectives all about the Disgusting Sneaker Contest.

The event raised money for charity through entrance fees and sponsors. There were only two rules. Sneakers had to belong to the child whose feet were in them, and damage couldn't be caused by anything but natural wear.

"The judges grade sneakers on a scale of one to twenty," Phoebe said. "They look at eyelets, tongues, soles, heels, and overall condition."

The judging had begun when they reached South Park. Ann Little, Phoebe's classmate, hurried over to her.

"I was getting worried," Ann said. "I thought something happened to you."

"Something did," Phoebe replied sadly. "Somebody stole my right sneaker while I was clipping my nails."

"I don't see Bugs Meany," Sally remarked, glancing around. "He's been bragging all week that he's a 'shoe-in.'"

"Bugs was thrown out on his ear," Ann answered happily. "He beat up his sneakers with an electric weed cutter, but he didn't fool the judges."

"Have you been judged?" Phoebe asked.

"At the moment I'm in the lead," Ann said. "But Stinky Redmond, Tessie Bottoms, and lots of others haven't had their turn."

"Tessie's just been called," Sally said.

Tessie, an eighth-grader, strutted up confidently. She removed both sneakers and laid them on the table in front of the judges.

All the judges wore rubber gloves for protection. They picked up each sneaker and examined it at arm's length.

Tessie received seventeen points, putting her in the lead. She paraded over to Phoebe.

"Top that, kiddo!" she gloated.

"Knock it off, Tessie," Ann said. "Phoebe's not in the contest this year. Somebody stole her right sneaker while she was clipping her toenails."

"If she ever learns what socks are for, she won't have to worry about her toenails," Tessie jeered.

Suddenly there was a big fuss by the table. Mrs. Carstairs, one of the judges, had swooned and couldn't continue.

"You've got to smell this contest to believe it," she muttered as she was helped away. "I should have brought a gas mask."

"Maybe the judges should get prizes," Sally observed.

Encyclopedia mumbled. His mind was on something else.

Something he had heard or seen bothered him. He was trying to remember what it was when Stinky Redmond's name was called.

"Stinky could have dressed up as a girl and stolen Phoebe's sneaker," Sally said. "He's tricky enough to slip a full moon past a werewolf."

Stinky wore black-and-white jogging sneakers. He laid them on the judges' table and looked cockily at Tessie.

"Did you see that?" Phoebe exclaimed. "He looked at Tessie as if she were his biggest rival, not me. He knows I can't defeat him because I have only one sneaker!"

"Phoebe's right," Ann said. "Stinky gave himself away. He's the thief!"

"Someone ought to wrinkle his chin," Sally said.

"Wait," Encyclopedia cautioned. He was still trying to remember.

The winners were announced at three o'clock. Stinky won. Tessie finished second.

Sally and Phoebe and Ann cheered an instant later. Ann had taken third.

Encyclopedia didn't groan or cheer. He had remembered.

"You're the thief," he said to . . .

WHO WAS THE THIEF?

Try These On!

Make a Poster

Step Right Up

Doesn't the Disgusting Sneaker Contest sound like a great way to spend an afternoon? Make a poster advertising the event. Include the rules as well as where and why the contest is held. Add your own ideas for prizes. Include a time and date. Make it seem like a contest everyone will want to enter!

Role-play

You Be the Judge

Being a judge at the Disgusting Sneaker Contest must be quite an experience! With a group of classmates, act out the judging of the contest. Play the roles of a few contestants and two or three judges. Add some words and actions to what's in the story, and perform your scene for your class.

What's the result of all this hard work?

An episode of GHOSTWRITER — like the one below called "A Crime of Two Cities"

Jamal and his family are on vacation in England. One day he and his new British friend Becky are almost run over by a strange, creepy bicycle messenger. The cyclist drops an envelope containing a coded message. When Jamal and Becky decipher the code, they discover the plan for a kidnapping — which is about to take place in New York! Jamal needs to get in touch with the rest of the team, so he contacts Ghostwriter.

Ghostwriter alerts the team in the U.S., and they pursue codes and clues in New York. Meanwhile, Jamal and Becky chase suspects through the streets of London — where Jamal's curiosity eventually puts him in danger!

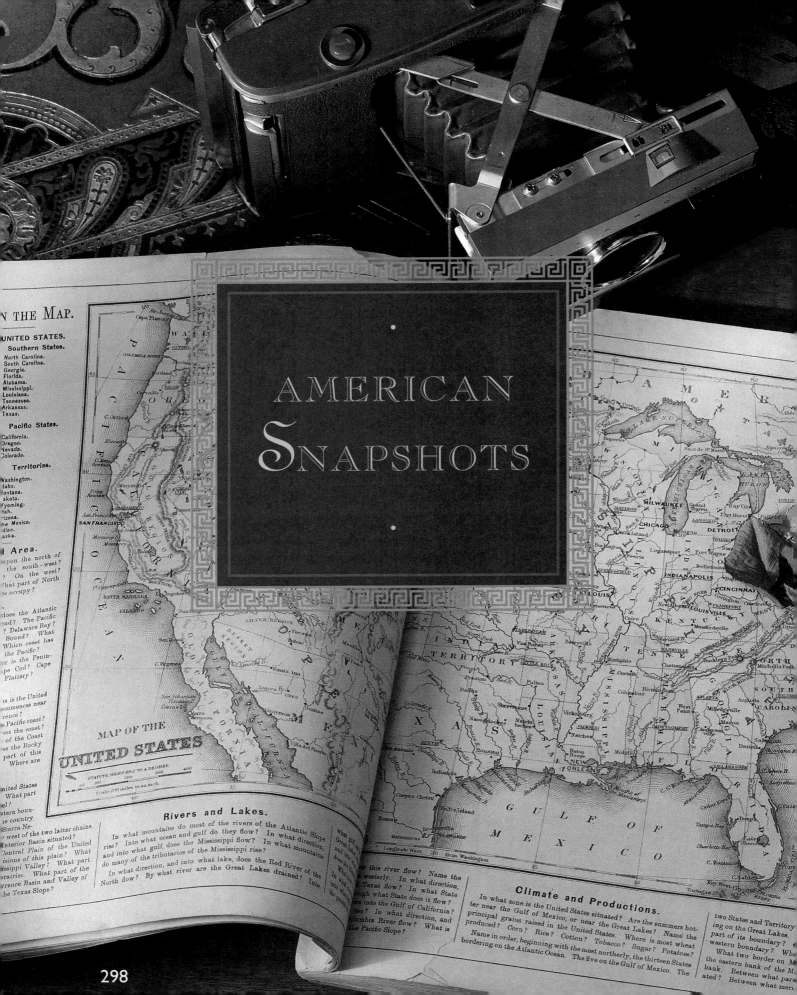

AMERICAN SNAPSHOTS

299

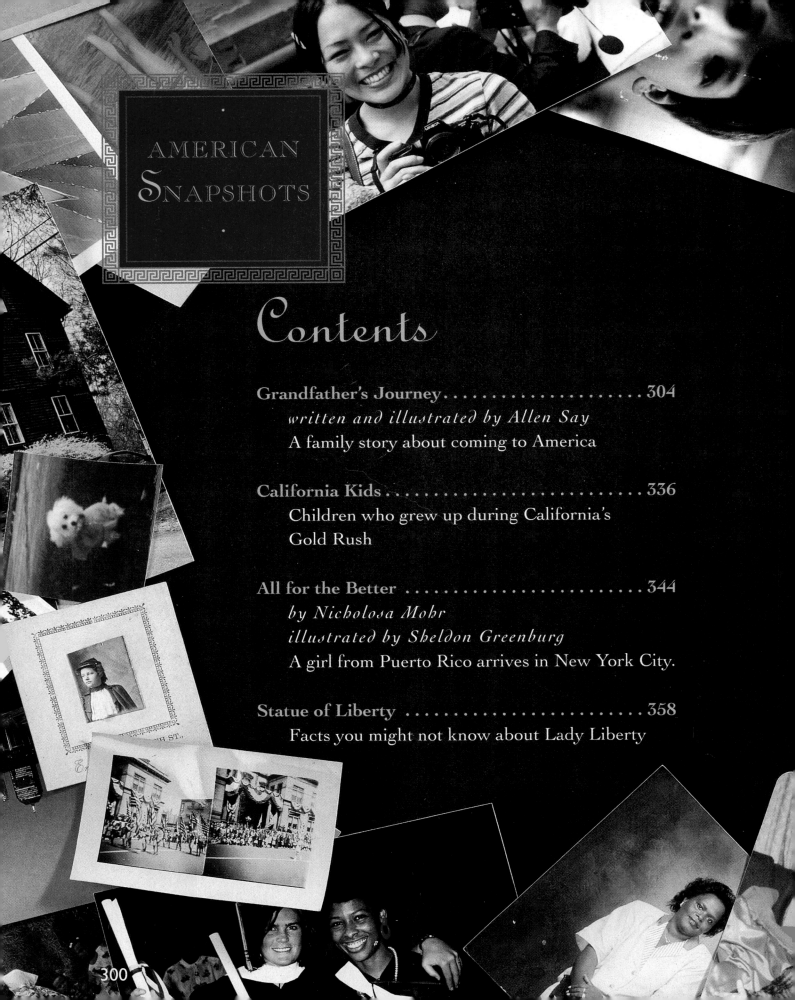

AMERICAN SNAPSHOTS

Contents

Read on Your Own!

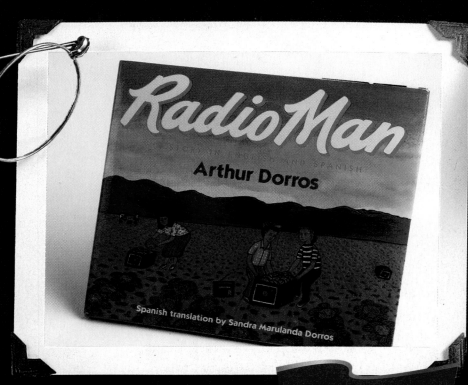

PAPERBACK PLUS

Radio Man/Don Radio

A Story in English and Spanish by Arthur Dorros

As Diego and his migrant farm worker family travel from state to state, the voices on his radio remind him of the places he's been.

In the same book . . .

More to read about migrant farm workers and a radio station run by and for children.

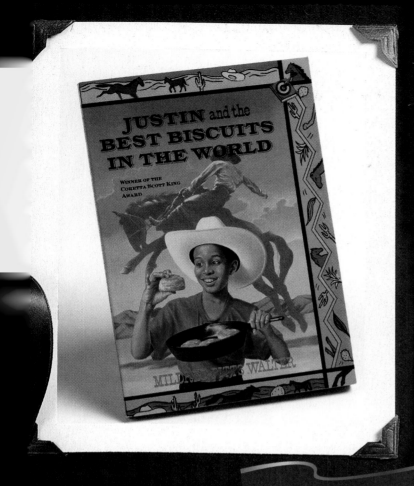

PAPERBACK **PLUS**

Justin and the Best Biscuits in the World

by *Mildred Pitts Walter*

When Justin visits his grand-father's ranch in Missouri, he learns what it really means to be a cowboy.

In the same book . . .

More about African American cowboys and cowboy life.

Grandfather's Journey

ALLEN SAY

My grandfather was a young man when he left his
home in Japan and went to see the world.

He wore European clothes for the first time and
began his journey on a steamship. The Pacific Ocean
astonished him.

For three weeks he did not see land. When land
finally appeared it was the New World.

He explored North America by train and river-
boat, and often walked for days on end.

Deserts with rocks like enormous sculptures amazed him.

The endless farm fields reminded him of the
ocean he had crossed.

Huge cities of factories and tall buildings
bewildered and yet excited him.

He marveled at the towering mountains and
rivers as clear as the sky.

He met many people along the way. He shook
hands with black men and white men, with yellow men
and red men.

The more he traveled, the more he longed to see
new places, and never thought of returning home.

Of all the places he visited, he liked California
best. He loved the strong sunlight there, the Sierra
Mountains, the lonely seacoast.

After a time, he returned to his village in Japan to marry his childhood sweetheart. Then he brought his bride to the new country.

They made their home by the San Francisco Bay
and had a baby girl.

As his daughter grew, my grandfather began to
think about his own childhood. He thought about
his old friends.

He remembered the mountains and rivers of his
home. He surrounded himself with songbirds, but
he could not forget.

Finally, when his daughter was nearly grown, he
could wait no more. He took his family and returned
to his homeland.

Once again he saw the mountains and rivers
of his childhood.

They were just as he had remembered them.

Once again he exchanged stories and laughed
with his old friends.

But the village was not a place for a daughter
from San Francisco.

So my grandfather bought a house in a large
city nearby.

There, the young woman fell in love, married, and
sometime later I was born.

When I was a small boy, my favorite weekend
was a visit to my grandfather's house. He told me
many stories about California.

He raised warblers and silvereyes, but he could not forget the mountains and rivers of California. So he planned a trip.

But a war began. Bombs fell from the sky and
scattered our lives like leaves in a storm.

When the war ended, there was nothing left of the
city and of the house where my grandparents had lived.

So they returned to the village where they had
been children.

But my grandfather never kept another
songbird.

The last time I saw him, my grandfather said that
he longed to see California one more time. He never
did.

And when I was nearly grown, I left home and
went to see California for myself.

After a time, I came to love the land my grandfather had loved, and I stayed on and on until I had a daughter of my own.

But I also miss the mountains and rivers of my childhood. I miss my old friends. So I return now and then, when I cannot still the longing in my heart.

The funny thing is, the moment I am in one country, I am homesick for the other.

I think I know my grandfather now.
I miss him very much.

Allen Say

As a child in Japan, Allen Say was fascinated by his grandfather's stories of travel and of America. Like his grandfather, Say was born in Japan. He moved to America when he was sixteen.

It took Allen Say two years to complete *Grandfather's Journey*. He explains that his favorite illustration from the book is the one of

himself as a sixteen year old, just arrived in the United States for the first time. (See page 330.) "I love that painting," Say admits.

Today Allen Say continues his work as an artist, author, and photographer. He has written and illustrated a number of popular books for children, including *Tree of Cranes*, about his childhood in Japan, and *A River Dream*, about his favorite hobby, fly-fishing.

AFTER THE JOURNEY

Tell It With Pictures

What did you think about the illustrations in *Grandfather's Journey*? How did they help you understand the story? Discuss the illustrations with a group of classmates. Then take turns trying to retell the story using just the illustrations.

An Amazing Country

Think about how the author's grandfather felt when he first saw the sights of America. Have you ever felt the same way when visiting a new place? Write a paragraph describing your visit and your feelings. Try to use some of the words from the story that described how the grandfather felt.

334

Create a Postcard

Greetings from America!

Create a postcard showing one of the spots in America that the author's grandfather first visited. Draw your own picture for the postcard or find a clipping from an old magazine. Then write what the grandfather might have written on the postcard to send to a friend back home in Japan.

Make a Collage

Your Home

The author's grandfather remembered the mountains and rivers of Japan. What are the things that remind you of where you live? Make a collage that shows where you live and what home means to you. When you are finished, display your collage and discuss with a classmate how the things on your collage are similar to or different from the things that reminded the grandfather of home.

335

CALIFORNIA

This poster advertised passage by boat
▼ from Massachusetts to the gold region.

Some forty-niners came by land
in covered wagon trains. ▼

Miners used pans like
this to discover gold. ▼

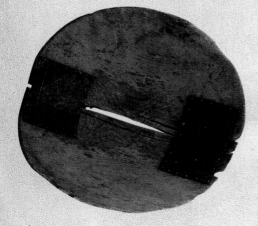

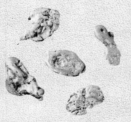

nuggets   *dust*   *flakes*

Most gold was found in one of these three forms. ▲

KIDS

IN 1848 *the cry rang out: Gold in California! Within ten years, over three hundred thousand hopeful fortune hunters arrived on the west coast. They came by sea and over land. They were called the Forty-niners because 1849 was the first big year of the California Gold Rush. Ygnacio Villegas and Eleanor Swinnerton were two California Kids who wrote about growing up during this exciting time.*

EN 1848 *se oyó el grito: ¡Hay oro en California! Dentro de diez años llegaron a la costa del oeste más de trescientas mil personas que soñaban con hacerse ricas. Viajaron por tierra y por mar. Se les llamó los viajeros del 49 porque el año 1849 era el año clave de la fiebre del oro en California. Ygnacio Villegas y Eleanor Swinnerton eran dos niños de California que escribieron acerca de sus experiencias durante esta emocionante época.*

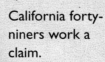

◄ California forty-niners work a claim.

Tall boots were made to keep the miners dry. ►

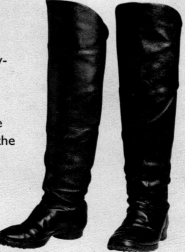

A miner poses with his tools and his bag of gold. ▶

YGNACIO

BOY RANCHO

The Villegas family traveled to Alta California in 1848. In Monterey the Villegas family became friends with Francisco Pacheco, who owned several huge ranchos covering many thousands of acres. They moved to Rancho San Felipe, where they opened a store on Pacheco Pass Road. During the 1850s, hungry miners traveled that road on their way to the gold fields, so the Villegas family added a restaurant to their store. As an old man Ygnacio wrote his boyhood adventures during the 1850s in California.

YGNACIO WRITES ABOUT 1850

A STAGECOACH RIDE

I remember in the early 1850s. I was being sent by my father to San Francisco to collect a bill. It was the first time I had ever ridden in a stage-coach or any other vehicle of that class. On account of the tiring work for the horses, there were stations along the road. In two hours we reached the first station and eating house. As the stage stopped in front of the eating house, three men stood by, ready to unhitch the horses and put on a fresh team.

A storefront scene in Sonora, California. *Botica* is Spanish for drugstore.

◀

a "pinch"	one ounce
$1	**$15**

small glass	large glass
$100	**$1000**

YGNACIO

UN MUCHACHO RANCHERO

La familia Villegas viajó a Alta California en 1848. En Monterey la familia Villegas se hizo amiga de Francisco Pacheco, quien poseía varios ranchos enormes que abarcaban muchos miles de acres. Ellos se mudaron a Rancho San Felipe donde abrieron una tienda en Pacheco Pass Road. Durante los años del 1850, muchos mineros hambrientos pasaban por ese camino en su ida a los yacimientos de oro, así que la familia Villegas agregó un restaurante a su negocio. En su vejez Ygnacio escribió sus aventuras de muchacho durante los años del 1850 en California.

> **YGNACIO ESCRIBE ACERCA DEL AÑO 1850**

UN VIAJE EN DILIGENCIA

Recuerdo que mi padre me envió a San Francisco a cobrar una cuenta, a principios de los años del 1850. Era la primera vez que yo andaba en diligencia o en cualquier otro vehículo de esa clase. Debido al trabajo cansador de los caballos, había paradas a lo largo del camino. En dos horas nosotros llegamos a la primera parada y lugar de comida. Tan pronto como la diligencia se detuvo enfrente de la casa de comidas, hubo tres hombres listos para desenganchar los caballos y poner un tiro fresco.

ELEANOR

A GOLD RUSH GIRL

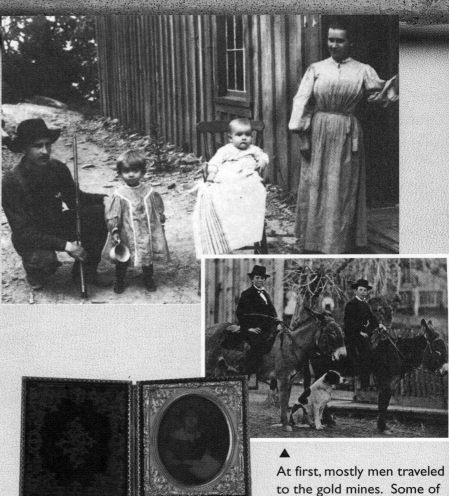

Eleanor Josephine Harvey Swinnerton was born in Butte County on May 27, 1853.

Eleanor's childhood was unusual. As a baby, her cradle was a small rocker that had been used for mining gold. On visits to Marysville, Eleanor stayed at a hotel and sometimes attended the theatre. Goldminers gave her nuggets to play with. Although she lived far from town, Eleanor went to school with her sister Fronie. She studied French and Algebra among other subjects. Education and culture had been highly valued by her family for generations.

When she was old, Eleanor wrote her childhood memoirs for her grandchildren.

▲ At first, mostly men traveled to the gold mines. Some of them were eventually joined by the rest of their families.

ELEANOR WRITES ABOUT 1856

LIFE IN MARYSVILLE

Father took the family to Marysville to spend the winter of 1856. He had an interest in the hotel "Great Western" and the theatre building across the street. There was always some troupe playing in the theatre.

Miners used wooden rockers like this one as one way to separate gold from earth. ◄

A family takes a break on their journey west. ▲

ELEANOR

UNA NIÑA DE LA ÉPOCA DE LA FIEBRE DEL ORO

Eleanor Josephine Harvey Swinnerton nació en el Condado de Butte, el 27 de mayo de 1853.

La infancia de Eleanor fue insólita. De bebé, su cuna fue un balancín que había sido usado en la explotación del oro. En sus visitas a Marysville, Eleanor se quedaba en un hotel y a veces asistía al teatro. Los mineros le daban pepitas de oro para que jugara con ellas. A pesar de que vivía lejos del pueblo, Eleanor fue a la escuela con su hermana Fronie. Ella estudió francés y álgebra, entre otras materias. Educación y cultura habían sido valoradas en su familia por generaciones.

Cuando envejeció, Eleanor escribió las memorias de su infancia, para sus nietos.

ELEANOR ESCRIBE ACERCA DEL AÑO 1856

LA VIDA EN MARYSVILLE

Papá llevó la familia a Marysville a pasar el invierno de 1856. Él tenía acciones en el hotel "Great Western" y en el edificio del teatro, del otro lado de la calle. Siempre había alguna compañía actuando en el teatro.

A GIRL ACTRESS

Sue Robinson and her father and step-mother were playing in Marysville that winter. Sue was about 12 years old then. She didn't like the stage, but wanted to live in a home and to go to school. My father offered to adopt her, but her father thought her too valuable in the theatre. At last he agreed she could go to school if she would dance and sing Wednesday nights and take part in plays on Tuesday and Saturday nights. She would come out dressed in a simple home dress and sing old-fashioned songs. The audience would toss money and gold nuggets to her — particularly when she sang "Good News From Home." She would gather up the stuff in a funny little apron and one night it came untied and let the money and gold go rolling on the floor. Then the audience went crazy and laughed and stamped and applauded until I was frightened.

Actors and actresses like this woman provided popular entertainment in the mining towns. ◄

Gold mining in Marysville, California, in 1850

342

Una niña actriz

Sue Robinson, su padre y su madrastra estaban actuando en Marysville ese invierno. Sue tendría unos doce años en ese entonces. A ella no le gustaba actuar y sólo quería un hogar e ir a la escuela. Mi padre ofreció adoptarla pero su padre pensaba que ella era demasiado valiosa para el teatro. Finalmente su padre accedió a que fuera a la escuela, siempre que bailara y cantara los miércoles por la noche y tomara parte en obras, también, los martes y sábados por la noche. Ella salía vestida con un sencillo vestido de casa y cantaba canciones del pasado. La audiencia le arrojaba dinero y pepitas de oro, especialmente cuando cantaba "Good News From Home", que ella juntaba en un delantalcito muy curioso. Una noche se le desató permitiendo que el dinero y el oro salieran rodando por el piso. Esto enloqueció a la audiencia que rió, pateó y aplaudió tanto que me asustó.

▲ "I come to California with a banjo on my knee..." Words from a popular song among the forty-niners.

MEET THE AUTHOR

Much of Nicholasa Mohr's writing is based on her own experiences in the section of New York City called *El Barrio*.

Nicholasa Mohr

After Mohr graduated from high school, she became a successful artist. When an art collector asked her to tell the story of a Puerto Rican girl growing up on the United States mainland, she began to write. Since then, Mohr has devoted most of her time to writing. Her well-known books for children include *The Magic Shell* and *Felita*, both about children who, like Mohr, find strength from their families and their own creativity.

All for the Better is the true story of Evelina Lopez, a Puerto Rican girl who arrived in New York City in the 1930s. Evelina grew up to become a leader in New York's Puerto Rican community.

MEET THE ILLUSTRATOR

Sheldon Greenburg

Sheldon Greenburg decided he wanted to be an artist when his second grade teacher paid him a big compliment. Greenburg had drawn a picture of a story the teacher had told his class, and she singled out his

drawing as an excellent example of what the story was about. Years later, Greenburg studied painting and drawing in California and New York.

When Greenburg illustrates stories, he tries to put himself in the main character's shoes. He also thinks about the kinds of images he would like to see if he were looking at the story for the first time. Greenburg grew up in Wichita, Kansas, and now lives in Berkeley, California, where he enjoys drawing, reading, biking, and skiing — on snow and on water.

All for the Better

A STORY OF EL BARRIO

BY NICHOLASA MOHR

ALL FOR THE
BETTER
A Story of El Barrio

by Nicholasa Mohr
Alex Haley, General Editor

Leaving Home

Cuidate mi hijita. "Take good care of yourself, my little daughter." It was **September 11, 1933,** and eleven-year-old Evelina Lopez was leaving her family for the first time. Evelina struggled to hold back her tears as she said good-bye. She asked for her mother's blessing. *Bendición Mami,* she whispered.

Her mother held her a long time, then said, "Be brave, my sweet Evelina. God willing, we will all be together someday. I promise."

Her mother, Eva Cruz Lopez, had faced an impossible decision — to part with her oldest daughter. Eva Lopez was raising three children by herself. In ordinary years that is hard enough to do, but in the years of the Great Depression it had become a hopeless task.

Worried about her children's future, Eva Lopez decided to send Evelina to live in New York City with Eva's older sister, Vicenta. Vicenta had recently married. She and her husband had no children yet and were willing to take Evelina in to help the family. The Depression had brought hard times to New York City, but things were much worse in Puerto Rico. Sending Evelina to live with her Tía Vicenta was the best thing to do.

Evelina kissed her little sisters, eight-year-old Lillian and baby Elba, for the last time.

"You will grow so fast, little Elba," Evelina said sadly to her baby sister. "I won't be able to see you take your first steps."

She kissed baby Elba again as the ship's shrill whistle blew. It was time to board. Evelina had to hurry. She hugged Lillian and then her mother. "I'll

miss my best friend and sister and you, too, Mami. I'll miss all of you so much and think of you every day."

Then she rushed to board the ship *El Ponce*, which was ready to embark on its five-day journey across the sea to New York City. Once on the ship, Evelina quickly made her way through all the people crowded on the deck and reached the railing. She looked down on the docks where people were waving good-bye to their relatives.

Evelina saw her mother and sister. They waved farewell to her. She grasped the railing, and leaning forward, waved and blew kisses in their direction.

The shrill whistle blared again as the ship
slowly pulled away from the dock and out into San
Juan Harbor. Evelina watched as first her mother
and sisters and then her beautiful Island disappeared from view. Soon the soft green-blue of the
Caribbean Sea and the cloudless bright sunny sky
were all she was able to see.

She wondered if she would ever again see the
abundant flowers and tall palm trees glistening in
the bright sunshine. Would she ever again bathe in
Puerto Rico's blue waters or walk along its white
sandy beaches? Would she ever again bask in the
warmth of her beautiful tropical Island of Puerto
Rico? It was scary to think the answer to these questions might be no.

But the scariest part was being without her family. Evelina hardly remembered her Tía Vicenta, who had left Puerto Rico several years earlier. And she had never even met her aunt's new husband. She felt as if she was going to live with strangers. Evelina tried hard not to be too fearful about the future. Mami, she told herself, had done what was best for *la familia*. So she would do what she must to be brave.

Doña Clara, an acquaintance of her mother's, was also sailing on *El Ponce*. She had agreed to share a cabin with Evelina and to take charge of her during their voyage.

During the first day at sea, Doña Clara was very attentive. She saw to it that Evelina was safely settled in her bunk and had all she needed to be comfortable. But the following day the sea grew rough and Doña Clara became seasick. She remained sick the entire voyage and never once left their cramped little cabin.

It was Evelina who ended up taking care of Doña Clara. "You're an angel," Doña Clara whispered from her sickbed. "I'm the one who is supposed to take care of you." Then she insisted that Evelina mingle with the other passengers. Since Doña Clara slept most of the time, Evelina took her advice. But she always checked in on Doña Clara to make sure she was all right.

Everyone remarked on what a thoughtful and responsible girl Evelina was. Her outgoing personality and good looks endeared her to all she met. "Evelina, come have dinner with us," they would say. Or, "Evelina, join us for a game of checkers." She was always sought after, and by the time the journey was over, Evelina had made many friends on board ship.

To her surprise, on the last day of the voyage
Evelina felt sad. Sad about leaving *El Ponce*. Sad
about saying goodbye to Doña Clara and all her
new friends. Everyone had been so kind! They had
taken her mind away from her own sorrow. They
had made the separation from her mother and
sisters seem less terrible, less fearful.

But now the voyage was coming to an end.
Evelina came up on deck. With all her might she
wished that *El Ponce* was entering San Juan Harbor,
not New York Harbor. She wanted to be back in
Puerto Rico.

Evelina watched as this strange new city
loomed gray and forbidding. She cringed at the
sight of the tall buildings crowding across the hori-
zon. Her heart sank as she looked around. The city
skies were dreary. The water had a foul, oily smell.

A tug guided *El Ponce* to the dock. Evelina
watched the workmen move around the dock shouting strange words at one another. They looped
heavy ropes from the ship around the dock's iron

posts. Quickly *El Ponce* was tied fast and the five-day journey was over. Doña Clara, who had recovered as soon as they had neared land again, took Evelina's hand to lead her ashore. They went down the gangplank onto the docks of South Brooklyn.

"Now I must make sure that you find your aunt and uncle," she said. Many of the passengers hugged Evelina. "Keep in touch," they said. *Que Dios te bendiga.* "God bless," they said.

"Wait here and don't move," said Doña Clara. "First, I have to make sure we have all our luggage. Then we'll find your aunt and uncle."

Evelina stood by herself and waited in these strange new surroundings. She watched as everyone bustled about, gathering their luggage and looking for their kinfolk. Suddenly she felt lost and bewildered. Where was Doña Clara? Where was Tía Vicenta? She was close to tears when she heard her name being called.

"Evelina! Evelina! Here we are!"
She turned to see her Tía Vicenta waving
eagerly in her direction. Beside her aunt
stood a man who must be her new uncle.
He, too, was waving at her.

Her aunt gave her a great big hug.
"This," she said, "is Enrique Godreau, my
husband and your uncle. But everybody
calls him Godreau."

Godreau smiled at his new niece.

"Your Tío Godreau is glad to see that
you did not get seasick, fall overboard, and
get eaten by sharks," her uncle said with a
wink. "So you must be as smart and as
tough as your aunt!" Evelina had to laugh
and immediately felt less sad.

Meanwhile, Doña Clara had returned
with the luggage. Vicenta and Doña Clara
knew each other from Puerto Rico. They
greeted each other warmly. "You have a
very special niece there," said Doña Clara.
"Evelina will bring joy to your life."

Doña Clara's brother and his wife were
somewhere in the growing crowd on the
dock. She had to go find them. Before she
left she gave Evelina a long hug. Everyone
quickly exchanged addresses and then said
good-bye.

A little while later, Evelina took her first
ride on a New York City subway. The
crowded subway crossed a bridge and then
rode high above the streets on its way to
Spanish Harlem. Evelina had to hold her

ears when the train shrieked its way around turns. She stared out the window at the vast city filled with brick and concrete buildings.

The train rumbled uptown until they reached their stop. Her aunt and uncle had an apartment on 117th Street and Madison Avenue. "Here we are in *El Barrio*," said her aunt. "Home at last."

The community of Spanish Harlem was called *El Barrio*, which means "The Neighborhood." *El Barrio* was the largest community of Spanish-speaking people in New York City. The majority of these people were Puerto Ricans. And most of them were newly arrived from the Island, just like Evelina.

There were no skyscrapers here, and most of the buildings were not so very tall. Just like home, small shops lined the avenues. Grocery stores were called *bodegas*. Even bakeries and luncheonettes had Spanish names, *Bodega de Santurce* and *Rivera's Luncheonette — Comidas Criollas*. There were also *botánicas*, which sold religious articles just like the ones back in Puerto Rico. Evelina felt more at ease. *El Barrio* had a familiar feeling.

"Here's our building," said her uncle. "Now instead of climbing a hill like we do back home, we climb lots of steps."

Evelina followed as they went up three flights of stairs.

"Welcome," said her aunt, holding the door to their small apartment open. "This is your home." She took Evelina to her bedroom. "Someday, God willing, your mother and sisters will be here with us, too."

Evelina settled down in her small bedroom. She put away her few items of clothing and gently placed the photographs of her mother and sisters on her bureau. She missed them so much her heart ached. Her eyes brimmed with tears.

Evelina wiped away her tears and stood looking out her bedroom window. Outside, traffic filled the streets and people scurried around in every direction. She wondered if they also missed home and if they were away from their families, too. Maybe some of them would be going back someday.

She saw a woman walking with two girls about the same ages as Lillian and herself. All three held hands. They are happy and they are together, she thought.

"Please, dear God," she prayed, "if I am never to go back to my beloved Puerto Rico, then, like Tía Vicenta says, bring Mami, Lillian, and baby Elba here to me soon."

Evelina understood that no matter what happened in her future, right now she was starting a brand-new life.

> **Evelina does settle into her new home in *El Barrio*. In fact, she goes on to become respected as someone who helps and cares for her neighbors. Read the rest of *All for the Better* to find out more about Evelina's remarkable childhood.**

Home at Last

Write a Dialogue

Hello, My Name Is Evelina

During Evelina's journey she was very popular. What do you suppose she talked about with her new friends on the ship? Write a dialogue between Evelina and one of the passengers she makes friends with. Show how they get to know each other and what they expect to find when they get to New York. When you are done, act out your dialogue with a classmate.

Make a List

Travel Tips

During Evelina's journey to New York, she kept busy by meeting the other passengers and playing checkers. Have you ever been on a long trip? What are some of the things you did to keep from being bored? Discuss your ideas with a group of classmates and write a list of "Things to Do on a Long Trip."

Draw a Picture

New York, New York

Think about the sights that Evelina saw when she first arrived in New York. Pick a scene from that part of the story and draw a picture showing what Evelina might have seen.

Compare Journeys

Coming to the U.S.

Both Evelina and the grandfather in *Grandfather's Journey* come to the United States when they are young. How are their reactions to this new land the same? How are they different? Write a paragraph that compares how these two characters feel in their new land.

Statue of Liberty

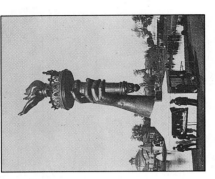

Liberty's hand and torch came to America first in 1876. Visitors could climb up to the torch for a fifty-cent fee. This section eventually went back to Paris before returning with the finished statue in 1885.

The seven rays of Liberty's crown represent the seven seas and seven continents of the world.

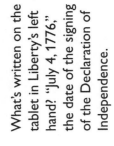

What's written on the tablet in Liberty's left hand? "July 4, 1776," the date of the signing of the Declaration of Independence.

S HE STANDS WATCH over New York Harbor — Liberty Enlightening the World. Best known simply as the Statue of Liberty, she was a gift to the people of the United States from the people of France in 1886 to honor the friendship and love of liberty shared by the two countries. Before long, waves of immigrants who passed the statue on their way to nearby Ellis Island came to revere Lady Liberty as a symbol of the freedom and opportunity they sought. Today she remains a beacon of freedom to the world.

The statue was completed in France in 1884. In the spring of 1885, it was taken apart and shipped to New York in 214 wooden packing crates. It was re-assembled on a base and pedestal built by American workers.

STATUE STATS

Height of statue, toe to torch: 151 feet, 1 inch

Total height with base and pedestal: 305 feet, 1 inch

Weight of statue: 225 tons

Number of steps to obser-vation deck in crown: 354

Liberty was designed and built by French sculptor Frédéric-Auguste Bartholdi. It was said that he created the statue's stern face to look like his mother, shown in the portrait at left.

The metal framework under Liberty's copper skin was de-signed by Alexandre-Gustave Eiffel, the man who built the famous Eiffel Tower in Paris.

Sarah, Plain and Tall

Patricia MacLachlan

Sarah,
Plain and Tall

BY PATRICIA MACLACHLAN

Caleb's mother died the day after he was born. His sister Anna remembers how Mama and Papa used to sing all the time. But with Mama gone, Papa doesn't sing anymore. Now Papa has placed a newspaper advertisement for a wife, and from far away in Maine, a woman named Sarah has answered.

Caleb and Papa and I wrote letters to Sarah, and before the ice and snow had melted from the fields, we all received answers. Mine came first.

Dear Anna,

Yes, I can braid hair and I can make stew and bake bread, though I prefer to build bookshelves and paint.

My favorite colors are the colors of the sea, blue and gray and green, depending on the weather. My brother William is a fisherman, and he tells me that when he is in the middle of a fogbound sea the water is a color for which there is no name. He catches flounder and sea bass and bluefish. Sometimes he sees whales. And birds, too, of course. I am enclosing a book of sea birds so you will see what William and I see every day.

Very truly yours,
Sarah Elisabeth Wheaton

Caleb read and read the letter so many times that the ink began
to run and the folds tore. He read the book about sea birds over and over.

"Do you think she'll come?" asked Caleb. "And will she stay? What if
she thinks we are loud and pesky?"

"You *are* loud and pesky," I told him. But I was worried, too. Sarah
loved the sea, I could tell. Maybe she wouldn't leave there after all to come
where there were fields and grass and sky and not much else.

"What if she comes and doesn't like our house?" Caleb asked. "I told
her it was small. Maybe I shouldn't have told her it was small."

"Hush, Caleb. Hush."

Caleb's letter came soon after, with a picture of a cat drawn on
the envelope.

Dear Caleb,

My cat's name is Seal because she is gray like the seals that swim offshore in Maine. She is glad that Lottie and Nick send their greetings. She likes dogs most of the time. She says their footprints are much larger than hers (which she is enclosing in return).

Your house sounds lovely, even though it is far out in the country with no close neighbors. My house is tall and the shingles are gray because of the salt from the sea. There are roses nearby.

Yes, I do like small rooms sometimes. Yes, I can keep a fire going at night. I do not know if I snore. Seal has never told me.

Very truly yours,
Sarah Elisabeth

"Did you really ask her about fires and snoring?" I asked, amazed.

"I wished to know," Caleb said.

He kept the letter with him, reading it in the barn and in the fields and by the cow pond. And always in bed at night.

One morning, early, Papa and Caleb and I were cleaning out the horse stalls and putting down new bedding. Papa stopped suddenly and leaned on his pitchfork.

"Sarah has said she will come for a month's time if we wish her to," he said, his voice loud in the dark barn. "To see how it is. Just to see."

Caleb stood by the stall door and folded his arms across his chest.

"I think," he began. Then, "I think," he said slowly, "that it would be good — to say yes," he finished in a rush.

Papa looked at me.

"I say yes," I told him, grinning.

"Yes," said Papa. "Then yes it is."

And the three of us, all smiling, went to work again.

The next day Papa went to town to mail his letter to Sarah. It was rainy for days, and the clouds followed. The house was cool and damp and quiet. Once I set four places at the table, then caught myself and put the extra plate away. Three lambs were born, one with a black face. And then Papa's letter came. It was very short.

Dear Jacob,

 I will come by train. I will wear a yellow bonnet. I am plain and tall.

           Sarah

"What's that?" asked Caleb excitedly, peering over Papa's shoulder. He pointed. "There, written at the bottom of the letter."

Papa read it to himself. Then he smiled, holding up the letter for us to see.

Tell them I sing was all it said.

Sarah came in the spring. She came through green grass fields that bloomed with Indian paintbrush, red and orange, and blue-eyed grass.

Papa got up early for the long day's trip to the train and back. He brushed his hair so slick and shiny that Caleb laughed. He wore a clean blue shirt, and a belt instead of suspenders.

He fed and watered the horses, talking to them as he hitched them up to the wagon. Old Bess, calm and kind; Jack, wild-eyed, reaching over to nip Bess on the neck.

"Clear day, Bess," said Papa, rubbing her nose.

"Settle down, Jack." He leaned his head on Jack.

And then Papa drove off along the dirt road to fetch Sarah. Papa's new wife. Maybe. Maybe our new mother.

Gophers ran back and forth across the road, stopping to stand up and watch the wagon. Far off in the field a woodchuck ate and listened. Ate and listened.

Caleb and I did our chores without talking. We shoveled out the stalls and laid down new hay. We fed the sheep. We swept and straightened and carried wood and water. And then our chores were done.

Caleb pulled on my shirt.

"Is my face clean?" he asked. "Can my face be *too* clean?" He looked alarmed.

"No, your face is clean but not too clean," I said.

Caleb slipped his hand into mine as we stood on the porch, watching the road. He was afraid.

"Will she be nice?" he asked. "Like Maggie?"

"Sarah will be nice," I told him.

"How far away is Maine?" he asked.

"You know how far. Far away, by the sea."

"Will Sarah bring some sea?" he asked.

"No, you cannot bring the sea."

The sheep ran in the field, and far off the cows moved slowly to the pond, like turtles.

"Will she like us?" asked Caleb very softly.

I watched a marsh hawk wheel down behind the barn.

He looked up at me.

"Of course she will like us." He answered his own question. "We are nice," he added, making me smile.

We waited and watched. I rocked on the porch and Caleb rolled a marble on the wood floor. Back and forth. Back and forth. The marble was blue.

We saw the dust from the wagon first, rising above the road, above the heads of Jack and Old Bess. Caleb climbed up onto the porch roof and shaded his eyes.

"A bonnet!" he cried. "I see a yellow bonnet!"

The dogs came out from under the porch, ears up, their eyes on the cloud of dust bringing Sarah. The wagon passed the fenced field, and the cows and sheep looked up, too. It rounded the windmill and the barn and the windbreak of Russian olive that Mama had planted long ago. Nick began to bark, then Lottie, and the wagon clattered into the yard and stopped by the steps.

"Hush," said Papa to the dogs.

And it was quiet.

Sarah stepped down from the wagon, a cloth bag in her hand. She reached up and took off her yellow bonnet, smoothing back her brown hair into a bun. She was plain and tall.

"Did you bring some sea?" cried Caleb beside me.

"Something from the sea," said Sarah, smiling. "And me." She turned and lifted a black case from the wagon. "And Seal, too."

Carefully she opened the case, and Seal, gray with white feet, stepped out. Lottie lay down, her head on her paws, staring. Nick leaned down to sniff. Then he lay down, too.

"The cat will be good in the barn," said Papa. "For mice."

Sarah smiled. "She will be good in the house, too."

Sarah took Caleb's hand, then mine. Her hands were large and rough.
She gave Caleb a shell — a moon snail, she called it — that was curled and
smelled of salt.

"The gulls fly high and drop the shells on the rocks below," she told
Caleb. "When the shell is broken, they eat what is inside."

"That is very smart," said Caleb.

"For you, Anna," said Sarah, "a sea stone."

And she gave me the smoothest and whitest stone I had ever seen.

"The sea washes over and over and around the stone, rolling it until it
is round and perfect."

"That is very smart, too," said Caleb. He looked up at Sarah. "We do
not have the sea here."

Sarah turned and looked out over the plains.

"No," she said. "There is no sea here. But the land rolls a little like the sea."

My father did not see her look, but I did. And I knew that Caleb had seen it, too. Sarah was not smiling. Sarah was already lonely. In a month's time the preacher might come to marry Sarah and Papa. And a month was a long time. Time enough for her to change her mind and leave us.

Papa took Sarah's bags inside, where her room was ready with a quilt on the bed and blue flax dried in a vase on the night table.

Seal stretched and made a small cat sound. I watched her circle the dogs and sniff the air. Caleb came out and stood beside me.

"When will we sing?" he whispered.

I shook my head, turning the white stone over and over in my hand. I wished everything was as perfect as the stone. I wished that Papa and Caleb and I were as perfect for Sarah. I wished we had a sea of our own.

◆——◆——◆

How will Sarah adjust to life with her new family? Find out by reading the rest of Sarah, Plain and Tall.

Meet the Author

PATRICIA MACLACHLAN

When Patricia MacLachlan was a
young girl in Minnesota, her mother told
her about the real Sarah, a woman who
had moved from Maine to the prairie to
become the mother to children in an
existing prairie family. As an adult, Mac-
Lachlan decided to write a book based
on her mother's stories. "I wished to
write my mother's story with spaces, like
the prairie, with silences that could say
what words could not," says the author.
The book that she wrote was *Sarah, Plain
and Tall*. MacLachlan is now a popular
author of books for children, including
Three Names and *Skylark*, the sequel to
Sarah, Plain and Tall. The busy author
also finds time to play cello and, like Sarah
in her books, to sing.

Meet the Illustrator

LESLIE WU

Leslie Wu was born in Syracuse, New
York, in 1950. She says that as a child
she was a "goofy, singing, dancing, drawing,
lonely child who never quite fit in. Nature
was where I felt most comfortable. I loved
camping, my grandmother's farm, listening
to whispers of wildflowers and animals."
For her illustrations of *Sarah, Plain and Tall*
she studied nature books on the wildflowers and landscape of the prairie. An avid
gardener, she loves studying and drawing
the colorful flowers that grow there.
About her work as an artist, Wu says "I'm
happiest when I'm drawing and painting."

Return to the Prairie

Write a Letter

Dear Brother William . . .

Sarah and the children tried to describe themselves to each other in letters. Write a letter to Sarah's brother William in Maine as if you were Sarah. Describe your new home on the prairie. Be sure to let William know about your new family, too.

Paint a Picture

How You See It

In her letters, Sarah tried to "paint a picture" of Maine in words. Draw or paint a picture that shows what you think Sarah's home in Maine might have looked like. Show your picture to a classmate and explain why you think Sarah's home looks the way you drew it.

372

Role-play a Scene

Sarah Finally Arrives

With a group of classmates, act out the scene when Sarah finally arrives at Caleb and Anna's home. Think about how each character felt at that moment. How would those feelings affect the way they acted and what they said?

Compare Characters

Why Did They Do That?

Think about the stories *Grandfather's Journey* and *All For the Better*. In those stories, the main characters made a journey. Sarah also made a journey to join Caleb and Anna. Write a paragraph or two explaining the different reasons that each character decided to go on a journey.

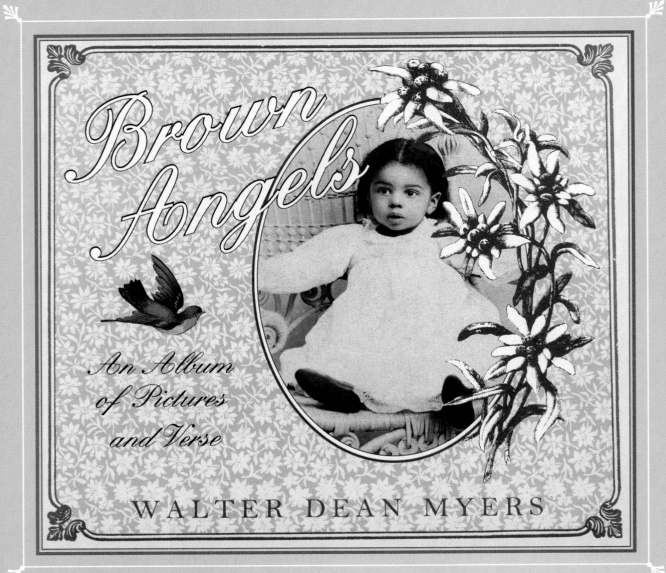

Brown Angels

An Album
of Pictures
and Verse

WALTER DEAN MYERS

Blossoms

I never dreamt
that tender blossoms
would be brown
Or precious angels
could come down
to live in the garden
of my giving heart
But here you are
brown angel

Friendship

There is a secret thread that makes us friends
    Turn away from hard and breakful eyes
    Turn away from cold and painful lies
That speaks of other, more important ends
There are two hard yet tender hearts that beat
    Take always my hand at special times
    Take always my dark and precious rhymes
That sing so brightly when our glad souls meet

Summer

I like hot days, hot days
Sweat is what you got days
Bugs buzzin from cousin to cousin
Juices dripping
Running and ripping
Catch the one you love days

Birds peeping
Old men sleeping
Lazy days, daisies lay
Beaming and dreaming
Of hot days, hot days,
Sweat is what you got days

Jeannie Had a Giggle

Jeannie had a giggle just beneath her toes
She gave a little wiggle and up her leg it rose

She tried to grab the giggle as it shimmied past her knees
But it slid right past her fingers with a "'scuse me if you please"

It slipped around her middle, it made her jump and shout
Jeannie wanted that giggle in, that giggle wanted out!

Jeannie closed her mouth, but then she heard a funny sound
As out that silly giggle flew and jumped down to the ground

Jeannie caught it with her foot just beneath her toes
She gave a little wiggle and up her leg it rose

Pride

The sound of their steps
has long been gone
Black foot, strong foot,
stumbling on
Oh follow the memory!

The sound of their song
has long been gone
Black song, strong song,
souls singing on
Oh cherish the memory!

The depth of their pride
will never be gone
Black hearts, strong hearts,
hearts beating on
Oh honor the memory!

Meet the AUTHOR

Virginia Driving Hawk Sneve

Virginia Driving Hawk Sneve (the name rhymes with "navy") was born in South Dakota in 1933. She is a member of the Rosebud Sioux Tribe, and her childhood was spent on the Rosebud Sioux reservation. She now lives in Rapid City, South Dakota, where she writes, teaches, and counsels students.

Sneve's writings for children include magazine articles, short stories, and picture books. "In my writing," she says, "I try to present an accurate portrayal of American Indian life as I have known it." You might also enjoy reading Sneve's books *The Sioux* and *The Navajo*.

Meet the ILLUSTRATOR

Ronald Himler

Ronald Himler is a painter, illustrator, and sculptor. At one time in his life, he worked as a toy designer. He was born in Cleveland, Ohio, and lived in New York City for a time. After attending some ceremonial Native American dances during a visit to the Southwest, Himler and his family moved to Tucson, Arizona. Today he is well-known for his paintings of Native American subjects. He has also illustrated over seventy-five books for children.

THE SEMINOLES
A First Americans Book
Virginia Driving Hawk Sneve

illustrated by Ronald Himler

THE FIRST SEMINOLES

Why cannot we live here in peace?
COACOOCHEE (WILDCAT)

Opothleyohola
(Creek leader)

The Seminoles once belonged to the Muskogee tribe that lived along streams in what are now southern Georgia and Alabama. In about 1708 white men came to this country and called these Indians "Creeks" because of where they lived. The white men drove the Creeks away from the streams and took their land. To escape the white men, a group of Indians moved south to territory that later became northern Florida, and settled around what is now Tallahassee. The Creeks called this group "Seminoles" which has been translated as "runaways" or "separatists," but has also been interpreted to mean "lovers of freedom" or "lovers of the wilds." The Seminoles did not want to live among white people, or with other Indians who accepted the white men's way of life.

Timucuan slave auction

Burial mounds found on Florida's west coast show that Indians were in the area 10,000 years ago. In the 1500s the Spanish, the first white men to come to Florida, found more than 10,000 Timucua Indians living there. The Spanish killed most of these Indians or sold them as slaves to landowners in Cuba and the West Indies. The remaining few joined the Seminoles.

In northern Florida the Seminoles farmed the rich land and raised horses and cattle they had gotten from the Spanish. The men hunted wild game, and the women made pottery.

The Seminoles built large dugout canoes, sturdy enough for ocean voyages. Some explored the Gulf of Mexico and went as far south as Cuba and the Bahamas. Their fearlessness in exploring unknown places would later help them make a home in the Everglades, a large swampy area in southern Florida.

SECOND SEMINOLE WAR

*We were all made by the same great Father
and are like his children.*
HOLATA MICO

In 1819 Spain sold Florida to the United States. Slave catchers from Georgia and other southern states came to reclaim the slaves who had escaped earlier. The owners not only caught former slaves, but they also took blacks who had been born free in Florida, and even captured mixed-blood and full-blood Seminoles. The Indians and blacks who escaped fled into the swamps.

In 1823 the Seminoles signed a treaty giving up most of their land. They had to leave the good farming country of north Florida and move into a reservation in the central part of the state. Despite the government's promise that the Seminoles would be safe from attacks if they obeyed U.S. laws, they were not safe. More settlers were moving into Florida and wanted Seminole land. They attacked the Indians and destroyed their crops.

Seminoles being attacked by white soldiers

The settlers wanted the Seminoles to be moved out of
Florida. In 1828 Andrew Jackson, now president of the
United States, signed the Indian Removal Act that required
all Indians in the southeastern United States to be removed to
the Indian Territory, which later became the state of
Oklahoma.

The majority of the Seminoles refused to go. They did
not want to leave the black slaves who had married into the
tribe, nor their mixed-blood children. For seven years the
Seminoles resisted by striking at the white soldiers, then van-
ishing into the swamps where the enemy could not follow.
This was the Second Seminole War. It was led by Osceola
and Coacoochee who was called Wildcat by the white men.

LIFE IN THE EVERGLADES

Close to nature, my brother, your thoughts ring softly
on the quiet air . . .
YA-KA-NES/PATTY L. HARJO

chickees

The Seminoles in Florida explored every part of the Everglades by traveling over the swampy waterways in dugout canoes. They quickly adapted to this swampland called a "river of grass" because of the tall, sharp-edged saw grass that grew in the water. The Everglades covered an area one hundred miles long and seventy miles wide from Lake Okeechobee to the Gulf of Mexico.

Scattered throughout the Everglades were hummocks, dry islands or mounds of rock with rich soil. The Seminoles found that they were good, safe places to live because few white men ventured near them.

Not only did the Everglades protect the Seminoles, but its dense forests provided shelter. The Indians erected *chickees,* open houses thatched with palmetto leaves, that stood about three feet off the ground. The slanting roof gave protection from the sun and rain, and the chickee was pleasantly cool and dry.

The Seminoles planted gardens in the fertile hummock soil. They grew sweet potatoes, pumpkins, melons, and corn, their most important crop.

From the corn the women made hominy by soaking the kernels in water and ashes. They ground the hominy into flour and made *sofkee*, a porridge that was a favorite dish. Another favorite was *coontie*, a kind of pudding made from the ground-up roots of the arrowroot plant.

The Seminoles used palm leaves or shells to hold their food. The women wove baskets from the cane and palmetto stalks that grew up in the swamp. Before the Seminoles moved into the Everglades, they had learned to use metal from the Spanish. The women had knives, iron pots, and kettles, but they also used shells for knives and garden hoes.

Each family did its cooking over a big open fire in the center of the village. This fire burned day and night.

CLOTHING

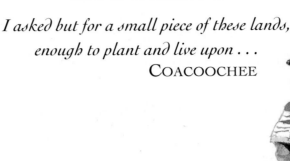

*I asked but for a small piece of these lands,
enough to plant and live upon . . .*
COACOOCHEE

"flat roll" hairstyle

The Seminoles dressed differently from other southern Indians such as the Creeks and Choctaws. The style of their clothes was influenced by Spanish cotton garments that were more comfortable than buckskin in the warm Florida climate.

The women made cool, loose-fitting clothes for their families. They wore long skirts and capelike blouses. The men's shirts reached their knees. Both men and women wore leather moccasins and leggings to protect their feet and legs from the sharp grass and spiny plants found in the Everglades.

After the women acquired sewing machines from the white men, they made bright patchwork designs that they sewed into colorful clothing. The women wore necklaces made of several strands of beads. The necklaces looked like a collar around their necks. The women combed their long hair into a wide, flat roll on the top of their heads. The men wore turbans and bandannas.

THE SEMINOLES TODAY

I never wish to tread upon my land unless I am free.

COACOOCHEE

The Florida Seminoles never signed a formal peace treaty with the United States. Up to the 1920s the Seminoles still lived by hunting, fishing, and farming. Over the years the Seminoles divided into two groups: the Miccosukees and Cow Creek Seminoles or Muskogees.

The Miccosukees' home is the Big Cypress Reservation. The Muskogees' reservation is called Brighton. The Seminole Tribe of Florida, Inc., has its headquarters in Hollywood, Florida, where there is a replica of a traditional chickee village. Seminoles also live on the State and Orient Road Reservations and at Immokalee Farms.

The "river of grass" is no longer as abundant or as large as it once was. The Seminoles can no longer survive living off the bounty of the Everglades. Much of the swampland has been land-filled and covered with the suburban homes of Florida's cities.

Today, Seminole men hunt and fish in the Everglades, but do so as sportsmen. Others serve as guides to white hunters and fishermen, but use airboats, not dugout canoes. Seminoles still farm and raise cattle on their reservations, but they all need other employment in order to support their families. Men and women earn income by selling their beautiful arts and crafts, logging, grass planting, and wrestling alligators. Tribal bingo halls and casinos also provide jobs for the Seminoles. Children attend reservation schools or go to public schools in Florida towns and cities. More and more Seminole young people are going on to college to become doctors, nurses, teachers, lawyers, and engineers.

Both the Oklahoma and Florida Seminoles retain an awareness of the sacredness of the land and teach their children the responsibility of caring for it. Few Seminoles depend on farming for survival, but they still celebrate the Green Corn Dance to cleanse and renew their lives. It is a sacred ritual and is not open to the public. The Seminoles remember that they are still one people who shared a sacred fire.

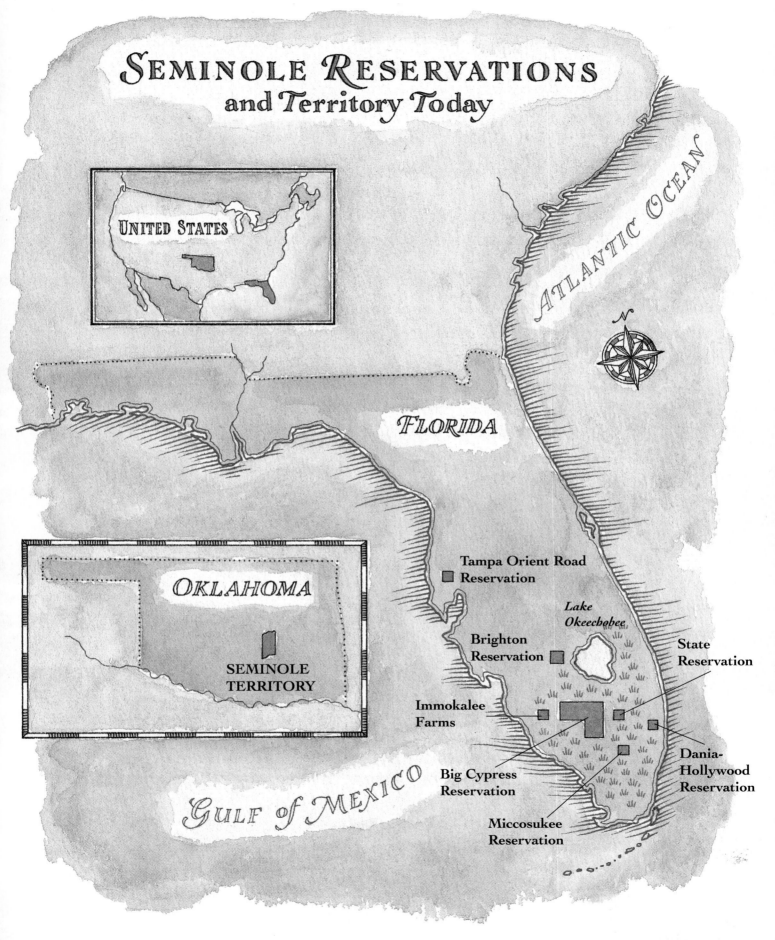

SEMINOLE RESERVATIONS
and Territory Today

UNITED STATES

ATLANTIC OCEAN

FLORIDA

OKLAHOMA

SEMINOLE TERRITORY

Tampa Orient Road Reservation

Lake Okeechobee

Brighton Reservation

State Reservation

Immokalee Farms

Big Cypress Reservation

Dania-Hollywood Reservation

Miccosukee Reservation

GULF of MEXICO

SHARE THE HERITAGE

Write a TV Editorial

In My Opinion . . .

In this selection, you learned that the Seminoles were forced off their land in the southeastern United States. How did you feel about that? Write an editorial that you might read on television that gives your opinion. When you're done, practice reading your editorial out loud to a partner.

Make a Poster

The Way They Lived

What did the Seminoles wear in the 1800s? What did they eat? What were their houses like? Pick an aspect of Seminole life described in the selection. Make a poster that shows what you have learned about this topic.

Create a Chart

Chart the Changes

Think about how the Seminoles' way of life has changed from the 1800s to today. Make a chart that compares Seminole life today with Seminole life in the 1800s. You might want to include comparing the way they dressed, the way they traveled, and so on.

Compare Histories

Visions of the Past

The Seminoles presents the history of a Native American tribe. *Grandfather's Journey* presents the history of a family in a very different way — as a personal narrative. Discuss the two books with a group of classmates. How does each account tell you about life in the past?

393

The Algonquians of Maryland

A Research Report by Briana Taylor

What is a *wiso*? a *matchacomico*? Briana learned the meaning of those words when she wrote this research report about the first Native Americans who lived in her area.

Briana Taylor
Hammond Elementary School
Laurel, Maryland

Briana wrote this report for her fourth-grade social studies class. "It wasn't very hard for me to write this report. I used information from different books and put it in my own words," she said.

Briana enjoys dancing, singing, reading, drawing, gymnastics, and collecting trolls. She would like to be a doctor someday so that she can help people.

enter

The Algonquians of Maryland

The Algonquians were one of the main groups of Native Americans who lived in the eastern woodlands. The Algonquians who lived in Maryland had certain characteristics. These characteristics included the food they ate, the clothing they wore, their housing, and the names for their leaders.

The Algonquians ate many different types of foods. They grew a lot of their food, such as corn, beans, peas, squash, pumpkins, and sunflowers. They caught some of their food. They caught fish, crabs, shrimp, eels, oysters, and clams. These particular people also hunted turkeys, partridges, pigeons, squirrels, raccoons, opossum, deer, and bears.

The Algonquians used animal skins, such as deerskin and bearskin, to make clothes. In the summer they wore little clothing, and some children wore almost none. Men and women both wore clothes that looked like aprons.

Clothes for the warm months were made from animal skins without the fur. They did not remove the fur from the skins for their winter clothing. In the winter they wore cloaks and leggings to keep warm. They wore moccasins on their feet all year.

The Algonquians lived in wigwams. They made them by setting saplings, or young trees, into the ground and bending the tops toward each other. They tied the tops together and covered the saplings with bark, animal skins, or woven grass mats. Usually the wigwams were about twelve to fifteen feet wide. Sometimes, the wigwams were larger for the important people.

The names of the leaders and groups were very interesting. The chief of a tribe was called a werowance. A tyak was the name for the leader and the most important chief of a group of tribes. A cockarouse was a member of the war council, and a wiso was a member

of the peace council. A council called a
matchacomico made decisions.

The food, clothes, shelter, and names of
leaders were some of the characteristics of
the Algonquians of Maryland that made them
different from Native Americans in other
parts of the country.

Bibliography

Boyce-Ballweber, Hettie. The First People of
    Maryland. Lanham: Maryland Historical
    Press. 1987.
Manakee, Harold R. Indians of Early
    Maryland. Baltimore: Maryland Historical
    Society. 1959.
Ruskin, Thelma. Indians of the Tidewater
    Country of Maryland, Virginia, Delaware
    and North Carolina. Lanham: Maryland
    Historical Press. 1986.

Indian Artist
Visits
New York,
New York

from *This Land Is My Land*

BY GEORGE LITTLECHILD

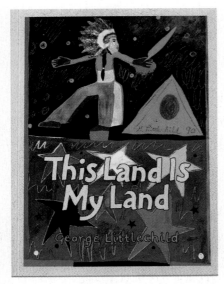

This painting is about my first visit to New York City. What a great time I had! I loved the tall buildings, the crowds of people, the huge stores, the fancy restaurants. And the art! It was amazing. There were paintings that had photographs in them. Others had fabric and buttons. There were paintings on canvas with wood and straw.

When I returned home I began to experiment with mixed media. My paintings became multi-layered, with beads, feathers, and photographs. In ten days my world had changed.

Yes, that is a photograph of me, standing ever so small beside the large towers.

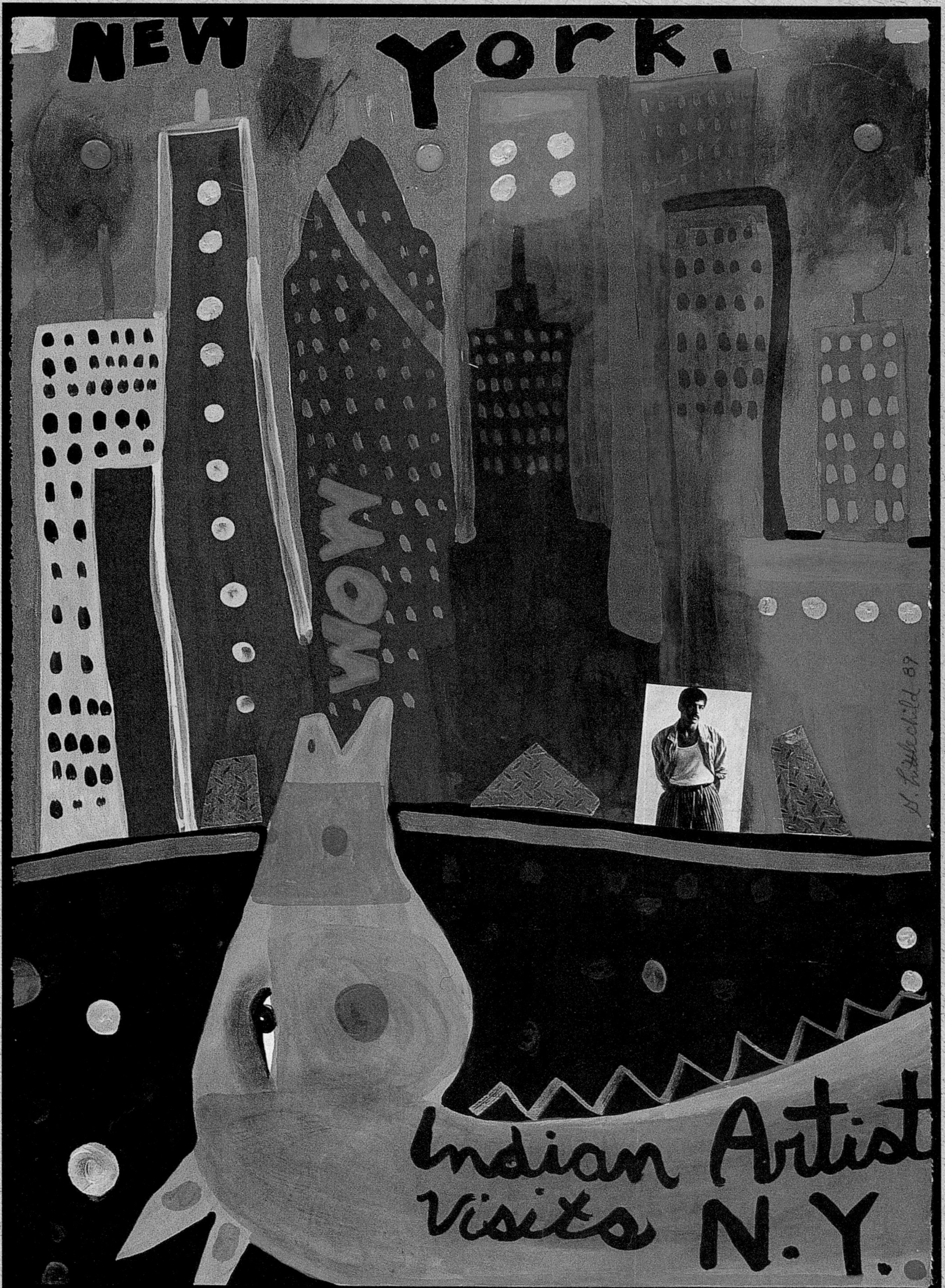
NEW York,
WOW
Indian Artist
Visits N.Y.

Meet the Challenge

Meet the Challenge

CONTENTS

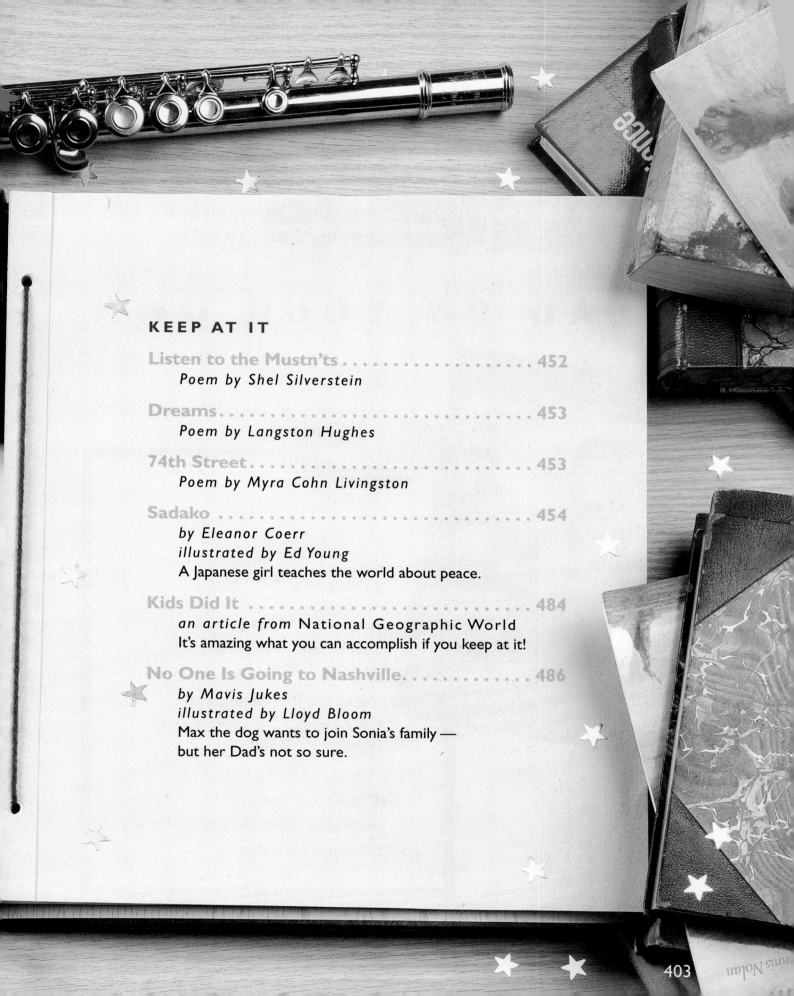

KEEP AT IT

Meet the Challenge

READ ON YOUR OWN

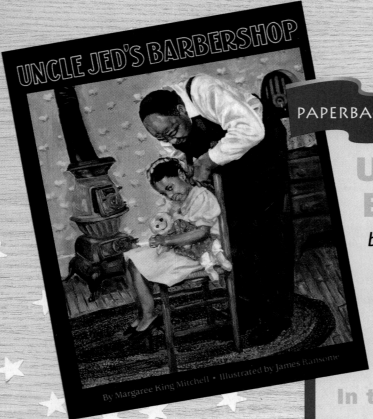

PAPERBACK **PLUS**

Uncle Jed's Barbershop

by Margaree King Mitchell

Sarah Jean's Uncle Jed is a traveling barber who dreams of owning his own shop. How will Sarah Jean's illness affect his dream?

In the same book . . .

More about hairstyles through the ages, as well as kids whose dreams of starting their own businesses came true, and a poet's view of dreamers.

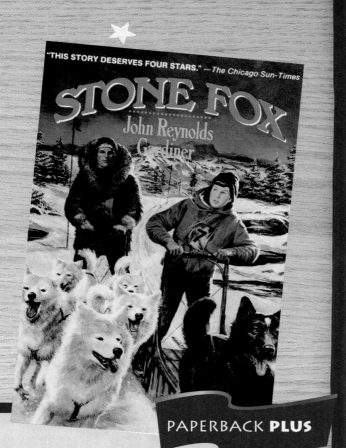

"THIS STORY DESERVES FOUR STARS." —*The Chicago Sun-Times*

STONE FOX
John Reynolds Gardiner

PAPERBACK **PLUS**

Stone Fox

by John R. Gardiner

Little Willy and his dog Searchlight *really need* to win this race — but how can they beat the famous Stone Fox?

In the same book . . .

Lots more about dog heroes and dogsledding — including races for kids and a visit with a former racer whose handmade sleds are real winners.

Meet More Books

Amazing Grace
by Mary Hoffman

Who says you can't play Peter Pan if you're an African American girl? Grace knows she can be anything she wants to be.

Beans on the Roof
by Betsy Byars

Sitting on the roof inspires the Bean family to write poems — except George "String" Bean, who has trouble thinking of something to write.

Class President
by Johanna Hurwitz

Who will succeed in becoming the next class president: class clown Lucas Cott or teacher's pet Cricket Hoffman?

The Courage of Sarah Noble
by Alice Dalglish

Sarah proves her courage when she helps her father build a home in the wilderness of colonial America.

Martin Luther King, Jr., and His Birthday
by Jacqueline Woodson

A look at the life of Martin Luther King, Jr., and the reasons his birthday became a national holiday.

Centerfield Ballhawk
by Matt Christopher

José Mendez is the best fielder on the Peach Street Mudders. But will he ever be the slugger that his father was?

Meet the Author
Gary Soto

Gary Soto played a lot of baseball, soccer, and four-square when he was a boy. "I was a playground kid," he says. The story of Lupe comes from Soto's own playground experiences. "The Marble Champ" is from his book, *Baseball in April*. That book contains short stories about the everyday life of Mexican American children growing up in California. Soto himself grew up in Fresno, California, where he went to Jefferson

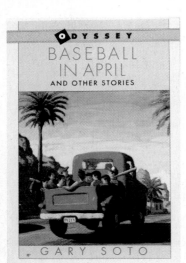

Elementary School. Two of his other books for children are *Local News* and *The Skirt*. Gary Soto now lives in Berkeley, California, where he writes and teaches college students.

Meet the Illustrator
Mike Reed

Mike Reed first studied music and later engineering. Then, he says, "I realized that my real calling was art." He even earned much of his money for college by doing illustrations. Eventually, Reed did get an art degree. His first "real job" as an illustrator was as a film animator. He worked on *Sesame Street*, cartoons, and commercials. Now Reed does illustrations for books and newspapers and teaches art. He even painted the self-portrait shown above.

The Marble CHAMP

LUPE MEDRANO, A SHY GIRL WHO SPOKE IN WHISPERS,

was the school's spelling bee champion, winner of the reading contest at the public library three summers in a row, blue ribbon awardee in the science fair, the top student at her piano recital, and the playground grand champion in chess. She was a straight-A student and — not counting kindergarten, when she had been stung by a wasp — never missed one day of elementary school. She had received a small trophy for this honor and had been congratulated by the mayor.

But though Lupe had a razor-sharp mind, she could not make her body, no matter how much she tried, run as fast as the other girls'. She begged her body to move faster, but could never beat anyone in the fifty-yard dash.

The truth was that Lupe was no good in sports. She could not catch a pop-up or figure out in which direction to kick the soccer ball. One time she kicked the ball at her own goal and scored a point for the other team. She was no good at baseball or basketball either, and even had a hard time making a hula hoop stay on her hips.

It wasn't until last year, when she was eleven years old, that she learned how to ride a bike. And even then she had to use training wheels. She could walk in the swimming pool but couldn't swim, and chanced roller skating only when her father held her hand.

"I'll never be good at sports," she fumed one rainy day as she lay on her bed gazing at the shelf her father had made to hold her awards. "I wish I could win something, anything, even marbles."

At the word "marbles," she sat up. "That's it. Maybe I could be good at playing marbles." She hopped out of bed and rummaged through the closet until she found a can full of her brother's marbles. She poured the rich glass treasure on her bed and picked five of the most beautiful marbles.

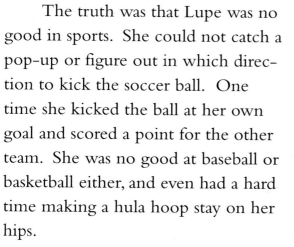

She smoothed her bedspread and practiced shooting, softly at first so that her aim would be accurate. The marble rolled from her thumb and clicked against the targeted marble. But the target wouldn't budge. She tried again and again. Her aim became accurate, but the power from her thumb made the marble move only an inch or two. Then she realized that the bedspread was slowing the marbles. She also had to admit that her thumb was weaker than the neck of a newborn chick.

She looked out the window. The rain was letting up, but the ground was too muddy to play. She sat cross-legged on the bed, rolling her five marbles between her palms. Yes, she thought, I could play marbles, and marbles is a sport. At that moment she realized that she had only two weeks to practice. The playground championship, the same one her brother had entered the previous year, was coming up. She had a lot to do.

To strengthen her wrists, she decided to do twenty push-ups on her fingertips, five at a time. "One, two, three . . ." she groaned. By the end of the first set she was breathing hard, and her muscles burned from exhaustion. She did one more set and decided that was enough push-ups for the first day.

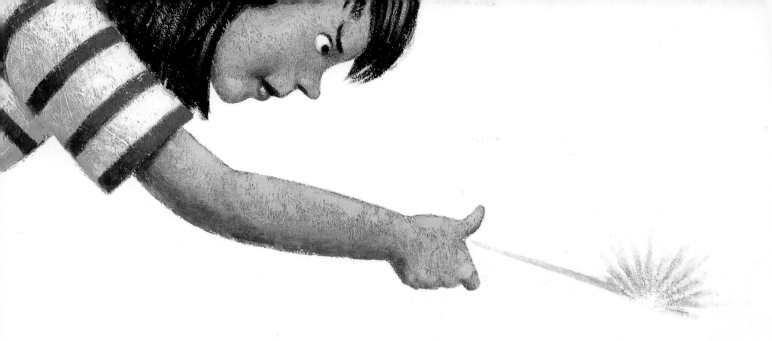

She squeezed a rubber eraser one hundred times, hoping it would strengthen her thumb. This seemed to work because the next day her thumb was sore. She could hardly hold a marble in her hand, let alone send it flying with power. So Lupe rested that day and listened to her brother, who gave her tips on how to shoot: get low, aim with one eye, and place one knuckle on the ground.

"Think 'eye and thumb' — and let it rip!" he said.

After school the next day she left her homework in her backpack and practiced three hours straight, taking time only to eat a candy bar for energy. With a popsicle stick, she drew an odd-shaped circle and tossed in four marbles. She used her shooter, a milky agate with hypnotic swirls, to blast them. Her thumb *had* become stronger.

After practice, she squeezed the eraser for an hour. She ate dinner with her left hand to spare her shooting hand and said nothing to her parents about her dreams of athletic glory.

Practice, practice, practice. Squeeze, squeeze, squeeze. Lupe got better and beat her brother and Alfonso, a neighbor kid who was supposed to be a champ.

"Man, she's bad!" Alfonso said. "She can beat the other girls for sure. I think."

The weeks passed quickly. Lupe worked so hard that one day, while she was drying dishes, her mother asked why her thumb was swollen.

"It's muscle," Lupe explained. "I've been practicing for the marbles championship."

"You, honey?" Her mother knew Lupe was no good at sports.

"Yeah. I beat Alfonso, and he's pretty good."

That night, over dinner, Mrs. Medrano said, "Honey, you should see Lupe's thumb."

"Huh?" Mr. Medrano said, wiping his mouth and looking at his daughter.

"Show your father."

"Do I have to?" an embarrassed Lupe asked.

"Go on, show your father."

Reluctantly, Lupe raised her hand and flexed her thumb. You could see the muscle.

The father put down his fork and asked, "What happened?"

"Dad, I've been working out. I've been squeezing an eraser."

"Why?"

"I'm going to enter the marbles championship."

Her father looked at her mother and then back at his daughter. "When is it, honey?"

"This Saturday. Can you come?"

The father had been planning to play racquetball with a friend Saturday, but he said he would be there. He knew his daughter thought she was no good at sports and he wanted to encourage her. He even rigged some lights in the back-yard so she could practice after dark. He squatted with one knee on the ground, entranced by the sight of his daughter easily beating her brother.

413

THE DAY OF THE CHAMPIONSHIP began with a cold blustery sky. The sun was a silvery light behind slate clouds.

"I hope it clears up," her father said, rubbing his hands together as he returned from getting the newspaper. They ate breakfast, paced nervously around the house waiting for 10:00 to arrive, and walked the two blocks to the playground (though Mr. Medrano wanted to drive so Lupe wouldn't get tired). She signed up and was assigned her first match on baseball diamond number three.

Lupe, walking between her brother and her father, shook from the cold, not nerves. She took off her mittens, and everyone stared at her thumb. Someone asked, "How can you play with a broken thumb?" Lupe smiled and said nothing.

She beat her first opponent easily, and felt sorry for the girl because she didn't have anyone to cheer for her. Except for her sack of marbles, she was all alone. Lupe invited the girl, whose name was Rachel, to stay with them. She smiled and said, "OK." The four of them walked to a card table in the middle of the outfield, where Lupe was assigned another opponent.

She also beat this girl, a fifth-grader named Yolanda, and asked her to join their group. They proceeded to more matches and more wins, and soon there was a crowd of people following Lupe to the finals to play a girl in a baseball cap. This girl seemed dead serious. She never even looked at Lupe.

"I don't know, Dad, she looks tough."

Rachel hugged Lupe and said, "Go get her."

"You can do it," her father encouraged. "Just think of the marbles, not the girl, and let your thumb do the work."

The other girl broke first and earned one marble. She missed her next shot, and Lupe, one eye closed, her thumb quivering with energy, blasted two marbles out of the circle but missed her next shot. Her opponent earned two more before missing. She stamped her foot and said "Shoot!" The score was three to two in favor of Miss Baseball Cap.

The referee stopped the game. "Back up, please, give them room," he shouted. Onlookers had gathered too tightly around the players.

Lupe then earned three marbles and was set to get her fourth when a gust of wind blew dust in her eyes and she missed badly. Her opponent quickly scored two marbles, tying the game, and moved ahead six to five on a lucky shot. Then she missed, and Lupe, whose eyes felt scratchy when she blinked, re-lied on instinct and thumb muscle to score the tying point. It was now six to six, with only three marbles left. Lupe blew her nose and studied the angles. She dropped to one knee, steadied her hand, and shot so hard she cracked two marbles from the circle. She was the winner!

"I DID IT!" LUPE SAID UNDER HER BREATH. She rose from her knees, which hurt from bending all day, and hugged her father. He hugged her back and smiled.

Everyone clapped, except Miss Baseball Cap, who made a face and stared at the ground. Lupe told her she was a great player, and they shook hands. A newspaper photographer took pictures of the two girls standing shoulder-to-shoulder, with Lupe holding the bigger trophy.

Lupe then played the winner of the boys' di-vision, and after a poor start beat him eleven to four. She blasted the marbles, shattering one into sparkling slivers of glass. Her opponent looked on glumly as Lupe did what she did best — win!

The head referee and the President of the Fresno Marble Association stood with Lupe as she displayed her trophies for the newspaper photographer. Lupe shook hands with everyone, including a dog who had come over to see what the commotion was all about.

That night, the family went out for pizza and set the two trophies on the table for everyone in the restaurant to see. People came up to congratulate Lupe, and she felt a little embarrassed, but her father said the trophies belonged there.

Back home, in the privacy of her bedroom, she placed the trophies on her shelf and was happy. She had always earned honors because of her brains, but winning in sports was a new experience. She thanked her tired thumb. "You did it, thumb. You made me champion." As its reward, Lupe went to the bathroom, filled the bathroom sink with warm water, and let her thumb swim and splash as it pleased. Then she climbed into bed and drifted into a hard-won sleep.

Champion

Write a Journal Entry

I Did It!
Lupe sure had a big day! What aspect of her experience do you think was most important to her? Write a journal entry in which Lupe describes how she feels about being the new marble champ.

Carry Out a Plan

Thumbs Up!
Lupe dreamed of being a marble champ. She made her dream come true by creating a plan and practicing, practicing, practicing. Is there some goal you dream of reaching? Think up a plan for reaching that goal. Put your plan up on the wall, and try to stick to it. Check off your progress every day.

Ideas

Act Out a Scene

Live . . . from Your Playground!

Act out Lupe's final match as though it were a television sports show. You don't need a camera — just your imagination. Get together with a few classmates and decide which story characters you will portray. Include interviews and play-by-play commentary to capture the action and excitement of the match.

Have a Discussion

Up Close and Personal

Do you think Lupe is a new person by the end of the story? Could winning a marble tournament really change her life? If so, how? Meet with a few classmates, and discuss how you think Lupe changes in the story.

419

THE UNKNOWN FORESTERS
A Story by Nathan A. Cox

What helps a team meet a challenge?
Nathan based his story on that question.

Nathan A. Cox
**Taylors Elementary School
Taylors, South Carolina**

Nathan's keen interest
in sports inspired him to
write this story in the
fourth grade. When he
grows up, Nathan wants to
play professional basketball or football
or be a successful businessman.

Nathan also likes to read and
draw, and he sings in the church choir.

The Unknown Foresters

In Australia the Unknown Forest is where the animals go to play. One day Kris the koala, Ron the rabbit, and Dan the dingo went to the forest. They wanted to form a sports team. They saw Karl the kangaroo reading a sports magazine.

Ron said, "I can run the fastest."

Kris said, "I can throw the farthest."

Dan said, "I can catch the best."

"What do you do best?" they asked Karl.

"I don't know," said Karl.

Kris, Ron, and Dan asked Karl to play baseball with them, but Karl couldn't catch as well as Dan. They later ran track, but Karl couldn't run faster than Ron. Finally, they played football, but Karl couldn't throw farther than Kris.

One day they noticed Karl jumping up and down. Karl could jump the highest of all! Together they said, "Basketball!" They all practiced every day. Because he jumped so high, Karl played forward so that he could slam the ball.

They decided to enter the annual basketball tournament. They were the Unknown Foresters. They beat the Desert Team, the Plateau Team, and the Lowland Team and went to the championship game. It would be against the Highlanders, who had been the champs for three years.

The game began with the Highlanders scoring six straight points. The Highlanders led 42–31 at halftime. At the end of the third quarter, the Highlanders were still leading 68–63. The fourth quarter was about to end as the Foresters had the ball. Ron ran down the court faster than ever! Kris threw the ball farther than ever! Dan caught the ball better than ever! Karl got the ball behind the three-point line. The score was 99–97 with the Highlanders leading. Karl took a big leap! The clock was running out. 3 . . . 2 . . . 1 . . . . Karl dunked the ball just before the last second! The final score was 99–100. The Foresters won! With all of their strengths, Kris, Dan, Ron, and Karl were a winning team.

ON A ROLL

Jim Knaub and Jean Driscoll wheel into the record books

BY DONNA M. TOCCI Train hard, rest hard, race hard. That is one motto Jim Knaub lives by.

Jean Driscoll spends many hours training for the next big race. In fact, she gives up most of her free time.

If you think these sound like the stories of many top athletes you have read about, you are right. Knaub and Driscoll are both world-class American athletes. They're Boston Marathon champions. Jean Driscoll has won all four times she has raced in Boston, and Jim Knaub has won five times over eleven years. Both athletes have set world records four times.

THEY'VE COME A LONG WAY

Wheelchair racing in the Boston Marathon has come a long way since it began in 1975. That year, Bob Hall was the only racer. For all 26.2 miles, he pushed his heavy, old-fashioned wheelchair. Most people probably thought how brave and touching this new entry was. Oh, how times have changed! Hall is still racing — but he is also the coordinator of the top wheelchair race in the world. The race that started with one entry now draws more than 80 athletes from around the world. And it is gaining fans. In Boston, crowds yell out the names of the wheelchair racers as they fly by.

Winner's Circle: Driscoll and Knaub bask in the glow of their 1993 Boston Marathon wins.

Wheelchair racing has gone through many changes. The biggest change is in the public's feelings about the event. Most people no longer see it as a special race for disabled people before the stars of the main event run down the road. They now see just what they should see — fine athletes who are out to win. These athletes want to show the world that their sport is just that — a sport.

DIFFERENT TRAINING STYLES

Jean Driscoll trains with her old school, the University of Illinois. For speed, Driscoll works out with the men. She likes to train with them even though they are far ahead of her some days. "I can use them as goals," she says. "It's good to have others push you."

Pioneering wheelchair racer Bob Hall in a racing chair he designed himself

Driscoll believes her success is due to two things. One is the support she gets from the team. The other is the careful attention of Marty Morse, her coach. He plays a big role in her racing. For example, he might help her to decide on the size of her chair. He might also help to design the gloves she uses when pushing.

Jim Knaub's thinking is quite different. He is his own coach. "I get the best results alone," says the Southern Californian. It

Jean Driscoll can be seen in the foreground, keeping up with the men.

Wheelchair athletes from all over the world race in the Boston Marathon. Heinz Frei of Switzerland won in 1994.

shows in the way he races. He moves quickly to the front, usually all alone. This is just the way he likes it.

Knaub trains on the streets six days a week. He lifts weights about three days a week. To prepare for the Boston Marathon, he does a lot of hills. He believes his climbing skill is a main reason for his wins in Boston. The Boston downhills are tricky. With all the potholes after bad winters, a racer can't just fly down the hills with ease. Thus, the race may be won or lost on the uphill climb.

LONG ROAD AHEAD

Wheelchair racing has come a long way, but it still has a long way to go. Both Driscoll and Knaub are working to make sure the sport succeeds. As with their training, they are going about it in different ways.

"I love kids. Every time I have the chance, I talk to them," Driscoll says. Urging young wheelchair athletes to try racing is one way to help keep the sport alive. This year she attended the Junior Nationals to watch the kids and to boost the girls' interest in racing.

Knaub at the finish line of the 1992 Boston Marathon

Knaub agrees that more women are needed in the sport. But he believes there is a need for more wheelchair athletes in general. This includes juniors and masters.

As successful racers, Knaub and Driscoll have gotten a lot of attention. Driscoll has been pictured in *Time* magazine. She was also the subject of a lead story in the *Boston Globe* before the 1993 race. Knaub was featured on MTV. "The media have caught on and allowed people to look at wheelchair racing as sport," says Driscoll. This is just how racing should be looked at. It's daring and different. It's exciting, fast, colorful, and dangerous. It is thrilling to watch a racer zooming along, downhill and around a corner, at more than 40 mph.

LOOKING TOWARD THE FUTURE

Interest in wheelchair racing keeps on growing. Therefore, the people making it happen must look to the future. Driscoll thinks the athletes should give back to the sport. "I'd like to do something, but it is hard as an active athlete," she says. She adds, though, that her racing career will one day be over. Then she may work on the political side of racing.

Knaub, like Driscoll, would like to see a strong ruling body unite the sport and its racers. He is working toward it every time he races. "I try to boost the sport along with myself," he says.

No matter how long Knaub and Driscoll keep racing, they will work to make the sport better. They will work to educate people. Knaub urges, "Don't put the wheelchair before the athlete."

"I'm not a disabled anything. I'm a super-able athlete," he goes on. When he screams down the hills in the Boston Marathon with the best of the best pushing to catch him, you wouldn't dare argue.

Racers negotiate the famous hills of the Boston Marathon.

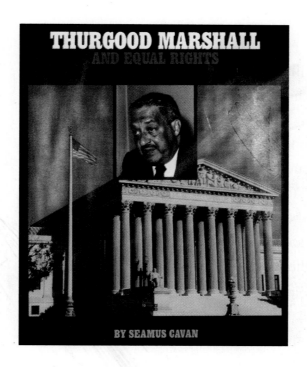

THURGOOD MARSHALL

and Equal Rights

by Seamus Cavan

Like many young boys, Thurgood Marshall often got into mischief. He was never a serious troublemaker, but he liked to have fun, and he didn't always do exactly what his parents told him to do.

Years later, Marshall remembered those early days. "We lived on a respectable street, but behind us there were back alleys where roughnecks and the tough kids hung out. When it was time for dinner, my mother used to go to the front door and call my older brother. Then she'd go to the *back* door and call me."

Thurgood caused a little trouble in school, too. He was smart, but he liked talking with his friends more than listening to the teacher.

Sometimes Thurgood's teachers just could not keep him quiet. On those days, he was sent to sit by himself on a chair in the school's basement.

It was boring in the basement. There was nothing there but some old, broken desks, some leaky pipes, a pile of coal, and the noisy boiler that heated the school. Even class was more fun than sitting alone down there. But the principal of the school had a rule. No student could return to class until he or she had read part of the United States Constitution and understood it well enough to explain it to him.

Even though he was a fun-loving boy, Thurgood Marshall had a serious, thoughtful side, too. When the principal gave him the Constitution to read, Thurgood thought of it as a chance to learn. By the time he left school, he knew the entire Constitution by heart.

But as he studied this document, Thurgood was puzzled. Over and over again, he read the words of the Fourteenth Amendment, which promises that all American citizens have equal rights under the law. He had no trouble understanding what the words meant, but when he thought about what life was like in his hometown, he knew that black Americans did not in fact have equal rights.

Under segregation, this school for African American children did not receive as much money and supplies as schools for white children did.

430

At segregated movie theaters, African Americans had to use the so-called "colored" entrance in the back.

Thurgood Marshall
as a toddler

Thurgood Marshall was born on July 2, 1908, in West Baltimore, Maryland. When he was growing up in the early part of the twentieth century, segregation — the separation of different races of people — was common throughout the United States. In many places, it was the law of the land.

Even the lessons Thurgood learned about the meaning of the Constitution took place in the basement of an all-black school. White children went to another, better, school in the white part of town.

In other parts of the United States, blacks were not allowed to buy houses in white neighborhoods. They had to ride in separate railroad cars or at the backs of buses, while whites rode up front. They could not eat at the same restaurants as white people, or sit in the same sections at movie theaters or ballparks. Blacks had to drink from water fountains marked COLORED, while whites drank from fountains marked WHITE. Blacks were often even kept from voting.

Thurgood Marshall could not understand how segregation could exist when the Constitution promised *everyone* equal rights. He went home from school one day and asked his father, Will Marshall, how this could be. The Constitution is the way things ought to be, not the way they are, Will Marshall told his son. This answer made young Thurgood very sad and angry. He decided that when he grew up he was going to change things.

And he did just that. Thurgood Marshall became a very influential lawyer and then a Supreme Court Justice. He dedicated his life to defending the civil rights of his fellow human beings.

Two elementary schools in the same Virginia town, around 1930. White children attended the school above. The school below was for African American children.

The Way Things Ought to Be

Thurgood Marshall never forgot the lesson his father taught him about the Constitution. Will Marshall made his living as a waiter, but his great love was for the law. He read about all the important court cases, and in his spare time he went to court to watch interesting trials in person. Many times, he brought Thurgood with him. At home, he and his son would discuss what they had heard in court. Will Marshall also made sure that Thurgood read the newspaper each day. Then he would ask his son questions about the articles he had read.

Thurgood Marshall's family was a strong influence on him. At left are his parents, Norma and William Marshall. Below, Marshall's mother (left) is shown with his aunt.

Thurgood Marshall at seventeen

Thurgood's mother, Norma Marshall, was a schoolteacher. She told Thurgood again and again that education was important, and she made sure that his fooling around with his friends never interfered with his schoolwork. She wanted Thurgood to become a dentist, but all that time spent reading the Constitution and talking to his father had given him a different idea. He thought that he might like to become a lawyer instead. It seemed that a lawyer might have a good chance of making the way things *were* more like the way things *ought to be.*

In 1925, when he was seventeen years old, Thurgood graduated from high school. Because most colleges did not accept black students, Marshall enrolled in Lincoln University in Pennsylvania, the nation's oldest black college. The four years he spent there were good ones. He worked hard and learned a lot. He also fell in love with a young woman named Vivian Burey, and they got married. Most important, he decided for certain that he wanted to be a lawyer.

Because he was black, Marshall was not accepted at the University of Maryland, the first law school he chose. He wound up going to Howard University in Washington, D.C., where most of the nation's black professionals were trained. It turned out to be a very wise choice.

Howard was proud to accept a student of Marshall's ability, and Marshall was eager to prove himself. After a week of classes there, he knew that Howard was the right place for him and that the law was the right course of study. The work was hard, and the days were long. But Marshall knew that what he wanted to do was important, and that the only way to succeed was through hard work. By the end of his first year, he was the top student in his class.

Marshall's favorite teacher at Howard was a brilliant lawyer named Charles Hamilton Houston. Houston taught his students that the law was the tool that black Americans could use to end segregation and to win all the rights promised them by the Constitution.

Marshall's favorite teacher at Howard was a brilliant lawyer named Charles Hamilton Houston.

Charles Hamilton Houston worked hard for civil rights. In top photo, he speaks at a protest meeting. In lower photo, Houston (far right) works on a desegregation court case. Marshall stands at left.

The courts were the place where blacks could win equal justice, Houston told his students. But they had to be prepared, and they had to commit themselves to excellence. They could not allow themselves to use the prejudice they would face as an excuse for failure.

Marshall admired Houston, and he took his teacher's words very seriously. If Houston told the class to read five cases for the next day's lesson, Marshall read ten. He knew that because he was black, he would always have to be a little bit better than the white lawyers he would face. He would have to work harder than they did.

His hard work paid off. Marshall finished law school in the spring of 1933 as the top student in his class. He was ready now to go to court. Many lawyers practice law because it is a way to make a lot of money, but Marshall had different goals. He wanted to be what Charles Houston called a "social engineer," which meant someone who used the law to change society for the better. In late 1933, Thurgood Marshall opened a small law office in east Baltimore.

Marshall worked hard to end segregation. Here, he arrives at a District Court hearing in Little Rock, Arkansas, where the governor had threatened to block school integration.

As a young lawyer, Marshall (right) worked with his former teacher, Charles Hamilton Houston (left), on important civil rights cases.

Equal Justice

Thurgood Marshall was a very unusual lawyer. He used all his training and ability to help others, not to make himself rich. Most of his clients were poor blacks who could not afford to pay him much or even anything at all. They came to Marshall because they were homeless, or because they had been beaten up by policemen, or because they were too poor to pay their bills. He never said no to anyone who needed his help. Soon he was known as a "little folks' lawyer," someone to whom poor people could turn for help.

Marshall also worked with an organization called the National Association for the Advancement of Colored People (NAACP). The NAACP was the nation's most important civil rights organization. Its members were dedicated to ending segregation through peaceful means.

To speak out against segregation required a great deal of courage. For many years, blacks who had done so lost their jobs or were arrested or even killed. But Marshall was not afraid. He told his fellow blacks that it was time to claim their equal rights under the law. The NAACP had a bold plan to end segregation in the United States, and Marshall was eager to play a part.

In 1938, Marshall became the chief lawyer for the NAACP. For fourteen years, he drove hundreds of thousands of miles back and forth across the country arguing court cases against segregation. Though he never earned much money for his work, he won several important cases regarding segregation and the right of blacks to vote.

By the end of the 1940s, Marshall was known as one of the best lawyers in the country. Sometimes racists threatened to kill him if he continued his work, but to black Americans and to whites who wished to see an end to prejudice, he was a hero.

But Marshall was not satisfied. He and the NAACP decided that the most important place where segregation had to be ended was in education. They had several good reasons. Education was of great importance to the future of society. Children who were denied a fair chance to receive a quality education were denied an opportunity to better themselves and to build a better life. Marshall and the NAACP also believed that if black and white children could be educated together, side by side in the same classrooms, they would learn not to hate and fear each other, and prejudice would come to an end.

He and the NAACP decided that the most important place

Above, a six-year-old Louisiana girl who made history by entering a previously all-white school.
At right, Marshall outlines NAACP strategy for fighting segregation.

In 1953, Marshall argued a case called *Brown* v. *Board of Education of Topeka, Kansas* before the Supreme Court of the United States. The *Brown* case was about black schoolchildren in Kansas, Delaware, Virginia, South Carolina, and the District of Columbia who wanted to attend integrated public schools. An integrated school is one that children of all colors and races are free to attend. The case was one of the most important that had ever been argued in front of the Supreme Court. Everyone who was involved knew that the entire future of legal segregation in the United States was at stake.

Marshall easily proved that the segregated schools the black children went to were not equal to the ones attended by white students. There were fewer teachers for the black students, for example. The black schools were not given money to provide busing for their students. The all-white schools received more tax money from

where segregation had to be ended was in education.

At left, Marshall chats with students who tried to enter a Little Rock, Arkansas, school but were turned away. The NAACP took their case to court. Below, Marshall makes a point.

Above, Marshall, chief counsel for the NAACP, holds a press conference after the Supreme Court ruled segregation illegal.

the government, which meant that their buildings were in better shape. But Marshall did not end his argument there. If he had, those who supported segregation could have promised to improve the black schools and make them equal to the white ones. That way, black and white students would still have to attend separate schools.

Instead, Marshall tried to show the nine justices, or judges, of the Supreme Court that segregation was extremely harmful to black youngsters. He presented testimony from teachers, doctors, and other experts to prove that segregation caused black children to feel inferior and lessened their desire to learn. In this way, segregation denied black children the chance to reach their full potential. He also told the justices that the men who wrote the Fourteenth Amendment had meant for all citizens, black or white, to get equal rights under the law.

In the *Brown* case, Marshall used all the power and skills he had learned in a lifetime of hard work and dedication. The Supreme Court took five months to decide the case. On May 17, 1954, Chief Justice Earl Warren finally read the court's decision. "Education is the most important function of state and local governments," Warren said. Then he asked the question: "Does segregation of children in public schools solely on the basis of race deprive the children of the minority group of equal educational opportunities?" After a brief pause, he provided the court's answer, which an entire nation was waiting to hear.

"We believe that it does. To separate [black schoolchildren] from others solely because of their race generates a feeling of inferiority that may affect their hearts and minds in a way unlikely ever to be undone. We conclude unanimously that in the field of public education the doctrine of 'separate but equal' has no place. Separate educational facilities are inherently unequal."

After their victory in *Brown v. Board of Education* , NAACP lawyers George E. C. Hayes (left), Thurgood Marshall, and James M. Nabrit (right) pose on the Supreme Court steps in front of the motto "Equal Justice Under Law."

"The doctrine of 'separate but equal' has no place. Separate educational facilities are inherently unequal."

SEGREGATION IN PUBLIC SCHOOLS OUTLAWED BY U. S. SUPREME COURT

Atlanta Daily World

CITY EDITION

"NEWS WHILE IT IS NEWS"

Published Every Morning Except Monday
ATLANTA (3), GEORGIA, TUESDAY, MAY 18, 1954

PRICE FIVE CENTS

VOLUME 26, NUMBER 241

FHA To Honor Farm Families At Fort Valley State

Chief Justice Warren Reads Court's Unanimous Decision

By DARRELL GARWOOD

WASHINGTON—(INS)—The Supreme Court unanimously outlawed racial segregation in the public schools yesterday as a violation of the constitutional guarantee of equality to all.

While Marshall fought segregation in the courts, his friend Dr. Martin Luther King, Jr., rallied public support through peaceful protests and civil rights marches.

Little Folks' Lawyer on the High Court

Marshall had no time to rest after his historic victory in the *Brown* case. Many Americans were not happy that he had changed the way they were used to living. In many places people tried to keep black students from going to schools that had been for white children only. In the state of Arkansas, the governor even tried to use soldiers to keep the schools from being integrated. Blacks who tried to obtain their equal rights under the law were sometimes beaten or arrested or even killed. Black churches were bombed.

But men like Thurgood Marshall and his friend Dr. Martin Luther King, Jr., a famous civil rights leader, were not frightened. King and Marshall and many other Americans kept on working to make American society live up to the words of the Constitution. For Marshall, that meant more long hours working for the NAACP. He traveled around the country, standing up to threats of violence and death, to bring lawsuits against school districts that refused to obey the *Brown* decision.

Marshall (seated, third from left) talks with senators during his confirmation hearings for the U.S. Court of Appeals.

Marshall received the highest honor a lawyer can receive . . . to be a justice of the U.S. Supreme Court.

In 1967, the Supreme Court posed for this portrait that includes its newest member, Thurgood Marshall (standing, far right).

In 1961, President John F. Kennedy appointed Thurgood Marshall a judge on the U.S. Court of Appeals. Marshall proved to be an excellent judge. He was especially wise on those cases that involved civil rights. The Supreme Court did not change even one of Marshall's decisions. This was a remarkable record.

His outstanding work won him more honors. In 1965, he was asked by President Lyndon Johnson to become the solicitor general, the chief lawyer of the country. Two years later, Marshall received the highest honor a lawyer can receive when Johnson asked him to be a justice of the U.S. Supreme Court. Marshall was the first black man to serve on the Supreme Court. Becoming a Supreme Court justice was a great achievement for him and for all black Americans. The president said that Marshall had already earned a place in American history.

Marshall served on the Supreme Court until 1991, when he retired. Even on the Supreme Court he remained a lawyer for the little folks, a person who fought for the rights of all Americans. He always remembered that some people did not have the help of loving parents or concerned teachers, and he tried to make sure that the law looked out for these people, too. Thurgood Marshall devoted his life to making sure that American society gave a fair chance to all its citizens. Few Americans have done as much to make their country a better place.

Important Dates in the Life of
Thurgood Marshall

1908

Thurgood Marshall is born in West Baltimore, Maryland, on July 2.

1925

Marshall begins college at Lincoln University, Pennsylvania.

1929

Marshall begins law school at Howard University, Washington, D.C.

1900

1938

Marshall becomes chief lawyer for the NAACP.

1933

Marshall opens a law office in East Baltimore, Maryland.

446

1954

Marshall wins the case of *Brown* v. *Board of Education*, which makes segregation in public schools illegal.

1961

Marshall becomes a judge on the U.S. Court of Appeals.

1967

Marshall is appointed a justice on the U.S. Supreme Court.

1993

Thurgood Marshall dies on January 24, 1993.

2000

1991

Thurgood Marshall retires.

1965

Marshall becomes the solicitor general.

447

Meet the
AUTHOR

Seamus Cavan

Seamus Cavan is the pen name of Sean Dolan. A pen name is a name an author uses professionally instead of his or her real name. Dolan was born in New York State and lived there most of his life. Among the books he liked best as a child are *The Adventures of Robin Hood* and *King Arthur and the Knights of the Round Table*. To find more of Dolan's many books on American history for young readers, look under both names: Sean Dolan and Seamus Cavan.

Meet the
ILLUSTRATOR

Beatrice Brooks

Beatrice Brooks was born and grew up in France. As a child, she was playful and talkative. She was also a dreamer who spent many hours reading and drawing. "When I was little," she says, " my goal was to come to the United States and work with Walt Disney!" Today Brooks lives in Texas, where she works as an illustrator, writes poetry, collects "elephants" in all shapes and colors, and spends lots of time reading and drawing.

UPDATE: Linda Brown
Then and Now

Linda Brown was turned away from an elementary school in her neighborhood because she was African American. In the early 1950s, the schools in Topeka, Kansas, were segregated: black children could not attend the same schools as white children.

Linda Brown's father joined with other African American parents and challenged segregation in court. In 1954, in the famous *Brown* v. *Board of Education* case, the Supreme Court ruled that schools in the United States must be open to children of all races.

Today, Linda Brown Thompson is an educator. She gives speeches about civil rights, particularly about the *Brown* case. She is also helping to plan a museum showing the importance of *Brown* v. *Board of Education.* Her grandchildren attend integrated schools in Topeka.

449

JUDGE for Yourself

That's Not Fair!

Lawyers have to be good at changing people's minds. They have to persuade juries or judges to agree with them. Think of something unfair that you would like to change, and make your case to a "jury" of your classmates. See if you can get them to see things your way.

Follow the Leader

Magazines often print short, true stories to inspire their readers to be like the hero of the story. Write a brief magazine article that gives the highlights of Thurgood Marshall's life. Include a conclusion that shows how Marshall's example can help readers meet their own challenges. Add illustrations and a catchy title.

450

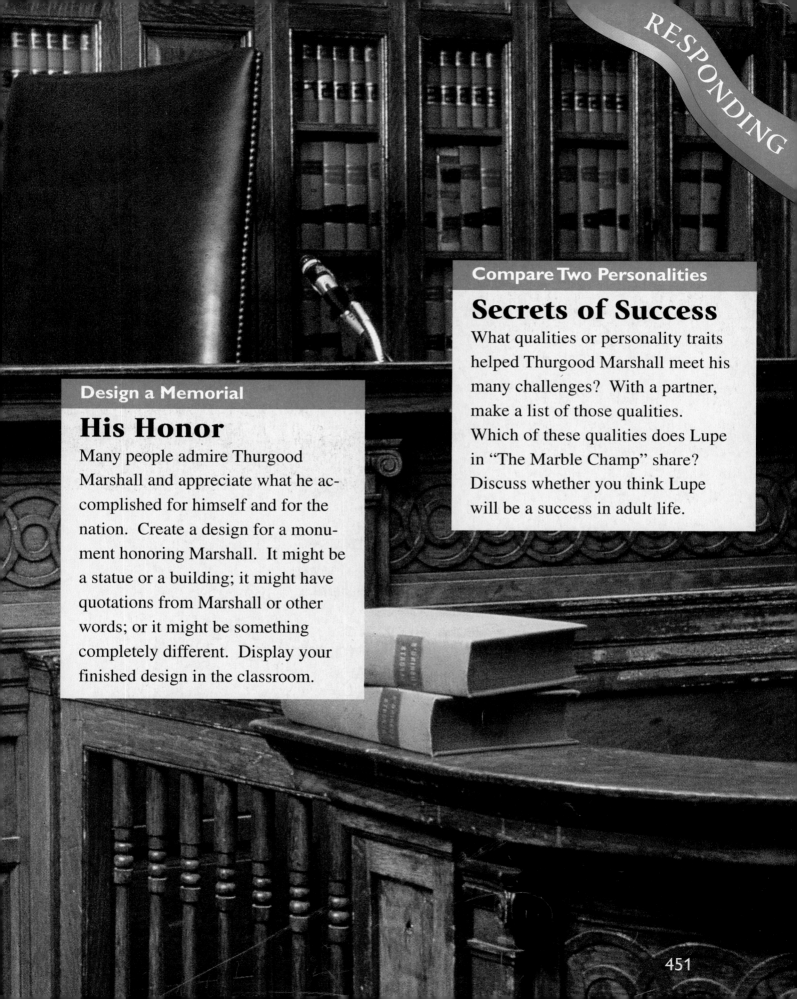

Compare Two Personalities

Secrets of Success

What qualities or personality traits
helped Thurgood Marshall meet his
many challenges? With a partner,
make a list of those qualities.
Which of these qualities does Lupe
in "The Marble Champ" share?
Discuss whether you think Lupe
will be a success in adult life.

Design a Memorial

His Honor

Many people admire Thurgood
Marshall and appreciate what he ac-
complished for himself and for the
nation. Create a design for a monument honoring Marshall. It might be
a statue or a building; it might have
quotations from Marshall or other
words; or it might be something
completely different. Display your
finished design in the classroom.

LISTEN TO THE MUSTN'TS

Listen to the MUSTN'TS, child,
Listen to the DON'TS
Listen to the SHOULDN'TS
The IMPOSSIBLES, the WON'TS
Listen to the NEVER HAVES
Then listen close to me —
Anything can happen, child,
ANYTHING can be.

— *Shel Silverstein*

Dreams

Hold fast to dreams
For if dreams die
Life is a broken-winged bird
That cannot fly.

Hold fast to dreams
For when dreams go
Life is a barren field
Frozen with snow.

— *Langston Hughes*

Golden Bird,
1919 bronze
sculpture by
Constantin
Brancusi

74th Street

Hey, this little kid gets roller skates.
She puts them on.
She stands up and almost
flops over backwards.
She sticks out a foot like
she's going somewhere and
falls down and
smacks her hand. She
grabs hold of a step to get up and
sticks out the other foot and
slides about six inches and
falls and
skins her knee.

And then, you know what?

She brushes off the dirt and the
blood and puts some
spit on it and then
sticks out the other foot

again.

— *Myra Cohn Livingston*

453

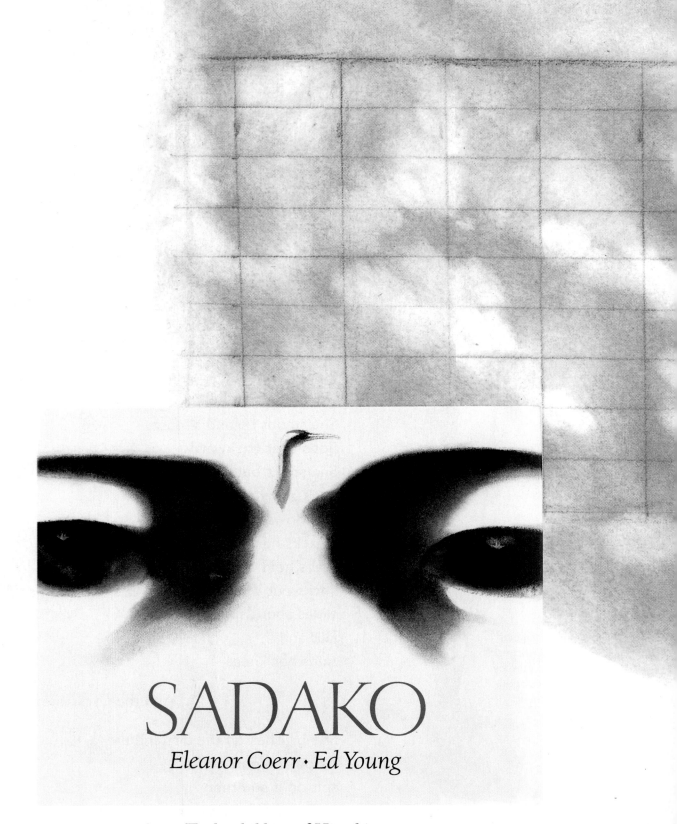

SADAKO

Eleanor Coerr · Ed Young

To the children of Hiroshima

One morning in August 1954, Sadako Sasaki looked up at the blue sky over Hiroshima and saw not a cloud in the sky. It was a good sign. Sadako was always looking for good-luck signs.

Back in the house, her sister and brothers were still sleeping on their bed quilts. She poked her big brother, Masahiro.

"Get up, lazybones!" she said. "It's Peace Day!"

Masahiro groaned, but when he sniffed the good smell of bean soup, he got up. Soon Mitsue and Eiji were awake, too.

Rushing like a whirlwind into the kitchen, Sadako cried, "Mother, can we please hurry with breakfast? I can hardly wait for the carnival!"

"You must not call it a carnival," her mother said. "It is a memorial day for those who died when the atom bomb was dropped on our city. Your own grandmother was killed, and you must show respect."

"But I do respect Obasan," Sadako said. "It's just that I feel so happy today."

At breakfast, Sadako fidgeted and wriggled her bare toes. Her thoughts were dancing around the Peace Day of last year — the crowds, the music, and the fireworks. She could almost taste the spun cotton candy.

She jumped up when there was a knock at the door. It was Chizuko, her best friend. The two were as close as two pine needles on the same twig.

"Mother, may we go ahead to the Peace Park?" Sadako asked.

"Yes, Sadako chan," her mother answered. "Go slowly in this heat!" But the two girls were already racing up the dusty street.

Mr. Sasaki laughed. "Did you ever see Sadako walk when she could run, hop, or jump?"

At the entrance to the Peace Park, people filed through the memorial building in silence. On the walls were photographs of the ruined city after the atom bomb — the Thunderbolt — had instantly turned Hiroshima into a desert.

"I remember the Thunderbolt," Sadako whispered.
"There was a flash of a million suns. Then the heat prickled
my eyes like needles."

"How could you possibly remember anything?"
Chizuko exclaimed. "You were only a baby then."

"Well, I do!" Sadako said stubbornly.

After a speech by the mayor, hundreds of white doves were freed from their cages. Then, when the sun went down, a dazzling display of fireworks lit up the dark sky.

Afterward, everyone carried rice-paper lanterns to the banks of the Ohta River. Written on the rice paper were the names of relatives and friends who had died because of the Thunderbolt. Sadako had written Obasan's name on hers.

Candles were lit inside the lanterns. Then they were launched on the river, floating out to sea like a swarm of fireflies.

461

It was the beginning of autumn when Sadako rushed into the house with the good news.

"The most wonderful thing has happened!" she said breathlessly. "The big race on Field Day! I've been chosen to be on the relay team!" She danced around the room. "If we win, I'll be sure to get on the team next year!"

That was what Sadako wanted more than anything else.

From then on, Sadako thought only of one thing — the relay race. She practiced every day at school and often ran all the way home. Masahiro timed her with their father's big watch.

Sadako dreamed of running faster. Maybe, she thought, I will be the best runner in the whole world.

At last the big day arrived. Parents, relatives, and friends gathered at the school to watch the sports events. Sadako was so nervous she was afraid her legs wouldn't work at all.

"Don't worry," Mrs. Sasaki said. "When you get out there, you will run as fast as you can."

At the signal to start, Sadako forgot everything but the race. When it was her turn, she ran with all the strength she had. Her heart thumped painfully against her ribs when the race was over.

It was then that a strange, dizzy feeling came over her. She scarcely heard when someone cried, "Sadako! Your team won!" The class surrounded Sadako, cheering and shouting. She shook her head a few times and the dizziness went away.

All winter long, Sadako practiced to improve her speed. But every now and then the dizziness returned. She didn't tell anyone about it, not even Chizuko. Frightened, Sadako kept the secret inside of her.

On New Year's Eve, Mrs. Sasaki hung good-luck symbols above the door to protect her family all throughout the year.

"As soon as we can afford it, I'll buy a kimono for you," she promised Sadako. "A girl your age should have one."

Sadako politely thanked her mother, but she didn't care about a kimono. She only cared about racing with the team next year.

For several weeks it seemed that the good-luck symbols were working. Sadako felt strong and healthy, and she ran faster and faster.

But all that ended one crisp, cold winter day in February when Sadako was running in the school yard. Suddenly everything seemed to whirl around her, and she sank to the ground.

Soon Sadako was in an examining room in the hospital, where a nurse took some of her blood. Dr. Numata tapped her back and asked a lot of questions.

Sadako heard the doctor say the word "leukemia." That was the sickness caused by the atom bomb! She put her hands over her ears, not wanting to hear any more.

Mrs. Sasaki put her arms around Sadako. "You must stay here for a little while," she said. "But I'll come every evening."

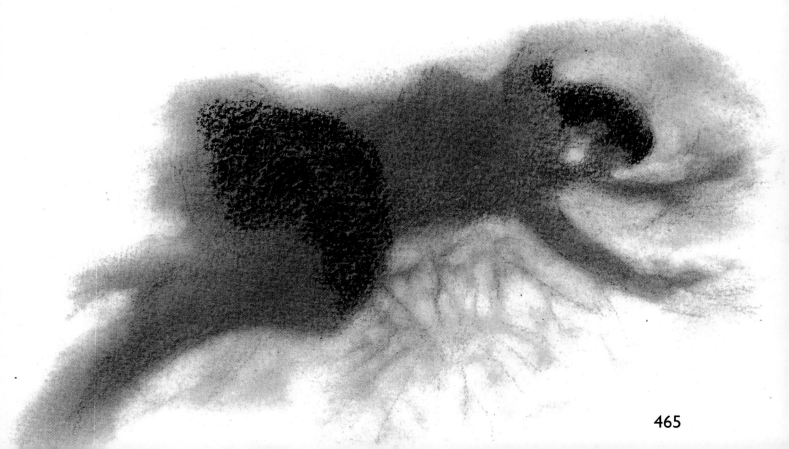

"Do I really have the atom-bomb disease?" Sadako asked anxiously.

"The doctors want to take some tests, that's all," her father told her. "They might keep you here a few weeks."

A few weeks! To Sadako it seemed like years. What about the relay team?

When her family had left for the night, Sadako buried her face in the pillow and cried for a long time. She had never felt so lonely.

The next day, Chizuko came to visit, smiling mysteriously.

"Close your eyes," she said. Sadako held her eyes tightly shut. "Now you can look!"

Sadako stared at the paper and scissors on the bed. "What's that for?"

"I've figured out a way for you to get well," Chizuko said proudly. "Watch!"

She cut a piece of gold paper into a large square and folded it over and over, until it became a beautiful crane.

Sadako was puzzled. "But how can that paper bird make me well?"

"Don't you remember that old story about the crane?" Chizuko asked. "It's supposed to live for a thousand years. If a sick person folds one thousand paper cranes, the gods will grant her wish and make her well again."

She handed the golden crane to Sadako. "Here's your first one."

"Thank you, Chizuko chan," Sadako whispered. "I'll never part with it."

That night, Sadako felt safe and lucky. She set to work folding cranes, and Masahiro hung them from the ceiling. Why, in a few weeks she would be able to finish the thousand cranes and go home — all well again.

Eleven . . . I wish I'd get better . . .

Twelve . . . I wish I'd get better . . .

One day Nurse Yasunaga wheeled Sadako out onto the porch for some sunshine. There Sadako met Kenji. He was nine and small for his age, with a thin face and shining dark eyes.

Soon the two were talking like old friends. Kenji had been in the hospital a long time, but his parents were dead and he had few visitors.

"It doesn't really matter," Kenji said with a sigh, "because I'll die soon. I have leukemia from the bomb."

Sadako didn't know what to say. She wanted so much to comfort him. Then she remembered. "You can make paper cranes like I do," she said, "so that a miracle can happen!"

"I know about the cranes," Kenji said quietly. "But it's too late. Even the gods can't help me now."

That night, Sadako folded a big crane out of her prettiest paper and sent it across the hall to Kenji's room. Perhaps it would bring him luck. Then she made more birds for her own flock.

One hundred ninety-eight . . . I wish I'd get better . . .

One hundred ninety-nine . . . I wish I'd get better . . .

One day Kenji didn't appear on the porch, and Sadako knew that Kenji had died.

Late that night, Sadako sat at the window, letting the tears come. After a while, she felt the nurse's gentle hand on her shoulder.

"Do you think Kenji is out there on a star island?" Sadako asked.

"Wherever he is, I'm sure he is happy now," the nurse replied. "He has shed that tired, sick body, and his spirit is free."

"I'm going to die next, aren't I?"

"Of course not!" Nurse Yasunaga answered with a firm shake of her head. "Come, let me see you fold another crane before you go to sleep. After you finish one thousand, you'll live to be an old, old lady."

Sadako tried hard to believe that. She folded birds and made the same wish. Now there were more than three hundred cranes.

In July it was warm and sunny, and Sadako seemed to be getting better.

"I'm over halfway to a thousand cranes," she told Masahiro, "so something good is going to happen."

And it did.

Her appetite came back and much of the pain went away. She was going to get to go home for O Bon, the biggest holiday of the year. O Bon was a special celebration for spirits of the dead who returned to visit their loved ones on earth.

Mrs. Sasaki and Mitsue had scrubbed and swept the house, and the air was filled with smells of delicious holiday food. Dishes of bean cakes and rice balls had been placed on the altar.

After they had eaten, Eiji handed Sadako a big box tied with a red ribbon. Slowly Sadako opened it. Inside was a silk kimono with cherry blossoms on it. Sadako felt hot tears blur her eyes.

"Why did you do it?" she asked, stroking the soft cloth. "Silk costs so much money."

"Sadako chan," her father said gently, "your mother stayed up late last night to finish sewing it. Try it on for her."

Mrs. Sasaki helped her put on the kimono and tie the sash. Everyone agreed that she looked like a princess.

Sadako let out a happy sigh. Perhaps — just perhaps — she was home to stay.

But by the end of the week Sadako was weak again and had to return to the hospital. The class sent her a Kokeshi doll to cheer her up. Sadako placed it on the bedside table next to the golden crane.

For the next few days, Sadako drifted in and out of a strange kind of half-sleep. Her parents sat beside the bed.

"When I die," she said dreamily, "will you put my favorite bean cakes on the altar for my spirit? And put a lantern on the Ohta River for me on Peace Day?"

Mrs. Sasaki could not speak. She took her daughter's hand and held it tightly.

"Hush!" Mr. Sasaki said. "That will not happen for many, many more years. Don't give up now, Sadako chan. You have to make only a few hundred more cranes."

As Sadako grew weaker, she wondered, Did it hurt to die? Or was it like falling asleep? Would she live on a heavenly mountain or star?

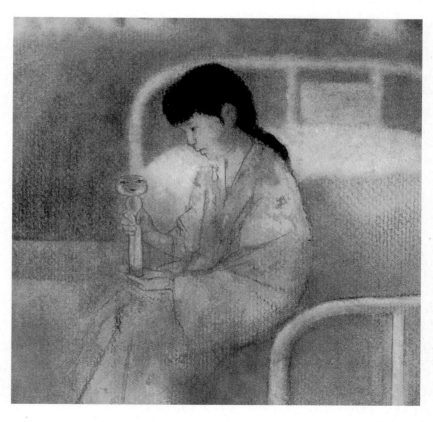

She fumbled with a piece of paper and clumsily folded one more bird.

Six hundred forty-four . . .

Her mother came in and felt her forehead. She gently took the paper away. As Sadako closed her eyes, she heard her mother whisper

"O flock of heavenly cranes,
Cover my child with your wings."

When she opened her eyes again, Sadako saw her family there beside the bed. She looked around at their faces and smiled. She knew that she would always be a part of that warm, loving circle.

Sadako looked up at the flock of paper cranes hanging from the ceiling. As she watched, a light autumn breeze made the birds rustle and sway. They seemed to be alive, and flying out through the open window.

Sadako sighed and closed her eyes. How beautiful and free they were.

Sadako Sasaki died on October 25, 1955.

Her friends and classmates worked together to fold 356 paper cranes, so that she would be buried with one thousand. In a way, she got her wish. She will live on in the hearts of all the people who hear her story.

The class collected Sadako's letters and writings and published them in a book called *Kokeshi*, after the doll they had given her. A Folded Crane Club was organized in her honor.

Sadako's friends began to dream of a monument to her and all the children who were killed by the bomb. Young people throughout the country helped collect money. They wrote letters and shared Sadako's story. Finally, in 1958, their dream came true.

479

Now there is a statue of Sadako in Hiroshima Peace Park. She is standing on the Mountain of Paradise, holding a golden crane in outstretched hands.

Every year, on Peace Day, children hang garlands of paper cranes under the statue. Their wish is engraved at its base:

This is our cry,
This is our prayer:
Peace in the world.

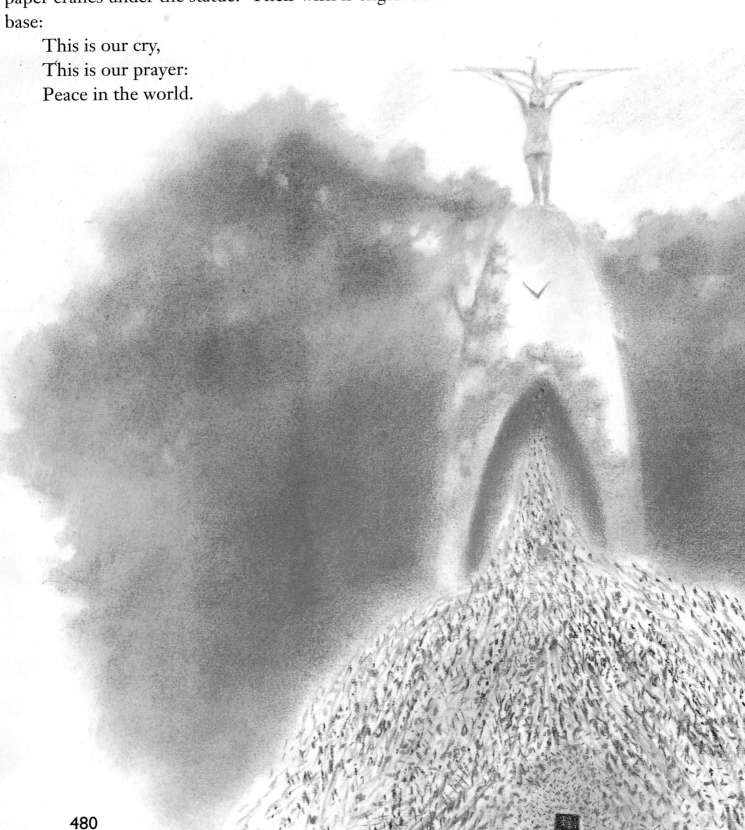

Meet the Author and the Illustrator
Eleanor Coerr and Ed Young

Canadian-born Eleanor Coerr has lived all over the world, from Asia to Ecuador. She first heard the story of Sadako Sasaki from young Japanese friends when she was living in Japan. "Sadako's story touched me so much I just had to write it," says Coerr. So, in 1977, Coerr wrote *Sadako and the Thousand Paper Cranes*. That book spread Sadako's story to children all over the world. Then, in 1989, Coerr had the chance to work with illustrator Ed Young to create a video about Sadako.

Ed Young was born in China and came to the United States at the age of nineteen. By 1989, he had illustrated over fifty children's books, but he had never worked on a video. Young spent over two years designing and drawing the illustrations. For part of this time, he visited Sadako's home, Hiroshima, to research the setting. By the time the video was finished, he had created over 250 pastel drawings! In the video, the camera moves across these drawings as Sadako's story is told.

In 1993, Young worked with Coerr one more time to make the picture book *Sadako*. It includes many of Young's drawings from the video. In this selection, you can see how well Coerr's words and Young's drawings work together.

Ideas
with
WINGS

Discuss the Story

A Special Gift

Receiving the kimono from her family made Sadako so happy she cried. Think of a favorite gift you've received or a special time you've shared with your family. Then meet with a few classmates and discuss why you think the cherry blossom kimono was so important to Sadako.

Brainstorm

Helping Hands

When Sadako needed her classmates, they helped her. With a group of classmates, discuss how people helped Sadako and how they helped to promote world peace. Then brainstorm ideas for ways you and your friends might continue their effort to create a peaceful world. Jot your ideas down on paper and share them with the rest of your class.

Write in Your Diary

I Met a New Friend Today

Reading about people in books is like meeting new friends. How do you feel about your newest friend, Sadako? Describe your thoughts and feelings in a diary entry. If you wish, add a drawing of your favorite part of the story.

Compare Two Biographies

Life Stories

Both Sadako and Thurgood Marshall were real people. They led very different lives, but each one had an important effect on people around them and on people who heard about them. In your group, discuss how and why each of them was important. Also talk about how their biographies — the stories of their lives — were similar and how they were different.

Kids Did It!

Diving Into the Big Time

FU MINGXIA, 13

In 1991, at age 12, Fu Mingxia became the women's platform diving world champ — the youngest ever. When she began diving, at age 7, she didn't even know how to swim. "The coach would tie a rope around my waist so she could pull me up after a dive," Mingxia said. Mingxia, from the Hubei Province of China, does about a hundred practice dives a day.

In major competitions platform divers sail off a ten-meter-high tower, about as tall as a three-story building. During two of her dives at the 1991 World Championships, Mingxia spun through three and a half somersaults before slicing the water cleanly. This was a major achievement for so young a diver.

School at Their Fingertips

CHRIS WALTERS, 17, AND EDEN FRICKE, 17

"Eden introduced herself to me one day and said, 'I'd like to do something to help handicapped students at our school,'" recalls Chris Walters (far left). "I answered, 'You're not the only one!'" Their partnership began right away. Eden Fricke (left) learned to type in Braille, then turned the floor plan of Linton High School, in Schenectady, New York, into a Braille wall map for blind students (small picture). Chris, who has been blind since birth, advised Eden on what to put on the map. Chris and Eden won first prize for their age group in the Aid for the Handicapped division of Ingenuity Challenge 300, a contest sponsored by General Electric. "We have more ideas," says Eden. "We want our school to set an example for others," Chris explains.

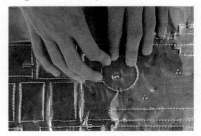

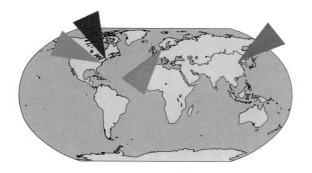

Keeping a Promise

Even before Chad Larkins started his freshman year at Friendly High School in Fort Washington, Maryland, he made himself a promise. "At a basketball game in the school gym I saw four murals of Revolutionary War soldiers," Chad recalls. "The school teams are called 'The Patriots.' The patriots in the murals were white, but blacks fought for the United States in every war. I said, 'Before I graduate, I'm putting up a mural of a black patriot.'" In 1991, Chad, with his principal's support, succeeded. Chad sketched, then painted the new mural himself (right). "I'm proud this change came about in a positive way," he says, adding that "people should learn their history."

Output Impact

What does the mayor of a Danish town have in common with a 13-year-old girl stunt driver? Not much — except both were guests on *Output*. That's a weekly radio show hosted by Ronnie Fridthjof of Hojbjerg, in Denmark. "The people I interview are different from each other, but they all appeal to kids," says Ronnie. "If I could interview anyone at all, I'd pick someone who works for peace." *Output* also includes music, call-in contests, and on-the-air computer games. Ronnie began broadcasting eight years ago, when Denmark first licensed local radio stations.

Max the dog is on his way to choose a new family.

Will he find a home?

They'll never get her to give up a great dog like Max!

No one is going to Nashville

by
MAVIS JUKES

pictures by
LLOYD BLOOM

No one is going to Nashville

It was six o'clock in the morning.

Sonia checked her alligator lizard. He was out of termites, and possibly in a bad mood. She decided to leave him alone. Nobody else was up except Ms. Mackey, the goose. She was standing on the back deck, talking to herself.

Sonia sat in the kitchen with her knees inside her nightgown. She peered out the window. The moon was still up above the rooftops. The houses were beginning to pale.

There was a dog on the stoop! He was eating radishes on the mat.

Sonia opened the door. "Hello doggy!" she said. She knelt down. "You like radishes?"

He licked her face.

"Have you been into the garbage?"

He signaled to her with his ears.

"Stay!" said Sonia. She went back in the house and clattered in the pot cupboard.

"What time is it, Sonia?" her father called from the bedroom.

Sonia didn't answer because he had forgotten to call her "Dr. Ackley." She filled the bottom of the egg poacher with water and left it on the stoop, then went into the house and to the bedroom. "Dad," she said. "What do you think is a good name for a dog?"

He was trying to doze. "I'm closing my eyes and thinking," he lied.

Sonia waited. "You're sleeping!" she said.

He opened one eye. "Names for dogs. Let's see. Dog names. Ask Annette. She's the dog lover. What *time* is it?"

"About six fifteen," said Annette. "I heard the train go by a few minutes ago." She rolled over.

Sonia went over to her stepmother's side of the bed. "Annette!" she said. "What name do you like for a dog?"

Annette propped herself up on her elbows. Her hair fell onto the sheets in beautiful reddish loops. "A dog name? My favorite? Maxine. Absolutely. I used to have a dog named Maxine. She ate cabbages." Annette collapsed on the pillow.

"Here, Maxine!" called Sonia.

"Oh no," said her father. He slid beneath the blankets. "I can't stand it! Not a dog at six o'clock in the morning!"

The dog padded through the door and into the bedroom.

"Maxine," said Sonia, "I want you to meet my father, Richard, and my Wicked Stepmother, Annette."

Annette got up. "That's not a Maxine," she reported, "that's a Max." She put on Richard's loafers and shuffled into the kitchen.

Richard got up and put on his pants. Sonia and Max watched him search for his shoes. Max's ears were moving so wildly they could have been conducting a symphony.

"Weird ears," said Richard. He went into the kitchen.

Ms. Mackey stared through the glass at his feet and started honking. He opened the door a couple of inches. *"Quiet!"* he whispered. "You're not even supposed to live inside the city limits!"

She puffed her feathers.

"Beat it!" said Richard. "Go eat some snails!"

Off she waddled.

Sonia came into the kitchen wearing white pants and a white shirt with DR. S. ACKLEY, D.V.M. printed on the pocket with a felt-tip pen. She took something from the refrigerator on a paper plate and left again.

"What are we going to do about Max?" said Annette.

"Send him packing," said Richard.

"Do you really think it's going to be that easy?" said Annette.

"Yes. Sonia knows I cannot stand dogs. Neither can her mother. We've been through this before. She accepts it."

Annette turned from Richard. "Well, don't be too sure," she said.

Richard went into the living room.

"Guess what," said Sonia. "Max ate all the meatloaf." She waved the paper plate at him.

"Great, I was planning to have that for lunch," said Richard dryly. "Dr. Ackley, may I have a word with you?"

Sonia sat on the couch and dragged Max up onto her lap. Annette stood in the doorway, looking on. Sonia carefully tore two slits in the paper plate. Richard watched, his hands clasped behind his back. His thumbs were circling each other.

"About this dog —" said Richard. He walked across the room.

"You're gorgeous," said Sonia to Max. She pushed each of Max's ears through a slit in the plate. "There!" she said. "Now you have a hat!"

Max licked her. She licked him back. Richard made an unpleasant face.

"That hat looks great!" said Annette. "Where's the camera?"

Richard began again. "I know you really like the dog, but he belongs somewhere."

"With me," said Sonia. "He's been abandoned. He came to me. He passed all the other houses. He's supposed to be mine." She pulled each ear out a little farther.

Richard turned and paced. "I don't like saying no," he said. "It's harder for me to say no than it is for other fathers because we only see each other on weekends."

492

Annette opened the closet to look for the camera.

"But," said Richard, "since we only see each other on weekends, I have more reasons to say no than other fathers." He put his hands in his pockets and jingled some change. "Number one: I don't like dogs and they don't like me." Richard pulled out a couple of coins and tossed them in the air. He caught them. "Number two: While you're at your mother's apartment, the dog becomes my responsibility."

Annette looked at him.

"And Annette's," he added. "Anyhow, since you're at your mother's house all week long, and I would have to walk the dog —"

"I could walk him," said Annette.

"— and feed him *and* pay the vet bills —" He dropped the coins into his pocket and glanced at Annette. "I feel that it's my decision." Richard looked at Sonia. "I'm the father. And I'm saying no."

Max jumped down. He shook off the hat and tore it up.

"You call me Dr. Ackley because you *know* I am planning to be a veterinarian," said Sonia, "yet you don't want me to have experience in the field by having pets."

"You're being unfair," said Richard. "I do let you have pets. Even though they abuse me. Have you forgotten this?" He displayed a small scar on the side of his finger.

"How could I forget that?" said Sonia. "Fangs bit you."

"Yes, Fangs the Killer Lizard bit me," said Richard.

"Do you remember *how* it happened?" said Sonia.

A smile crept across Annette's face. She sat down and opened the newspaper.

"I don't recall, exactly," said Richard. "And it's a painful memory. Let's not go through it."

"Well, *I* remember exactly what happened," said Sonia. "You said that you were so fast you once won a pie-eating contest, and that when you were a kid people used to call you Swifty."

Richard pretended to be bored with the story.

"And," continued Sonia, "you said you bet you could put a termite down in front of Fangs before he could snap it out of your fingers."

Richard folded his arms and looked at the ceiling.

"I said, 'I bet you can't,'" said Sonia. "Annette said, 'Don't try it.'"

Richard stared over at Annette, who was behind the newspaper trying not to laugh.

"And," said Sonia, "Fangs bit you."

"I know you're laughing, Annette," said Richard as she turned the page. "Is this my fault, too?" He pulled up his pant leg. "What do you see here?" he asked.

"A white leg with blue hairs," said Sonia.

"Wrong!" said Richard. "A bruise. Laugh it up, Annette, at my expense!"

Annette folded the newspaper. "You were teasing Ms. Mackey, and she bit you."

"Teasing Mrs. Mackey!" said Richard. "I was getting mud off my zoris!"

"Mizzzzzzzzz Mackey," said Sonia. "You were washing your feet in *her* pool, knowing she hates bare feet, and she bit you."

Richard threw up his hands. "*Her* pool. Now it's *her* pool. I built that for carp or goldfish!"

"*We* built that," said Annette.

"For whatever I wanted to put in it, and I chose a goose," said Sonia.

"No dog!" shouted Richard. He stalked into the kitchen, Annette and Sonia following him. "Send Weirdears home!" He crashed through the pot cupboard. "Where's the other half of the egg poacher?" He banged a griddle onto the stove. "No dog! Discussion closed!"

Sonia and Max went out on the stoop. They stood there a moment. Then Sonia bent down and gripped Max's nose with both hands. She looked into his eyes, frowning. "Go home!" said Sonia, knowing that he *was* home.

By the time breakfast was over and the dishes were done, Max had been sent away so many times by Richard that he moved off the stoop and into the hedge.

At noon, Richard called the pound. Sonia and Annette were listening.

Richard said, "You only keep strays five days? *Then* what? You must be kidding! Good-bye."

Sonia took the phone from him. She dialed her mother's number. "Hello, Mom?"

Annette left the room.

"Mom, can you and I keep a nice dog that Dad *hates* but I *love*?" Sonia glared at Richard and said to her mother, "Just a minute, someone's listening." She stepped into the closet with the telephone and closed the door. "Well, it would only be until we could locate the owner." Silence. "I *know* there are no dogs allowed in the apartment house, but nobody needs to know but us!" Silence, then mumbling. Sonia came out of the closet. "I know you were listening, Dad!"

"I admit it," said Richard. "And I'll tell you what. You really just want to locate the owner? Nobody told me that. Fair enough! You write a description of the dog. We'll run an ad in the classified section. We'll keep the dog as long as the pound would. By next weekend, we'll know something."

"Thanks, Dad!" Sonia gave him a hug.

Richard felt pleased with himself. He broke into a song.

Sonia ran to the freezer and took out four hot dogs. Then off she raced to her room for a pencil and paper. "Oops!" she said. She darted back into the kitchen and grabbed a handful of Cheerios out of the box. She opened the sliding door and threw the Cheerios onto the deck for Ms. Mackey. Then she said, "Dad? Will you please feed Fangs?"

"All right," said Richard. "I can deal with the lizard. Where's my leather glove?"

Sonia ran out the door. "Max!" she said. "Here!" She was breathless. "Here!" she fed him the hot dogs, one at a time.

Then Sonia wrote the ad:

> Found. Brown dog with a white background. Wearing paper hat. Misbehaves. Has radish breath. Answers to the name "Weirdears." Call 233-7161.

Sonia put the paper in her "DR. S. ACKLEY, D.V.M." pocket, and had a tumble with Max on the lawn. They spent the afternoon together, being pals. When it was time to go to her mother's house, Sonia hugged Max and told him: "I'll see you again, so I won't say good–bye."

Max wagged his tail in a circle.

Sonia went into the house and handed Richard the ad.

"Sonia!" said Richard.

"Dr. Ackley," said Sonia.

"This doesn't even sound like the same dog! Max isn't a 'brown dog with a white background.' He's a white dog with brown spots!"

"Same thing," said Sonia.

"Also, Max doesn't misbehave. He's very polite," said Richard.

"Then why don't you like him?" said Sonia.

Richard turned the paper over, took a pen from his shirt, and clicked it once. "Let's see."

Sonia read over his shoulder as he wrote:

> Found. White dog with brown spots.
> Vicinity Railroad Hill. Male. No tags.
> Medium-sized. Strange ears. Call 233-7161,
> through May 3rd.

"What does it mean, 'through May 3rd?'" she asked.

"After that," said Richard, "we're going to let someone adopt him."

Sonia fell into a swoon on the rug. "Us," she thought as she lay on the floor with her eyes shut.

"Now," said Richard. "Off we go to your mother's. We're already late."

As they were leaving, Annette picked up Max and waved his paw at Sonia. Sonia grinned.

"Ridiculous!" said Richard. He gave Annette a kiss. "Be right back!"

The week passed by slowly. Neither the newspaper ad nor calls to the pound and police station produced Max's owner. On Friday evening, Richard and Annette sat on the couch, waiting for Sonia to arrive. Max put his nose on Richard's knee.

Richard looked at Annette. "What does he want?" he asked.

"He's courting you," said Annette as Max licked Richard's hand.

"He's *tasting* me," said Richard. "He's thinking about sinking his teeth in my leg."

A horn beeped in the driveway. "Here she is now," Richard said. He went out on the stoop and waved.

"See you Sunday!" called Sonia's mother to Richard. She whizzed backward out of the driveway.

Sonia took the steps two at a time and ran past Richard. "Max!" she said. "I knew you'd be here!"

"Unfortunately," said Richard. "No owner."

"That's what I figured," said Sonia. "So" — she dug in her pack — "I wrote the ad" — she handed a note to Richard — "for Max to be adopted."

"Great!" said Richard. He felt relieved. "Then you *do* understand."

Neatly written, in multicolored ink, and decorated with pictures of iris and geraniums, Sonia had written:

> Free. We don't want him. A weird dog. Blotchy-colored. Has ear problems. Tears hats. Lives in hedges. Wags his tail in a circle instead of back and forth. Call 233-7161.

"Sonia!" said Richard.

She pointed to the name on her pocket.

"Dr. Ackley!" they both said at once.

"Nobody will want to adopt the dog if we say *this* in the paper."

"I know," said Sonia.

"Well, I also wrote one," said Richard. "I've already had it placed in tomorrow's paper." He opened his wallet and unfolded a piece of paper. He read it aloud:

"Free to a good home. Beautiful, medium-sized male, Shepherd-mix. Snow white with gorgeous brown dots. A real storybook dog that will be an excellent companion. Would prefer country environment. Loves children. Sweet disposition. Obedient. Expressive ears. Call 233-7161."

Sonia looked at Richard and said, "Don't call me Dr. Ackley anymore." She turned and stormed into the kitchen. She unbuttoned her shirt and balled it up. She stuffed it into a box under the sink that was filled with bottles for the recycling center.

Very late that night, Sonia woke up. She slipped from her bed and found Max in the living room. She searched for some cowboy music on the radio. She held Max in her arms.

Annette appeared in the doorway. "What are you two doing up?"

"It might be our last night," said Sonia. "We're dancing. He weighs a ton." She turned off the radio and put Max down. "What are you doing up?"

"Restless," said Annette. "I keep hearing the trains — listen!" She put her finger to her lips. She closed her eyes. A train was drawing closer through the darkness to the station. They heard the lonesome wail of the train whistle. "It must be midnight. The freight is coming in."

Max whined softly. Sonia and Annette knelt beside him.

"I knew Mom or Dad wouldn't let me keep him," began Sonia. "Neither one of them likes dogs."

Max pushed his nose into Sonia's hand. She smoothed his whiskers. Annette said nothing.

"And," continued Sonia, "animals are better off in the country. It's just that I really believed that Max could be mine."

Annette didn't speak.

The freight train clattered away into the night. The whistle sounded faint and lost. They listened until it was gone.

501

502

Max sat with his neck stretched way back and his nose pointed up while they scratched his throat. He looked something like a stork.

"Max reminds me of Maxine," said Annette quietly.

"Really?" said Sonia. "What happened to Maxine?"

"Nobody knows for sure," said Annette. "She went off one day and didn't come back."

"Oh," said Sonia.

"We lived near the tracks —"

"Oh," said Sonia.

"My father was an engineer. One night he came home looking very sad." Annette's eyes were filling. "And my father told me —"

Sonia clutched Annette's hand. "Don't tell me. You don't have to say it."

"And my father told me that Maxine —"
Sonia hid her face in Max's neck.

"— that Maxine may have hopped a freight," said Annette, "and gone to Nashville to be a country western star."

Richard appeared in the doorway. "What's going on?" he said. "Who's going to Nashville?"

"No one!" said Annette. She stood up. "No one is going to Nashville!"

"Okay!" said Richard. "No one is going to Nashville!"
Max and Sonia got up.
Everybody went back to bed.

At nine o'clock the next morning the telephone rang. Sonia heard her father say, "Between East Railroad and Grant. About eight blocks west of the station. Come on over and see how you like him."

Richard hung up the phone. "They're coming this morning."
Sonia said nothing.

"I don't expect to be here," said Annette. "I have errands to do."

An hour later a pickup pulled into the driveway. Max barked. A woman got out of the truck and stretched. A man wearing green cowboy boots got out too, carrying a little girl wearing a felt

jacket with cactuses on it and a red ballet skirt. She was holding an Eskimo Pie.

Richard walked down the steps with Max beside him. Sonia lingered in the doorway. Annette came out on the stoop, holding the box for the recycling center. Sonia's shirt was tucked between the bottles. Annette rested a corner of the box on the rail.

"Is this the dog?" said the woman. "He's a beauty!"

"Yes," said Richard.

The cowboy knelt down with his daughter. "Hey, partner!"

Max went over to them.

"Howdy boy!"

The little girl put out her hand, and Max licked it.

"Do you have a yard?" asked Richard.

"A ranch," said the cowboy. "With a lake." He patted Max. "What's your name, boy?"

"Max," said Richard.

"Why, you doggone pelican!" the cowboy told Max. "I have an uncle named Max!"

"We'll take him," said the woman. "For our little girl."

Sonia came out on the stoop. "Annette! Could you ask them about taking a goose, too?" She was blinking back tears. "And an alligator lizard?"

Annette heard a whistle. The train was coming in. "Listen!" she said. "No one is going to Nashville!" She pulled Sonia's shirt from the box. The box fell from her arms, and the bottles shattered on the cement.

"We're keeping the dog," said Annette. She almost choked on the words. She pressed the shirt into Sonia's hands.

Annette started down the steps. "We're keeping the dog!"

"Watch out for the glass!" said Richard.

Annette went to the little girl. "I'm sorry," she said. She picked up Max. She looked at Richard. "We're keeping this dog for our little girl." Tears were falling. She climbed the stairs.

"Okay! Okay! Watch out for the glass," said Richard.

Sonia was waiting. Annette put Max into her arms. "For Dr. Ackley," said Annette, "from your Wicked Stepmother and from your father, with love. Discussion closed."

505

Meet the Author
Mavis Jukes

Mavis Jukes gets much of the inspiration for her books from her own experiences with people, situations — and dogs. She says this about *No One Is Going to Nashville:* "I got the idea for the book when a spotted dog showed up at my house and claimed me as his owner." Jukes eventually found a home on a fishing boat for the dog, but she goes on to say, "I have often felt that I owe my writing career to the dog that tried to adopt me . . . ."

Also, like Annette in this story, Mavis Jukes is a step-mother. She has two adult stepsons as well as two daughters. Jukes and her family live in California.

Meet the Illustrator
Lloyd Bloom

Lloyd Bloom, who did the drawings for this book, lives in Brooklyn, New York. He studied drawing, painting, and sculpture to prepare for his career as a children's book illustrator. While working on another book by Mavis Jukes, *Like Jake and Me*, Bloom invented a new way of painting with pastels. Many of the books he has illustrated have won awards.

Pet Ideas!

Role-play a Dialogue

Guess What!?

Sonia probably can't wait to tell her mother about her new dog. How do you think she would explain how she got to keep Max? What might her mother say in return? With a partner, role-play a telephone conversation between Sonia and her mother.

Write a Letter

Pen Pal?

Max has an old friend, a cocker spaniel named Pal. Write a letter from Max to Pal in which Max explains how he found his new home. Include Max's opinions of his new family.

Compare Two Stories

If at First You Don't Succeed . . .

Both *No One Is Going to Nashville* and "The Marble Champ" are about girls who have a goal and a lot of will power. With your group, discuss how the two stories are similar and how they are different. Include the main characters, their families, the challenges they face, and the outcome.

Make a Poster

Lost and Found

Even before Max arrives, Sonia has some unusual pets. What if one of them got lost? Make a lost-pet poster for Sonia to hang up around her neighborhood. Describe the animal; draw a picture; offer a reward. *Or* make the poster Sonia's father would make if he really didn't want the animal to be returned.

509

COULD IT REALLY HAPPEN?

COULD IT REALLY HAPPEN?

CONTENTS

READ ON YOUR OWN

A RIVER DREAM

ALLEN SAY

PAPERBACK **PLUS**

A River Dream

by Allen Say

Mark looks out his bedroom window to find his neighborhood gone. In its place, there flows a beautiful river where his favorite uncle is fishing.

In the same book . . .

More unusual reading about fish and fishing.

PAPERBACK **PLUS**

The Enormous Egg

by *Oliver Butterworth*
illustrated by Louis Darling

Nate Twitchell has found an enormous egg. But Nate can't believe his eyes when he sees what's inside.

In the same book . . .

Fiction and nonfiction about dinosaurs, dinosaur tracks, and adventures in time.

It *Really* Happens In Books.

The Secret in the Matchbox
by Val Wallis

Bobby Bell has a secret: he has a dragon in a matchbox. What would happen if he let the dragon loose in the classroom?

The Pigs Are Flying!
by Emily Rodda

Rachel is bored. She wishes something exciting would happen. Suddenly, huge pink pigs fill the sky!

Death Trap: The Story of the La Brea Tar Pits
by Sharon Elaine Thompson

Are there really saber-toothed cats and mastodons in downtown Los Angeles?

Three Strong Women: A Tall Tale From Japan
by Claus Stamm

Maru-me, her mother, and her grandmother teach Forever-Mountain, the champion wrestler, what it really means to be strong.

Flat Stanley
by Jeff Brown

It's not always easy being flat. That's what Stanley Lambchop finds after a falling bulletin board flattens him like a pancake.

Catwings
by Ursula K. LeGuin

Cats with wings? You have to read it to believe it!

Meet Chris Van Allsburg

Chris Van Allsburg says that he was disappointed with most of the board games he played as a child: "Even when I owned Park Place with three hotels, I never felt truly rich . . . ." This was his inspiration for *Jumanji* — a game that provides all the excitement anyone could ask for, and more! In his books, Van Allsburg plays with the reader's point of view and perspective. Part of the fun of *Jumanji* is seeing things where they don't belong — a lion on the piano, rhinos in the living room, a python on the fireplace mantel. This kind of surprise occurs often in Van Allsburg's books, including his first book, *The Garden of Abdul Gasazi*, about a strange magician, and *The Stranger*, about a visitor who has a secret.

Written and Illustrated by

Chris Van Allsburg

"Now remember," Mother said, "your father and I are bringing some guests by after the opera, so please keep the house neat."

"Quite so," added Father, tucking his scarf inside his coat.

Mother peered into the hall mirror and carefully pinned her hat in place, then knelt and kissed both children good-bye.

When the front door closed, Judy and Peter giggled with delight. They took all the toys out of their toy chest and made a terrible mess. But their laughter slowly turned to silence till finally Peter slouched into a chair.

"You know what?" he said. "I'm really bored."

"Me too," sighed Judy. "Why don't we go outside and play?"

Peter agreed, so they set off across the street to the park. It was cold for November. The children could see their breath like steam. They rolled in the leaves and when Judy tried to stuff some leaves down Peter's sweater he jumped up and ran behind a tree. When his sister caught up with him, he was kneeling at the foot of the tree, looking at a long thin box.

"What's that?" Judy asked.

"It's a game," said Peter, handing her the box.

"'JUMANJI,'" Judy read from the box, "'A JUNGLE ADVENTURE GAME.'"

"Look," said Peter, pointing to a note taped to the bottom of the box. In a childlike handwriting were the words "Free game, fun for some but not for all. P.S. Read instructions carefully."

"Want to take it home?" Judy asked.

"Not really," said Peter. "I'm sure somebody left it here because it's so boring."

"Oh, come on," protested Judy. "Let's give it a try. Race you home!" And off she ran with Peter at her heels.

At home, the children spread the game out on a card table. It looked very much like the games they already had. There was a board that unfolded, revealing a path of colored squares. The squares had messages written on them. The path started in the deepest jungle and ended up in Jumanji, a city of golden buildings and towers. Peter began to shake the dice and play with the other pieces that were in the box.

"Put those down and listen," said Judy. "I'm going to read the instructions: 'Jumanji, a young people's jungle adventure especially designed for the bored and restless.

"'A. Player selects piece and places it in deepest jungle. B. Player rolls dice and moves piece along path through the dangers of the jungle. C. First player to reach Jumanji and yell the city's name aloud is the winner.'"

"Is that all?" asked Peter, sounding disappointed.

"No," said Judy, "there's one more thing, and this is in capital letters: 'D. VERY IMPORTANT: ONCE A GAME OF JUMANJI IS STARTED IT WILL NOT BE OVER UNTIL ONE PLAYER REACHES THE GOLDEN CITY.'"

"Oh, big deal," said Peter, who gave a bored yawn.

"Here," said Judy, handing her brother the dice, "you go first."

Peter casually dropped the dice from his hand.

"Seven," said Judy.

Peter moved his piece to the seventh square.

"'Lion attacks, move back two spaces,'" read Judy.

"Gosh, how exciting," said Peter, in a very unexcited voice. As he reached for his piece he looked up at his sister. She had a look of absolute horror on her face.

"Peter," she whispered, "turn around very, very slowly."

The boy turned in his chair. He couldn't believe his eyes. Lying on the piano was a lion, staring at Peter and licking his lips.

The lion roared so loud it knocked Peter right off his chair. The big cat jumped to the floor. Peter was up on his feet, running through the house with the lion a whisker's length behind. He ran upstairs and dove under a bed. The lion tried to squeeze under, but got his head stuck. Peter scrambled out, ran from the bedroom, and slammed the door behind him. He stood in the hall with Judy, gasping for breath.

"I don't think," said Peter in between gasps of air, "that I want . . . to play . . . this game . . . anymore."

"But we have to," said Judy as she helped Peter back downstairs. "I'm sure that's what the instructions mean. That lion won't go away until one of us wins the game."

Peter stood next to the card table. "Can't we just call the zoo and have him taken away?" From upstairs came the sounds of growling and clawing at the bedroom door. "Or maybe we could wait till Father comes home."

"No one would come from the zoo because they wouldn't believe us," said Judy. "And you know how upset Mother would be if there was a lion in the bedroom. We started this game, and now we have to finish it."

Peter looked down at the game board. What if Judy rolled a seven? Then there'd be two lions. For an instant Peter thought he was going to cry. Then he sat firmly in his chair and said, "Let's play."

Judy picked up the dice, rolled an eight, and moved her piece.

"'Monkeys steal food, miss one turn,'" she read. From the kitchen came the sounds of banging pots and falling jars. The children ran in to see a dozen monkeys tearing the room apart.

"Oh boy," said Peter, "this would upset Mother even more than the lion."

"Quick," said Judy, "back to the game."

Peter took his turn. Thank heavens, he landed on a blank space. He rolled again. " 'Monsoon season begins, lose one turn.' " Little raindrops began to fall in the living room. Then a roll of thunder shook the walls and scared the monkeys out of the kitchen. The rain began to fall in buckets as Judy took the dice.

"'Guide gets lost, lose one turn.'" The rain suddenly stopped. The children turned to see a man hunched over a map.

"Oh dear, I say, spot of bad luck now," he mumbled. "Perhaps a left turn here then . . . No, no . . . a right turn here . . . Yes, absolutely, I think, a right turn . . . or maybe . . ."

"Excuse me," said Judy, but the guide just ignored her.

". . . around here, then over . . . No, no . . . over here and around this . . . Yes, good . . . but then . . . Hm . . ."

Judy shrugged her shoulders and handed the dice to Peter.

"... four, five, six," he counted. "'Bitten by tsetse fly, contract sleeping sickness, lose one turn.'"

Judy heard a faint buzzing noise and watched a small insect land on Peter's nose. Peter lifted his hand to brush the bug away, but then stopped, gave a tremendous yawn, and fell sound asleep, his head on the table.

"Peter, Peter, wake up!" cried Judy. But it was no use. She grabbed the dice and moved to a blank. She rolled again and waited in amazement. "'Rhinoceros stampede, go back two spaces.'"

As fast as he had fallen asleep, Peter awoke. Together they listened to a rumble in the hallway. It grew louder and louder. Suddenly a herd of rhinos charged through the living room and into the dining room, crushing all the furniture in their path. Peter and Judy covered their ears as sounds of splintering wood and breaking china filled the house.

Peter gave the dice a quick tumble. "'Python sneaks into camp, go back one space.'"

Judy shrieked and jumped up on her chair.

"Over the fireplace," said Peter. Judy sat down again, nervously eyeing the eight-foot snake that was wrapping itself around the mantel clock. The guide looked up from his map, took one look at the snake, and moved to the far corner of the room, joining the monkeys on the couch.

Judy took her turn and landed on a blank space. Her brother took the dice and rolled a three.

"Oh, no," he moaned. "'Volcano erupts, go back three spaces.'" The room became warm and started to shake a little. Molten lava poured from the fireplace opening. It hit the water on the floor and the room filled with steam. Judy rolled the dice and moved ahead.

"'Discover shortcut, roll again.' Oh dear!" she cried. Judy saw the snake unwrapping himself from the clock.

"If you roll a twelve you can get out of the jungle," said Peter.

"Please, please," Judy begged as she shook the dice. The snake was wriggling his way to the floor. She dropped the dice from her hand. One six, then another. Judy grabbed her piece and slammed it to the board. "JUMANJI," she yelled, as loud as she could.

The steam in the room became thicker and thicker. Judy could not even see Peter across the table. Then, as if all the doors and windows had been opened, a cool breeze cleared the steam from the room. Everything was just as it had been before the game. No monkeys, no guide, no water, no broken furniture, no snake, no lion roaring upstairs, no rhinos. Without saying a word to each other, Peter and Judy threw the game into its box. They bolted out the door, ran across the street to the park, and dropped the game under a tree. Back home, they quickly put all their toys away. But both children were too excited to sit quietly, so Peter took out a picture puzzle. As they fit the pieces together, their excitement slowly turned to relief, and then exhaustion. With the puzzle half done Peter and Judy fell sound asleep on the sofa.

"Wake up, dears," Mother's voice called.

Judy opened her eyes. Mother and Father had returned and their guests were arriving. Judy gave Peter a nudge to wake him. Yawning and stretching, they got to their feet.

Mother introduced them to some of the guests, then asked, "Did you have an exciting afternoon?"

"Oh yes," said Peter. "We had a flood, a stampede, a volcano, I got sleeping sickness, and — " Peter was interrupted by the adults' laughter.

"Well," said Mother, "I think you both got sleeping sickness. Why don't you go upstairs and put your pajamas on? Then you can finish your puzzle and have some dinner."

When Peter and Judy came back downstairs they found that Father had moved the puzzle into the den. While the children were working on it, one of the guests, Mrs. Budwing, brought them a tray of food.

"Such a hard puzzle," she said to the children. "Daniel and Walter are always starting puzzles and never finishing them." Daniel and Walter were Mrs. Budwing's sons. "They never read instructions either. Oh well," said Mrs. Budwing, turning to rejoin the guests, "I guess they'll learn."

Both children answered, "I hope so," but they weren't looking at Mrs. Budwing. They were looking out the window. Two boys were running through the park. It was Danny and Walter Budwing, and Danny had a long thin box under his arm.

Get in the Game

Record a Telephone Message

Watch Out!!!!!!

Use a tape recorder to record a telephone message to Danny and Walter Budwing, as if you were talking to their answering machine. Warn them what will happen if they play Jumanji. Tell them what happened to Peter and Judy. Tell them to BEWARE!!!

Write a Description / Draw a Picture

Jumanji for Experts

Monkeys, snakes, lions, monsoons. What else could happen on the road to Jumanji? Make up more dangers that would make Jumanji really hard . . . and really weird. Write a description or draw pictures of what will happen when a player lands on each of your new danger spots.

Role-play a Conversation

How Was Your Day, Dears?

With three classmates, role-play the conversation Peter and Judy might have had with their parents after the guests have gone. How would Judy and Peter describe their day playing Jumanji? And what will their parents say?

Discuss an Author's Work

Van Allsburg's Views

In the biography of Chris Van Allsburg, you read that he likes to play with the reader's point of view in his illustrations. Discuss the illustrations in *Jumanji* with a partner. How do the unusual points of view help create the strange world of the story?

How to Play "Flip a Coin"

Instructions by Sofia Vilella

Have you ever thought about inventing your own game? Sofia created a new game and wrote these instructions for playing it. Try it!

Sofia Vilella
Calusa Elementary School
Miami, Florida

"It was a lot of fun creating a game that other people can learn how to play," said fourth-grader Sofia. "The hard part was thinking about how to do it." Sofia also enjoys writing stories.

Sofia's favorite sport is in-line skating, which she does with her family. She also likes to read, watch movies, and go to the beach. In the future Sofia wants to be a teacher.

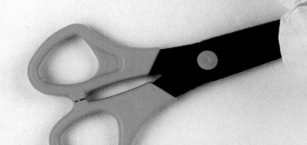

How to Play "Flip a Coin"

Let me introduce you to an exciting new game. It is called "Flip a Coin."

This game is for two to three players, ages six and up. It is an indoor game. The materials needed are two decks of cards and a coin. You can use a quarter, a dime, a nickel, or a penny.

When you have all the materials, all you need is to be alert and to have a little luck.

First, put the two decks of cards in one stack where all the players can reach it. Second, one player flips the coin, and each player calls heads or tails before it lands. Each player who calls the coin correctly gets to pick a card from the stack. For example, if the coin lands on heads, each player who calls heads picks a card from the stack.

As they play, all players will create two piles of cards. One pile is for "good" cards and the other pile is for "bad" cards. "Good" cards are nine and above (nine, ten, jack, queen, king, ace). "Bad" cards are eight and below (two through eight).

Players can take turns flipping the coin. Finally, the game ends when all the cards in the stack are gone. At the end of the game the player who has the most "good" cards wins.

You have just learned a new way to have fun!

Elliot's House

A Short Story By LOIS LOWRY

THE BIG BOOK FOR OUR PLANET

All of the children in Ms. McKreutzer's classroom drew pictures of their own homes. There were condos, apartments, farmhouses, ranch houses, and split-levels, and one little girl — her name was Alvinia — drew a mansion with seven chimneys and a gazebo.

"We certainly do live in all sorts of places, don't we, class?" Ms. McKreutzer said. She hung the pictures on the wall.

From time to time the children made changes on their pictures. "We got new curtains," Elizabeth said, and she added yellow curtains to the windows of her house.

"New car," Alvinia said. She added a stretch limo to the front of her mansion.

A boy named Elliot had drawn a picture of an ordinary house. Elliot's house had a chimney, a door, four windows, a fence, a front walk, and a tree. Now, beside the door, he added a lumpy mound of something brownish green.

"What's that?" the children asked.

"Garbage," Elliot told them.

"Is it waiting there to be collected?" Ms. McKreutzer asked.

"No," Elliot said. "It's where we keep it. We throw it out this window." He pointed to the window beside the door of the house. "We like to do it that way," he explained.

"My goodness," said Ms. McKreutzer.

A boy named David recolored his house one day. It had been white. Now it was red. "We painted our house," he explained.

Elizabeth added some flowering plants to her yard. "Zinnias," she said.

Alvinia added bushes around her swimming pool. "New landscaping," she announced.

Elliot added several more mounds. They covered the first window, and he added others below another window. "More garbage," he announced, even though no one had asked. He drew black dots above the mounds.

"Flies," he explained.

"My goodness," Ms. McKreutzer said.

Each day Elliot added something new to his picture. He added a large white rectangle. "Old broken-down refrigerator," he explained.

He added some silvery ovals near the front walk. "Dead fish," he said. Then he added cats.

Tires.

Cars without tires.

Mice. Or maybe they were rats.

And the garbage mounds grew higher.

"All of your windows are covered up now," Ms. McKreutzer said one day. "How do you get sunlight?"

"It's dark inside," Elliot said. "We like it that way."

"How do you get into your house?" the other children asked. "The front walk is covered with dead fish and broken appliances."

"We climb," Elliot explained. "And dig tunnels. We like it that way."

David added a baby carriage to his picture after his mom had a new baby. To hers, Alvinia added three gray curly-haired dogs, walking in a row. "Champion poodles," she said.

The rest of the class smiled politely and said, "Nice." But they weren't really interested in David's new baby brother or Alvinia's dogs. They were all very interested in Elliot's house. They watched his picture each day to see what Elliot would add next.

Carefully Elliot drew a round orange thing in the branches of his tree.

"Frisbee?" Ms. McKreutzer asked.

Elliot shook his head. "Pizza," he said. "It was on the kitchen table for a week and started getting moldy. So we threw it out of an upstairs window."

He took a pencil and made black dots all over the yard and the piles of garbage.

"More flies?" Ms. McKreutzer asked nervously.

"No," Elliot said. "Ants."

"My goodness," Ms. McKreutzer said. "Are they, ah, *inside* the house, too?"

Elliot nodded. "Yes," he said. "We —"

"I know. You like it that way," Ms. McKreutzer said.

One day Elliot didn't come to school. *Absent*, Ms. McKreutzer wrote in her book after Elliot's name.

The next day she wrote *Absent* again.

School was a little boring without Elliot there. The children wished he would come back so that they could see what he would add to his picture.

With an orange crayon Elizabeth added some new blossoms to the zinnias in her yard. "Nice," the other children said.

553

Alvinia used her set of deluxe acrylic paints and carefully painted pink hair ribbons on her three poodles. "Cute," Ms. McKreutzer said. She yawned a little bit, politely holding her hand in front of her mouth.

Everyone looked at the picture of Elliot's house and wished that Elliot would return.

"Ms. McKreutzer," one of the children said suddenly, looking very surprised, "there's no house left!"

It was true. They all stared at the picture and realized that it was true. Elliot's house had disappeared behind the mounds of garbage and trash. They could see a tiny chunk of chimney sticking out from behind a mountain of dirty laundry that had been tossed onto the roof. But that was the only thing left of the original house that Elliot had drawn.

"My goodness, class," Ms. McKreutzer said. "I think we should investigate this."

The entire class peered from the windows of the school bus that took them on their search. Ms. McKreutzer had Elliot's address written on an index card. She read it to the school-bus driver fourteen times as he drove around the block again and again.

Finally he stopped the bus. He sighed. He was a little annoyed because he had won first prize in navigation at bus driver's school. Never before had he failed to find an address.

"It should have been right here," he said in a peevish voice, "but it isn't." He pointed to a field between two houses.

The children stared. It was a messy vacant lot with some vehicles in it. A steam shovel was scooping dirt from one place and depositing it in another. A Caterpillar tractor was smoothing the mounds. A ragged corner of a pizza box fluttered in the breeze. Then it disappeared under a shovelful of dirt.

There was a sign tacked to the fence. The children read the sign together.

"*Landfill*," they all read aloud.

"Landfill is a compound word, class," Ms. McKreutzer pointed out. She was a teacher, after all.

"*Elliot* is landfill," the class replied. "He likes it that way," they added.

They missed him. But after a while he was only a dim memory. When his picture, hanging on the classroom wall, became faded and curled at the edges, someone took it down and threw it away. It was recycled.

Lois Lowry

Lois Lowry has been making up her own stories since she was a child. She can remember being eight years old, sitting for hours on her Aunt Kate's porch, making up long stories about a beautiful antique baby doll. "Unaware, I was beginning to be a writer," she now says. As an adult, Lowry didn't begin writing for children until her own children were in high school and college. She based her first book, *A Summer to Die*, on her own experience — the death of her sister Helen. Since then she has become an award-winning author. Two of her other books you might enjoy are *Anastasia Krupnik* and *All About Sam*.

KENNETH SPENGLER

Kenneth Spengler says he's always loved to draw, especially in school. "I liked school very much," he says. "I enjoyed the friends I made and my art classes." As a boy he loved to go on adventures in the woods around his home in Hatboro, Pennsylvania. He would act out historic and futuristic stories. What's Spengler's advice for children who might want to become illustrators? "If you like to draw and tell stories, keep practicing, then send your work to some publishers and see what happens." He also recommends learning from teachers and other friends who also enjoy art.

Make Some Weird Drawings

Strange Stuff at *Your* House

What weird things could happen in a drawing of your house? Draw three pictures of the place where you live. Make each drawing a little different to show some weird change happening. Make all three drawings so strange that people looking at them will ask, "Could this *really* happen?"

Have a Contest

What's in a Landfill?

Have a contest with a group of classmates to see who can list the most things that Elliot might have had in his landfill. Break up into two-person teams. Each team should write a list. Start with the items from the story, then make up your own.

MOUNDS OF IDEAS

Role-play a Family Scene

At Home with Elliot

Make up a family for Elliot. Then, with a group of classmates, act out scenes from an ordinary day at their not-so-ordinary home. How do they have dinner? How do they clean up their rooms? And don't forget Elliot's favorite saying, "We like it that way."

Compare Endings

Did You Expect *That*?

Think of the endings to "Elliot's House" and *Jumanji*. Discuss these two stories and their endings with a classmate. Which ending did you like better? What made it so unusual? How did the illustrations help you understand what was happening?

Jimmy Jet and His TV Set

by Shel Silverstein

I'll tell you the story of Jimmy Jet —
And you know what I tell you is true.
He loved to watch his TV set
Almost as much as you.

He watched all day, he watched all night
Till he grew pale and lean,
From "The Early Show" to "The Late Late Show"
And all the shows between.

He watched till his eyes were frozen wide,
And his bottom grew into his chair.
And his chin turned into a tuning dial,
And antennae grew out of his hair.

And his brains turned into TV tubes,
And his face to a TV screen.
And two knobs saying "VERT." and "HORIZ."
Grew where his ears had been.

And he grew a plug that looked like a tail
So we plugged in little Jim.
And now instead of him watching TV
We all sit around and watch him.

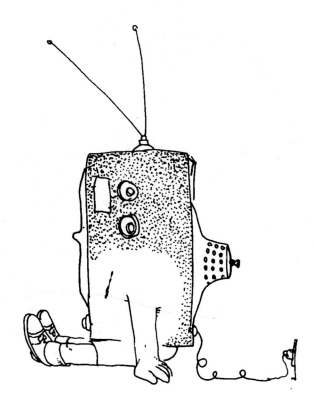

The place is Ho-Ho-Kus, New Jersey. The year is 1999. On May 11, after months of careful research and planning, Holly Evans launches vegetable seedlings into the sky.

On May 18, the young scientist reports on her experiment. Holly intends to study the effects of extraterrestrial conditions on vegetable growth and development. She expects the seedlings to stay aloft for several weeks before returning to earth.

Her classmates are speechless.

The date is June 29. Shortly after sunrise, a member of the Billings, Montana, Moose Lodge, hiking through the Rocky Mountains, makes a startling discovery.

Robert Bernabe is in a daze when he returns to camp. All he can say for the next several hours is, "TURNIPS!"

All over the country, the skies fill with vegetables.

567

Cucumbers circle Kalamazoo.

Lima beans loom over Levittown.

Artichokes advance on Anchorage.

Parsnips pass by Providence.

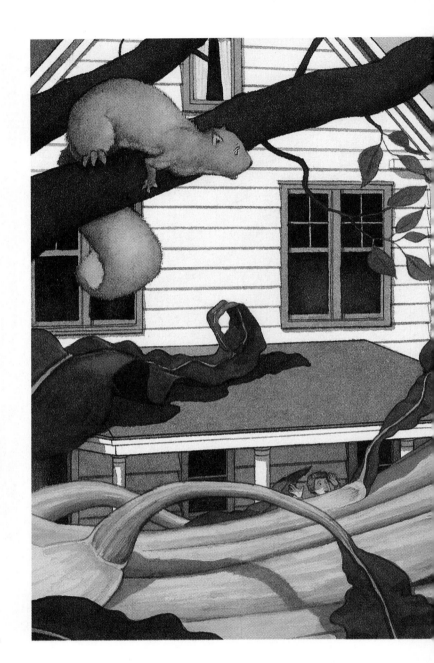

And broccoli lands with a big
bounce in Holly Evans's backyard.

In Ottumwa, Iowa, Tony Kramer emerges from his barn and shouts for joy. "At last, the blue ribbon at the state fair is mine!"

By midafternoon, all vegetables
float safely to the ground.
    Except for the peppers. For
some reason, they need a little help.

TV news channels broadcast twenty-four-hour coverage of the "airborne vegetal event." Cauliflower carpets California, spinach blankets Greenwich, and arugula covers Ashtabula.

Holly is puzzled. Arugula is not part of her experiment.

Vegetables become very big business. Peas from Peoria are shipped down the Mississippi to Mobile in exchange for eggplant.

Real estate booms in North Carolina.

Avocados bolster Vermont's economy.

Potatoland is wisely abandoned.

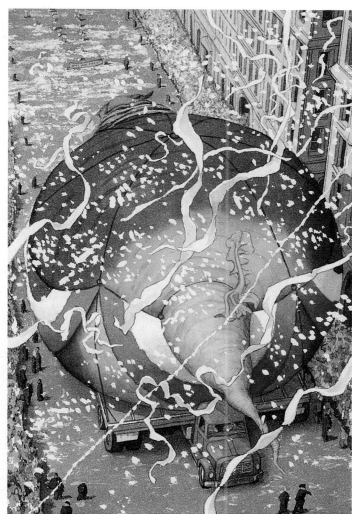

The Big Apple is renamed the Big Rutabaga.

Arugula, eggplant, avocado, and now rutabaga. As the list of vegetables that Holly did not plant grows longer, she concludes that the giant specimens are not the results of her experiment.

More curious than disappointed, Holly asks herself, "What happened to *my* vegetables?

"And whose broccoli is in my backyard?"

The place is the ionosphere. On June 29, the Arcturian star-cruiser *Alula Borealis* was touring its sixth planet in four days, and the captain had just pointed out the fjords of Norway off the port side.

In the galley an assistant fry cook accidentally jettisoned the entire food supply. As their vegetables drifted toward the small blue planet below, everyone on board had the same thought: Where would their supper come from?

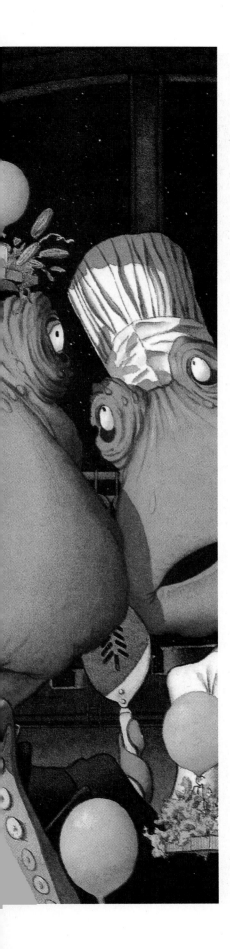

David Wiesner

David Wiesner has been an artist and storyteller for as long as he can remember. He began drawing as a young child. A television series in which an artist showed children how to draw inspired Wiesner to improve his talents. He was only six or seven at the time, but Wiesner bought all the instruction books that went with the TV show and he practiced all he could. Today Wiesner says, "I create books I think I would have liked to have seen when I was a kid." Wiesner likes to create ordinary worlds where not-so-ordinary things happen. "What I really find interesting is that opportunity to take a normal, everyday situation and somehow turn it on its end," he says. You will see that *June 29, 1999* isn't an ordinary summer day. You will also find the not-so-ordinary in two of Wiesner's other books, *Tuesday* and *Hurricane*.

HUGE *Idea*

Uh–Oh!

You're the cook on the spaceship and you've just lost the crew's dinner — and all the rest of the food supply. How do you tell the captain? With a partner, act out the conversation that might take place as the cook tries to explain this one. What will the captain say?

Write a TV News Bulletin

This Just In

Write a special TV News Bulletin for *June 29, 1999* that tells shocking news of the strange objects in the sky. Include what's happening, where it's happening, and what experts think the reasons might be. (You'll have to make up that last part.) Then read the news to classmates.

Compare Illustrations

When Weird Things Happen

Think about *June 29, 1999* and *Jumanji*. How would you compare the two fantasy stories? Discuss the two books with a partner. See if you can write a list of the similarities and differences between the books.

Write a Diary Entry

June 29, 1999

What will Holly Evans write in her diary for the date June 29, 1999? Write a diary entry for Holly, telling her thoughts and feelings about the incredible events on this day. Remember, Holly doesn't know about the spaceship. Or does she?

"LOOK, MA! There's an ALLIGATOR in the Toilet"

and Other Strange but Definitely, Positively, Absolutely Untrue Tales

by Anne Newgarden

ALLIGATORS
in the SEWERS

Many New Yorkers used to bring back baby alligators as souvenirs from Florida . . .

And years later, after lots of gators were flushed into the sewers . . .

You can never tell where an alligator will pop up next!

"It was a dark and rainy night," your friend whispers. "My friend's best friend's cousin and her father were driving along a road in Vermont, when they spotted a girl hitchhiking. They picked her up, and she told them where she lived. Then she just sat in the back seat, not saying a word. When they reached the house, the cousin and her father turned around . . . but the girl was gone!

"The two of them were really spooked, so they went to the door and-knocked. A couple invited them in. As they started to tell their story, the travelers saw a picture of the girl who vanished on the wall. 'That's our daughter,' the couple said. 'She was killed in an accident on that road three years ago. You're the seventh ones who've tried to bring her home.'"

Yikes! At this point, you're a little spooked. Thing is, you've heard that same story before. But you know for sure it happened to a friend of a friend of yours — in Iowa! What's going on?

Nothing too weird, answers Professor Jan Harold Brunvand. You've just run smack-dab into what he calls an "urban legend," or FOAF (Friend of a Friend) tale. Almost all of them are stories that start with "a friend of a friend told me . . ."

"An urban legend is a story that's passed along from person to person, and place to place," Brunvand told CONTACT. "It changes slightly along the way. But it's always told as if it really happened." Some of these amazing — *but absolutely untrue* — stories even show up in newspapers!

Although urban legends sound like stories that take place only in cities, Brunvand says they can take place in the country, as well. "The word 'urban' is used because the stories tell about present-day life," he explains.

Brunvand collects these "folk tales" from around the world. He studies where they come from and how they differ. Why does Brunvand study the stories? To find out what they say about the "folks" who pass them on.

ELEPHANT on the LOOSE!

Think you've never met up with an urban legend? Well, think again. Not all urban legends are ghost stories.

Some are downright funny. Take

the story Brunvand calls "The Elephant and the VW." A circus elephant mistakes a red VW Beetle for a stool and sits on it! Brunvand says the story sprung from people's fears in the early 1970s that small cars may be too flimsy.

"Whatever is new and puzzling or scary — but which eventually becomes

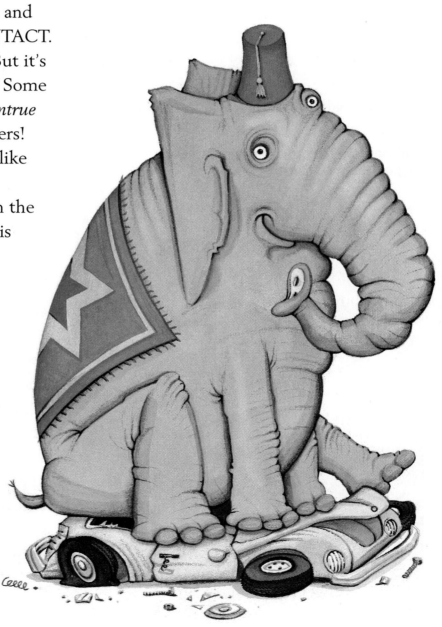

familiar — may turn up as an urban legend," Brunvand explains. "In the 1950s, for example, major highways were being built, and long-distance road travel was becoming more common. So urban legends started popping up behind the driver's seat." After all, out on that open road, anything might happen.

RATS! Another Legend

Nowadays, the urban legends that are most likely to make you shudder are fast-food horror stories. They pop up almost as quickly as fast-food restaurants.

Don't remember hearing any? How about the one about the dead mouse that turns up at the bottom of the soda pop bottle. Or the guy who bit into a piece of fast food "chicken" and found a southern fried rat! These distasteful stories, Brunvand says, show some people's fears about what fast food may be doing to us. Urban legends deliver the warning: "Watch out! This might happen to you!"

It seems that many folks are already on the lookout — for these weird whoppers, that is. People around the world send Brunvand up to 30 letters a week, passing on new legends they've heard. And Brunvand saves every story he gets: cobras in carpets, alligators in sewers, worms in hamburgers, spiders in plants — even fingers in pickle jars! All in a day's work, Brunvand shrugs.

The Quivering CACTUS

With Mom out of town, Junior is watering her plants.

The cactus is about to explode and it's filled with tarantulas!

PAUL BUNYAN
The Mightiest Logger of Them All

It seems an amazing baby was born in the state of Maine. When he was only two weeks old, he weighed more than a hundred pounds, and for breakfast every morning he ate five dozen eggs, ten sacks of potatoes, and a half-barrel of mush made from a whole sack of cornmeal. But the baby's strangest feature was his big, curly black beard. It was so big and bushy that every morning his poor mother had to comb it with a pine tree.

Except for that black beard, the big baby wasn't much trouble to anybody until he was about nine months old. That was when he first started to crawl, and since he weighed over five hundred pounds, he caused an earthquake that shook the whole town.

The baby's parents tried putting him in a giant floating cradle off the coast of Maine but every time he rolled over, huge waves drowned all the villages along the coast.

So his parents hauled the giant toddler to a cave in the Maine woods far away from civilization and said good-bye. His father gave him a fishing pole, a knife, some flint rocks, and an axe. "We'll think of you often, honey," his mother said, weeping. "But you can't come back home — you're just too big."

That's the story of how Paul Bunyan came to take care of himself in the Maine woods. And even though he lived alone for the next twenty years, he got along quite well.

In those times, huge sections of America were filled with dark green forests. It would be nice if those trees could have stayed tall and thick forever. But the pioneers needed them to build houses, churches, ships, wagons, bridges, and barns. So one day Paul Bunyan took a good look at all those trees and decided to invent logging.

"Tim-ber!" he yelled, and he swung the bright steel axe his father had given him in a wide circle. There was a terrible crash, and when Paul looked around, he saw he'd felled ten white pines with a single swing.

After that Paul traveled plenty fast through the untamed North Woods. He cut pine, spruce, and red willow in Minnesota, Michigan, and Wisconsin. He cleared cottonwoods out of Kansas so farmers could plant wheat and oaks out of Iowa so farmers could plant corn.

When next heard of, Paul was headed to Arizona. He dragged his pick-axe behind him on that trip, not realizing he was leaving a big ditch in his tracks. Today that ditch is called the Grand Canyon.

When Paul got back from the West, he decided to start a logging camp. Word spread fast. Since all the woodsmen had heard of Paul Bunyan, thousands of them hurried to Paul's headquarters at Big Onion on the Big Onion River in Minnesota to be part of his crew.

"There's only two requirements," Paul announced to the men who'd gathered to apply for the job. "All my loggers have to be over ten feet tall and able to pop six buttons off their shirts with one breath."

Well, about a thousand of the lumberjacks met those requirements, and Paul hired them all. Then he built a gigantic logging camp with bunkhouses a mile long and bunks ten beds high. The camp's chow table was so long that it took a week to pass the salt and pepper from one end to the other. Paul dug a few ponds to provide drinking water for everyone. Today we call those ponds the Great Lakes.

Things went pretty well at the Big Onion Lumber Company until the Year of the Hard Winter. One day Shot Gunderson, the crew boss, complained to Paul, "Boss, it's so cold that the flames for all the lanterns are freezing. And, Boss, when I give orders to the woods crew, all my words freeze in the air and hang there stiff as icicles."

"Well, haul away your frozen words and store them somewhere next to the lantern flames," Paul advised. "They'll both thaw out in the spring."

Sure enough, they did. The only problem was that, come spring, the melting lantern flames started some mean little brush fires. And when Shot's frozen words thawed, old cries of "Timber!" and "Chow time!" started to echo throughout the woods, causing all sorts of confusion. But other than that, things ran pretty smoothly.

Well, there's stories and stories about Paul Bunyan. For many years, old loggers sat around potbellied stoves and told about the good old times with Paul. Those loggers are all gone now, but many of their stories still hang frozen in the cold forest air of the North Woods, waiting to be told. Come spring, when they start to thaw, some of them might just start telling themselves. It's been known to happen.

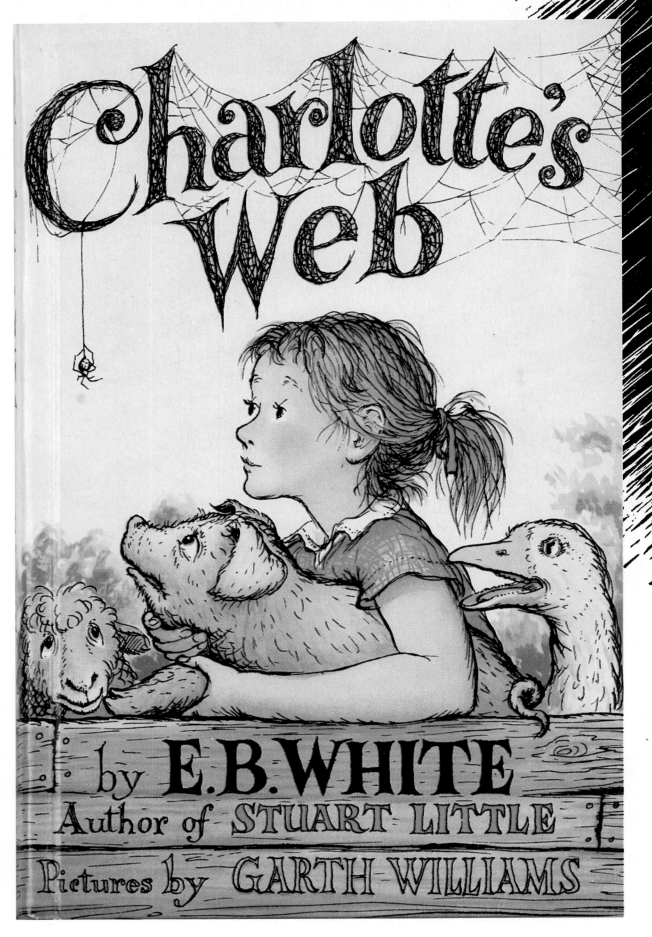

Charlotte's Web

by E. B. WHITE

Author of STUART LITTLE

Pictures by GARTH WILLIAMS

Wilbur is a friendly little pig. He was sad to be sold by his first owner, an eight-year-old girl named Fern. Now he has gotten used to his new home at Mr. Zuckerman's farm. And he has found a good friend — Charlotte, a clever, warm-hearted spider. But just when everything seems to be going well, bad news arrives. Mr. Zuckerman's plans for Wilbur include turning him into bacon and ham! When Charlotte comes to the rescue, her solution makes Mr. Zuckerman and the other humans in the story wonder, "Could it really happen?"

The Miracle

The next day was foggy. Everything on the farm was dripping wet. The grass looked like a magic carpet. The asparagus patch looked like a silver forest.

On foggy mornings, Charlotte's web was truly a thing of beauty. This morning each thin strand was decorated with dozens of tiny beads of water. The web glistened in the light and made a pattern of loveliness and mystery, like a delicate veil. Even Lurvy, who wasn't particularly interested in beauty, noticed the web when he came with the pig's breakfast. He noted how clearly it showed up and he noted how big and carefully built it was. And then he took another look and he saw something that made him set his pail down. There, in the center of the web, neatly woven in block letters, was a message. It said:

SOME PIG!

Lurvy felt weak. He brushed his hand across his eyes and stared harder at Charlotte's web.

"I'm seeing things," he whispered. He dropped to his knees and uttered a short prayer. Then, forgetting all about Wilbur's breakfast, he walked back to the house and called Mr. Zuckerman.

"I think you'd better come down to the pigpen," he said.

"What's the trouble?" asked Mr. Zuckerman. "Anything wrong with the pig?"

"N-not exactly," said Lurvy. "Come and see for yourself."

The two men walked silently down to Wilbur's yard. Lurvy pointed to the spider's web. "Do you see what I see?" he asked.

Zuckerman stared at the writing on the web. Then he murmured the words "Some Pig." Then he looked at Lurvy. Then they both began to tremble. Charlotte, sleepy after her night's exertions, smiled as she watched. Wilbur came and stood directly under the web.

"Some pig!" muttered Lurvy in a low voice.

"Some pig!" whispered Mr. Zuckerman. They stared and stared for a long time at Wilbur. Then they stared at Charlotte.

"You don't suppose that that spider . . ." began Mr. Zuckerman — but he shook his head and didn't finish the sentence. Instead, he walked solemnly back up to the house and spoke to his wife. "Edith, something has happened," he said, in a weak voice. He went into the living room and sat down, and Mrs. Zuckerman followed.

"I've got something to tell you, Edith," he said. "You better sit down."

Mrs. Zuckerman sank into a chair. She looked pale and frightened.

"Edith," he said, trying to keep his voice steady, "I think you had best be told that we have a very unusual pig."

A look of complete bewilderment came over Mrs. Zuckerman's face. "Homer Zuckerman, what in the world are you talking about?" she said.

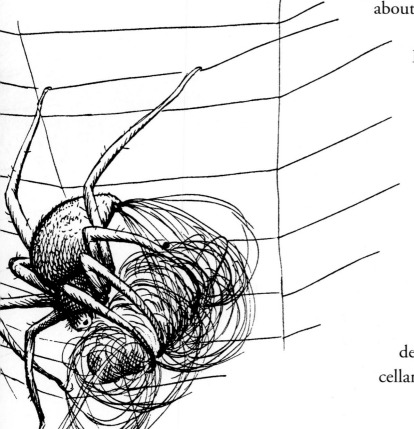

"This is a very serious thing, Edith," he replied. "Our pig is completely out of the ordinary."

"What's unusual about the pig?" asked Mrs. Zuckerman, who was beginning to recover from her scare.

"Well, I don't really know yet," said Mr. Zuckerman. "But we have received a sign, Edith — a mysterious sign. A miracle has happened on this farm. There is a large spider's web in the doorway of the barn cellar, right over the pigpen, and when

Lurvy went to feed the pig this morning, he noticed the web because it was foggy, and you know how a spider's web looks very distinct in a fog. And right spang in the middle of the web there were the words 'Some Pig.' The words were woven right into the web. They were actually part of the web, Edith. I know, because I have been down there and seen them. It says, 'Some Pig,' just as clear as clear can be. There can be no mistake about it. A miracle has happened and a sign has occurred here on earth, right on our farm, and we have no ordinary pig."

"Well," said Mrs. Zuckerman, "it seems to me you're a little off. It seems to me we have no ordinary *spider*."

"Oh, no," said Zuckerman. "It's the pig that's unusual. It says so, right there in the middle of the web."

"Maybe so," said Mrs. Zuckerman. "Just the same, I intend to have a look at that spider."

"It's just a common grey spider," said Zuckerman.

They got up, and together they walked down to Wilbur's yard. "You see, Edith? It's just a common grey spider."

Wilbur was pleased to receive so much attention. Lurvy was still standing there, and Mr. and Mrs. Zuckerman, all three, stood for about an hour, reading the words on the web over and over, and watching Wilbur.

Charlotte was delighted with the way her trick was working. She sat without moving a muscle, and listened to the conversation of the people. When a small fly blundered into the web, just beyond the word "pig," Charlotte dropped quickly down, rolled the fly up, and carried it out of the way.

After a while the fog lifted. The web dried off and the words didn't show up so plainly. The Zuckermans and Lurvy walked back to the house. Just before they left the pigpen, Mr. Zuckerman took one last look at Wilbur.

"You know," he said, in an important voice, "I've thought all along that that pig of ours was an extra good one. He's a solid pig. That pig is as solid as they come. You notice how solid he is around the shoulders, Lurvy?"

"Sure. Sure I do," said Lurvy. "I've always noticed that pig. He's quite a pig."

"He's long, and he's smooth," said Zuckerman.

"That's right," agreed Lurvy. "He's as smooth as they come. He's some pig."

When Mr. Zuckerman got back to the house, he took off his work clothes and put on his best suit. Then he got into his car and drove to the minister's house. He stayed for an hour and explained to the minister that a miracle had happened on the farm.

"So far," said Zuckerman, "only four people on earth know about this miracle — myself, my wife Edith, my hired man Lurvy, and you."

"Don't tell anybody else," said the minister. "We don't know what it means yet, but perhaps if I give thought to it, I can explain it in my sermon next Sunday. There can be no doubt that you have a most unusual pig. I intend to speak about it in my sermon and point out the fact that this community has been visited with a wondrous animal. By the way, does the pig have a name?"

"Why, yes," said Mr. Zuckerman. "My little niece calls him Wilbur. She's a rather queer child — full of notions. She raised the pig on a bottle and I bought him from her when he was a month old."

He shook hands with the minister, and left.

Secrets are hard to keep. Long before Sunday came, the news spread all over the county. Everybody knew that a sign had appeared in a spider's web on the Zuckerman place. Everybody knew that the Zuckermans had a wondrous pig. People came from miles around to look at Wilbur and to read the words on Charlotte's web.

The Zuckermans' driveway was full of cars and trucks from morning till night — Fords and Chevvies and Buick roadmasters and GMC pickups and Plymouths and Studebakers and Packards and De Sotos with gyromatic transmissions and Oldsmobiles with rocket engines and Jeep station wagons and Pontiacs. The news of the wonderful pig spread clear up into the hills, and farmers came rattling down in buggies and buckboards, to stand hour after hour at Wilbur's pen admiring the miraculous animal. All said they had never seen such a pig before in their lives.

When Fern told her mother that Avery had tried to hit the Zuckermans' spider with a stick, Mrs. Arable was so shocked that she sent Avery to bed without any supper, as punishment.

In the days that followed, Mr. Zuckerman was so busy entertaining visitors that he neglected his farm work. He wore his good clothes all the time now — got right into them when he got up in the morning. Mrs. Zuckerman prepared special meals for Wilbur. Lurvy shaved and got a haircut; and his principal farm duty was to feed the pig while people looked on.

Mr. Zuckerman ordered Lurvy to increase Wilbur's feedings from three meals a day to four meals a day. The Zuckermans were so busy with visitors they forgot about other things on the farm. The blackberries got ripe, and Mrs. Zuckerman failed to put up any blackberry jam. The corn needed hoeing, and Lurvy didn't find time to hoe it.

On Sunday the church was full. The minister explained the miracle. He said that the words on the spider's web proved that human beings must always be on the watch for the coming of wonders.

All in all, the Zuckermans' pigpen was the center of attraction. Fern was happy, for she felt that Charlotte's trick was working and that Wilbur's life would be saved. But she found that the barn was not nearly as pleasant — too many people. She liked it better when she could be all alone with her friends the animals.

What's to become of this famous, terrific pig? Read the whole story about Wilbur and his special spider friend Charlotte in the classic book, Charlotte's Web.

Meet the Author
E. B. White

PHOTOGRAPH © 1973 BY JILL KREMENTZ

Elwyn Brooks White was born in 1899 in Mount Vernon, New York. In 1938, White moved from New York with his wife and son to a farm in Maine. He quickly fell in love with farm life, and it was the farm that inspired him to write *Charlotte's Web*. "One day when I was on my way to feed the pig, I began feeling sorry for the pig because, like most pigs, he was doomed to die," he explained. "This made me sad. So I started thinking of ways to save a pig's life. I had been watching a big, gray spider at her work and was impressed by how clever she was at weaving. Gradually I worked the spider into the story . . ."

If you like *Charlotte's Web*, you might enjoy White's other classic books for children, *Stuart Little* and *The Trumpet of the Swan*.

Meet the Illustrator
Garth Williams

Garth Williams also used his experience living on a farm as the inspiration for illustrating *Charlotte's Web*. He especially liked drawing the animals: "I start with the real animal, working over and over until I can get the effect of human qualities and expressions and poses. I redesign animals . . . ." The hardest part was drawing Charlotte's face. After looking at a number of different sketches, E. B. White advised Williams just to draw two round dots for eyes and three straight lines for hairs. And that is what he did.

Garth Williams has illustrated over seventy books for children, including *Stuart Little* by E. B. White and Laura Ingalls Wilder's Little House books.

Some Ideas!

Write a Dialogue

"Well, Charlotte, You Did It!"

In this chapter of *Charlotte's Web* you don't get to hear the animals talking. Only the humans talk. Write a dialogue between Charlotte and Wilbur in which they discuss the excitement created by Charlotte's message "Some Pig!"

Conduct TV Interviews

I Couldn't Believe My Eyes

With a group of classmates, role-play TV interviews with the human characters from the story. What would a TV reporter ask these people? What will each person say about the wonderful pig at Zuckerman's?

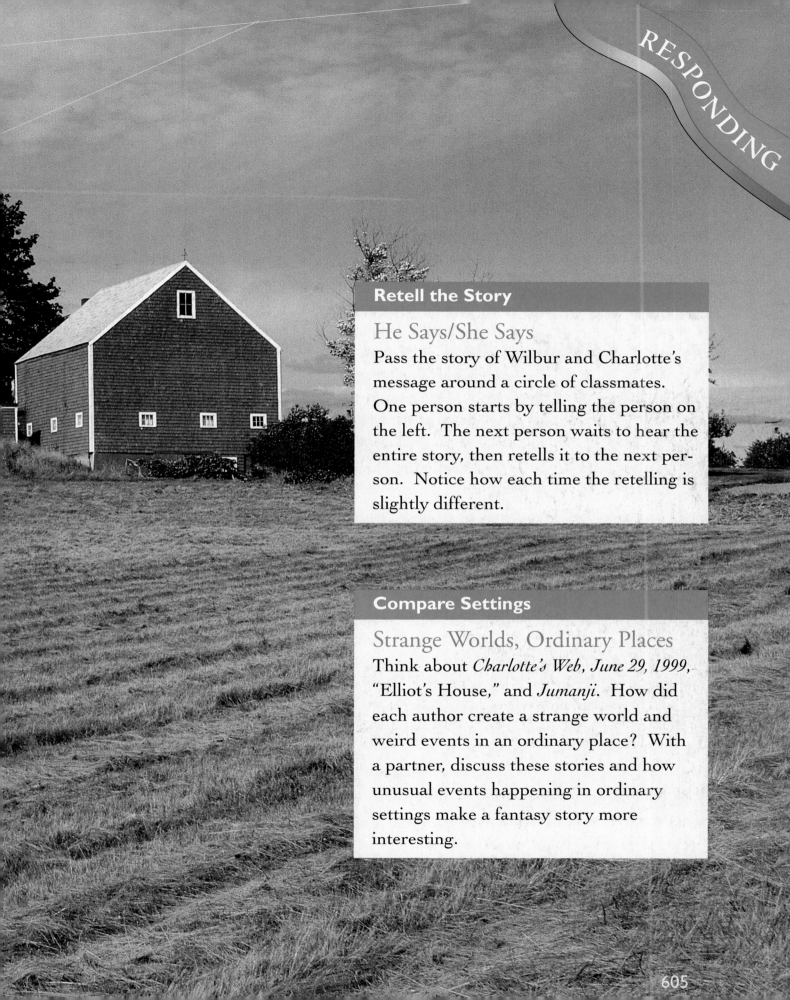

Retell the Story

He Says/She Says

Pass the story of Wilbur and Charlotte's message around a circle of classmates. One person starts by telling the person on the left. The next person waits to hear the entire story, then retells it to the next person. Notice how each time the retelling is slightly different.

Compare Settings

Strange Worlds, Ordinary Places

Think about *Charlotte's Web*, *June 29, 1999*, "Elliot's House," and *Jumanji*. How did each author create a strange world and weird events in an ordinary place? With a partner, discuss these stories and how unusual events happening in ordinary settings make a fantasy story more interesting.

Some of the words in this book may have pronunciations or meanings you do not know. This glossary can help you by telling you how to pronounce those words and by telling you the meanings with which those words are used in this book.

You can find out the correct pronunciations of any glossary word by using the special spelling after the word and the pronunciation key that runs across the bottom of the glossary pages.

The full pronunciation key opposite shows how to pronounce each consonant and vowel in a special spelling. The pronunciation key at the bottom of the glossary pages is a shortened form of the full key.

Full Pronunciation Key

Consonant Sounds

b	bib, cabbage	kw	choir, quick	t	tight, stopped
ch	church, stitch	l	lid, needle, tall	th	bath, thin
d	deed, mailed, puddle	m	am, man, dumb	*th*	bathe, this
f	fast, fife, off, phrase, rough	n	no, sudden	v	cave, valve, vine
		ng	thing, ink	w	with, wolf
g	gag, get, finger	p	pop, happy	y	yes, yolk, onion
h	hat, who	r	roar, rhyme	z	rose, size, xylophone, zebra
hw	which, where	s	miss, sauce, scene, see	zh	garage, pleasure, vision
j	judge, gem	sh	dish, ship, sugar, tissue		
k	cat, kick, school				

Vowel Sounds

ă	rat, laugh	ŏ	horrible, pot	ŭ	cut, flood, rough, some
ā	ape, aid, pay	ō	go, row, toe, though	û	circle, fur, heard, term, turn, urge, word
â	air, care, wear	ô	all, caught, for, paw		
ä	father, koala, yard	oi	boy, noise, oil	yo͞o	cure
ĕ	pet, pleasure, any	ou	cow, out	yo͝o	abuse, use
ē	be, bee, easy, piano	o͝o	full, took, wolf	ə	about, silent, pencil, lemon, circus
ĭ	if, pit, busy	o͞o	boot, fruit, flew		
ī	by, pie, high				
î	dear, deer, fierce, mere				

Stress marks

Primary Stress ': bi•ol•o•gy [bī ŏl´ə jē]
Secondary Stress ': bi•o•log•i•cal [bī´ ə loj´i kəl]

A

a•ban•doned (ə **băn′**dənd) *adj.*
Left behind or deserted: *The
abandoned puppy looked lost
and hungry.*

ac•cu•rate (**ăk′**yər ĭt) *adj.*
Exact, or free from mistakes:
*Because she had never played be-
fore, her first shots were not very
accurate.*

a•dapt (ə **dăpt′**) *v.* To adjust to
fit changing conditions: *The
Seminoles, who were used to living along streams, adapted to
living in the swamps.*

a•larmed (ə **lärmd′**) *adj.*
Excited or disturbed: *The horses
were alarmed by the noise of the
approaching train.*

al•i•bi (**ăl′**ə bī′) *n., pl.* **alibis.**
An excuse for proving that a per-
son was elsewhere when a crime
was committed: *She was not in
the cabin when the crime was
committed, and this alibi kept
her from being charged by the
police.*

am•a•teur (**ăm′**ə chər *or* **ăm′**ə
tər) *adj.* Relating to someone
who engages in an activity for fun
rather than for money: *Meg is an
amateur detective, not a professional one.*

a•maze (ə **māz′**) *v.* To fill with
wonder: *The beauty of the land
amazed the young man, and he
could not look away.*

a•mend•ment (ə **mĕnd′**mənt)
n. A change or added part to the
United States Constitution: *An
amendment to the Constitution
gave women the right to vote.*

an•ces•tor (**ăn′**sĕs′ tər) *n.* One
from which another is descended:
*His ancestors lived in the forest
long before he was born.*

ar•range (ə **rānj′**) *v.* To plan or
prepare for: *We arranged to
have our meetings twice a week
at my house.*

as•ton•ish (ə **stŏn′**ĭsh) *v.* To fill
with a great feeling of surprise;
amaze: *The size of the huge city
astonished Grandfather.*

ancestors

ă pat / ā pay / â care / ä father / ĕ pet / ē be / ĭ pit / ī ride / î fierce / ŏ pot / ō go
ô paw, for

a•tom bomb (ăt′əm bŏm) *n.* A powerful bomb whose great explosive force is a product of energy released by splitting atoms: *The **atom bomb** dropped on Hiroshima killed thousands of people.*

a•ward•ee (ə wôr dē′) *n.* Someone who receives an award: *Each **awardee** will be given a trophy at the ceremony.*

B

be•wil•der (bĭ wĭl′dər) *v.* To confuse or puzzle greatly: *All the loud sounds and bright lights of the city **bewildered** him.*

be•wil•der•ment (bĭ wĭl′dər mənt) *n.* The state of being puzzled or confused: *He looked around at the many people in the yard, and a look of total **bewilderment** crossed his face.*

bored (bôrd) *adj.* Made discontented; weary from lack of interest: *Eric was **bored** by the dull speaker, so he tried to find another way to amuse himself.*

bus•tle (bŭs′əl) *v.* To move in a hurried or busy way: *People **bustled** along the sidewalks, in a hurry to get home.*

C

cas•u•al•ly (kăzh′ōō əl ē) *adv.* Showing little concern; said or done without strong feeling or planning: *She mentioned the game **casually**, as if she didn't care whether or not they played.*

cham•pi•on (chăm′pē ən) *n.* The first-place winner in a competition: *The **champion** of the contest will win the biggest trophy.* —*v.* to fight for or support.

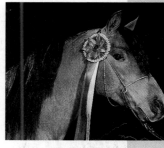

champion

charred (chärd) *adj.* Burned, but with parts still remaining: *The **charred** remains of the great trees stand guard over the burned forest.*

col•lect (kə lĕkt′) *v.* To gather or bring together: *The men **collected** the garbage from the neighborhood every morning and took it to the dump.*

oi **oi**l / ōō b**oo**k / ōō b**oo**t / ou **ou**t / ŭ c**u**t / û f**u**r / th ba**th** / *th* ba**the** / ə **a**go, it**e**m, penc**i**l, at**o**m, circ**u**s

Constitution of the United States

com•fort (**kŭm′**fərt) *v.* To make feel better when sad or scared: *I tried to* **comfort** *her, but she is still very sad.*

com•mit•tee (kə **mĭt′**ē) *n.* A group of people formed to complete a task: *Two* **committees**, *each with four members, will discuss the ideas this afternoon.*

com•mu•ni•ty (kə **myoo′**nĭ tē) *n., pl.* **communities.** A place where a group of people live: *The* **community** *of Spanish Harlem was a friendly, lively place.*

com•pan•ion (kəm **păn′**yən) *n.* One that keeps someone company: *A pet can be a good* **companion** *to keep a person from feeling lonely.*

com•pe•ti•tion (kŏm′ pĭ **tĭsh′** ən) *n.* A contest; a struggle to win: *We finally beat Johnston in the double-dutch* **competition** *this year.*

con•clude (kən **kloōd′**) *v.* 1. To come to a decision or form an opinion: *After much thought, he* **concludes** *that his project is not a success.* 2. To finish; to bring or come to an end.

con•di•tions (kən **dĭsh′**əns) *n.* Events or facts that affect a situation or activity: *The weather* **conditions** *on Friday will have an effect on Holly's experiment.*

Con•sti•tu•tion (kŏn′stĭ **toō′** shən) *n.* The document containing the basic laws of government of the United States, adopted in 1787 and put into effect in 1789: *The* **Constitution** *guarantees certain rights to all people of the United States.*

cus•toms (**kŭs′**təmz) *n.* The process of inspecting goods and baggage brought into a country: *When we went to Mexico, we had to go through* **customs** *before we could enter the country.*

de•duce (dĭ **doōs′**) *v.* To reach a conclusion by thinking and reasoning: *Can you* **deduce** *who stole the map by studying these clues?*

ă pat / ā pay / â care / ä father / ĕ pet / ē be / ĭ pit / ī ride / î fierce / ŏ pot / ō go ô paw, for

de•feat (dĭ **fēt′**) *v.* To beat in a contest: *Did you **defeat** Olivia and win the contest today?*

de•pos•it (dĭ **pŏz′**ĭt) *v.* To put or lay down, to place: *The truck driver spent all day **depositing** loads of garbage at the dump.*

de•vel•op•ment (dĭ **vĕl′**əp mənt) *n.* Changes that take place as a result of growth: *We tracked the plants' **development** for three weeks to see how high they would get.*

dis•ap•point•ed (dĭs′ə **poin′**ted) *adj.* Frustrated or let down: *The rainy weather **disappointed** the children, who wanted to play outdoors.*

dis•po•si•tion (dĭs′pə **zĭsh′**ən) *n.* One's usual way of acting, reacting, or behaving: *That friendly little puppy has a sweet **disposition**.*

drear•y (**drîr′**ē) *adj.* **drearier, dreariest.** Gray and depressing, gloomy: *The **dreary** sky made Clara miss the bright colors of her island.*

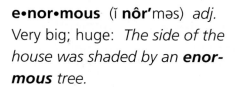

E

ef•fect (ĭ **fĕkt′**) *n.* The way one thing acts upon another; the result: *Our class will study the **effects** of water and sunlight on plant growth.*

e•nor•mous (ĭ **nôr′**məs) *adj.* Very big; huge: *The side of the house was shaded by an **enormous** tree.*

en•vi•ron•ment (ĕn **vī′**rən mənt) *n.* Surroundings and conditions that affect how living things grow and change: *The hot, steamy **environment** of the rain forest supports many plants and animals.*

ex•cite (ĭk **sīt′**) *v.* To arouse strong feelings in: *The new land and all its opportunities **excited** Grandfather.*

ex•haus•tion (ĭg **zôs′**chən) *n.* Very great tiredness: *His muscles shook with **exhaustion** after the long race.*

deposit

environment
Environ means "in a circle" in Latin. An environment is what surrounds, or circles, living things.

exhaustion
The Latin word *exhaurire* means "to draw out." Exhaustion draws all the strength from a person's body.

oi **oi**l / o͞o b**oo**k / o͞o b**oo**t / ou **ou**t / ŭ c**u**t / û f**u**r / th ba**th** / *th* ba**the** / ə **a**go, it**e**m, penc**i**l, at**o**m, circ**u**s

science experiment

ex•per•i•ment (ĭk **spĕr'**ə mənt) *n.* A test used to prove or find out about something: *Her* ***experiment*** *will show how vegetables grow in space.*

for•bid•ding (fər **bĭ'**dĭng) *adj.* Unfriendly or frightening: *The tall, dark buildings gave the city a* ***forbidding*** *appearance.*

foul (foul) *adj.* Dirty or unpleasant: *A* ***foul*** *odor reached Walter and made him wrinkle his nose in disgust.*

garbage

gar•bage (**gär'**bĭj) *n.* Unwanted or useless material; trash to be thrown away: *The* ***garbage*** *will be taken to the dump in the morning.*

gen•er•a•tion (jĕn' ə **rā'**shən) *n.* 1. Offspring that are at the same stage of descent from a common ancestor: *Several* ***generations*** *of that family live in the same town.* 2. The act or process of producing or bringing about.

haze

glare (glâr) *v.* To stare at in an angry way: *The man* ***glared*** *down at the children and demanded to know what they wanted.*

greet•ings (**grē'**tĭngs) *n.* Kind regards or best wishes: *They send* ***greetings*** *to you in their kind letter.*

haze (hāz) *n.* Dust, smoke, or other matter that makes the air less clear: *A brownish* ***haze*** *hung over the city, making it difficult to see the mountains.*

hes•i•tate (**hĕz'**ĭ tāt') *v.* To pause or stop in uncertainty: *The man* ***hesitated*** *and looked back at the tree before he walked away.*

home•sick (**hōm'**sĭk') *adj.* Missing one's home or a special place: *After traveling for three weeks, we were* ***homesick***.

ă pat / ā pay / â care / ä father / ĕ pet / ē be / ĭ pit / ī ride / î fierce / ŏ pot / ō go
ô paw, for

hon•or (ŏn'ər) *n.* Recognition, respect, or awards for showing special abilities or qualities: *They deserve high **honors** for all their good work.*

ig•nite (ĭg nīt') *v.* To catch fire quickly: *The dry bushes **ignited**, and the fire quickly spread.*

in•te•grat•ed (ĭn'tĭ grā tĭd) *adj.* Having people of all races together: *Thurgood Marshall believed children of all races should attend classes together in **integrated** schools.*

in•ves•ti•gate (ĭn vĕs'tĭ gāt') *v.* To study or examine closely: *Julian decided to **investigate** to find out who owned the dog in the car.*

judge (jŭj) *n.* A person who decides the winner of a contest: *The **judges** look for certain qualities as they choose the winner.*

kin•dle (kĭn'dl) *v.* To start a fire: *Sparks from the exploding trees **kindled** new fires.*

land•fill (lănd'fĭl) *n.* An area in which trash is buried beneath layers of dirt: *The trash is taken to the **landfill** every Thursday.*

leu•ke•mi•a (lōō kē'mē ə) *n.* A disease of the blood that is a form of cancer: *She is in the hospital with **leukemia**.*

long (lông) *v.* To wish for something very much: *They **longed** to see their old friends.*

loom (lōōm) *v.* To appear, often seeming huge and threatening: *The buildings of the big city **loomed** in the distance, making her feel small and scared.* — *n.* A frame or machine on which thread is woven into cloth.

ignite
Ignite comes from the Latin word *ignis*, which means "fire."

landfill

loom

oi **oi**l / ōō b**oo**k / ōō b**oo**t / ou **ou**t / ŭ c**u**t / û f**u**r / th ba**th** / *th* ba**the** / ə **a**go, it**e**m, p**e**ncil, at**o**m, circ**u**s

marvel/miracle

It's no wonder that *marvel* and *miracle* have similar meanings. They both come from the Latin word *mirari*, which means "to wonder."

monument

mar•vel (**mär′**vəl) *v.* To be filled with surprise or wonder: *He marveled at the wonderful countryside and the busy new cities.*

me•mor•ial (mə **môr′**ē əl) *adj.* Acting to honor the memory of a person or event: *We had a memorial ceremony to honor those who were killed in the war.*

meth•od (**měth′**əd) *n.* A plan or process for doing something: *I think a monorail is the best method of mass transportation.*

might•y (**mī′**tē) *adj.* **mightier, mightiest.** Powerful, large, or strong: *Crumbles gave a mighty bark to show that he was feeling better.*

mir•a•cle (**mĭr′**ə kəl) *n.* An amazing or marvelous thing that seems impossible: *The people on the farm thought Charlotte's beautiful web was a miracle.*

mir•a•cu•lous (mĭ **răk′**yə ləs) *adj.* Of or like a miracle: *The message in the spider's web was the most miraculous thing Lurvy had ever seen.*

mound

mis•chie•vous (**mĭs′**chə vəs) *adj.* Naughty; causing trouble: *That was a mischievous prank he played on the man.*

mon•u•ment (**mŏn′**yə mənt) *n.* Something created to help people continue to remember a person or event: *The children helped raise money to build the monument, a statue of Sadako.*

mo•tive (**mō′**tĭv) *n.* A reason for an action: *The thief had no money, so we know that was one of his motives in committing the crime.*

mound (mound) *n.* A pile or hill: *The mound of trash grew so high it reached the windows of the house.*

op•pon•ent (ə **pō′**nənt) *n.* A person who is against another person in a contest: *My opponent in tomorrow's game is a friend of my brother's.*

ă pat / ā pay / â care / ä father / ĕ pet / ē be / ĭ pit / ī ride / î fierce / ŏ pot / ō go
ô paw, for

op•por•tun•i•ty (ŏp'ər **too**'nĭ tē) *n., pl.* **opportunities.** A good chance: *Going to Howard University is an* **opportunity** *to get a good education.*

P

pa•pers (**pā**'pərs) *n.* Documents telling who or what one is: *To sign up for school, we brought our* **papers** *to show our names and where we were born.*

par•ti•ci•pant (pär **tĭs**'ə pənt') *n.* One who takes part: *There were more than 100* **participants** *in this year's soccer tournament.*

per•fect (**pŭr**'fĭkt) *adj.* Without any faults; completely pleasing; excellent: *The beautiful stone was the color of a* **perfect** *white rose.*

pes•ky (**pĕs**'kē) *adj.* **peskier, peskiest.** Causing trouble: *Perhaps those* **pesky** *little dogs will leave the cat alone now.*

poised (poizd) *adj.* Balanced: *The runners stood* **poised**, *ready to start the race when the whistle blew.*

pol•lin•ate (**pŏl**'ə nāt') *v.* To transfer pollen from one flower to another: *Flying from flower to flower, bees* **pollinate** *the plants in the forest.*

pre•fer (prĭ **fûr'**) *v.* To value more or like better: *I like living on the prairie, but I would* **prefer** *to live near the ocean.*

prej•u•dice (**prĕj**'ə dĭs) *n.* A strong feeling or opinion formed unfairly; hostility toward a member of a particular group: *Sending children of different races to separate schools is a result of* **prejudice**.

proj•ect (**prŏj**'ekt') *n.* A task to be done or a problem to be solved: *The* **project** *is to write a report and draw a poster about transportation.*

R

red her•ring (rĕd **hĕr**'ĭng) *n.* Something that draws attention away from the matter or issue: *The fake clue was a* **red herring** *that kept the detective from solving the mystery.*

poised

red herring
A red herring is really a type of smoked fish. It was originally used to draw hunting dogs off the trail of their prey.

oi **oi**l / o͞o b**oo**k / o͞o b**oo**t / ou **ou**t / ŭ **c**u**t / û f**u**r / th ba**th** / *th* ba**the** / ə **a**go, it**e**m, penc**i**l, at**o**m, circ**u**s

schedule

schedule

A sheet of papyrus, an ancient kind of paper, was called a *scheda* in Latin. *Scheda* became *schedule* over time. Many people write out their schedules on paper.

reg•is•ter (**rĕj'**ĭ stər) *v.* To place on an official list: *We met the principal when we went to **register** at our new school.*

re•lieved (rĭ **lēv'**d´) *adj.* Freed from worry or discomfort: *He was **relieved** that Sonia understood the need to find the dog's owners.*

res•er•va•tion (rĕz'ər **vā'**shən) *n.* Land set aside by the government for Native Americans: *The government insisted that the Native Americans give up their own land and move onto the **reservation**.* 2. The act of setting something aside for later use. 3. Something that restricts or causes doubt.

re•spon•si•bil•i•ty (rĭ spŏn'sə **bĭl'**ĭ tē) *n., pl.* **responsibilities.** Something a person has to do; a duty: *Taking care of a pet is an important **responsibility**.*

rest•less (**rĕst'**lĭs) *adj.* Unsettled; unable to relax: *The children were **restless** after being stuck inside all day.*

rhythm (**rĭth'**əm) *n.* An action or condition repeated in regular sequence: *The girls jumped in **rhythm** to the beat of the music.*

ri•val (**rī'**vəl) *n.* Someone who competes with another for the same object or goal: *Sally and her **rival**, Phoebe, will compete against each other today.*

rou•tine (rōō **tēn'**) *n.* 1. An act that is part of a piece of entertainment: *We added five new steps to our dance **routine**.* 2. A series of usual activities; regular procedure.

sa•cred (**sā'**krĭd) *adj.* Holy; deserving of great respect: *During the ritual, even the small children were quiet and respectful of the **sacredness** of the occasion.*

schedule (**skĕj'**ōōl *or* **skĕj'**əl) *n.* A plan with a time line for doing something: *By the third week, we had made up lost time and were ahead of **schedule**.*

ă p**a**t / ā p**ay** / â c**a**re / ä f**a**ther / ĕ p**e**t / ē b**e** / ĭ p**i**t / ī r**i**de / î f**ie**rce / ŏ p**o**t / ō g**o** ô p**aw**, f**or**

scorch (skôrch) *v.* To burn the surface with great heat: *Flames moved quickly, **scorching** the grass and leaves.*

scurry (skûr′ē) *v.* **scurried, scurrying.** To rush around in a hurried manner: *People **scurried** from shop to shop, hoping to get home before dark.*

sigh (sī) *v.* To take a deep breath and let it out with a sound expressing boredom: *Peter **sighed** heavily and wished again for something to do.*

singe (sĭnj) *v.* To slightly burn surface features such as hair or fur: *Animals moved quickly to avoid **singeing** their fur in the flames.*

slouch (slouch) *v.* To droop lazily: *He **slouched** in his chair until a sudden noise made him sit up straight.*

smol•der•ing (smōl′dər ĭng) *adj.* Burning slowly without a flame: *The **smoldering** ruins of the cabins burned for days.*

so•lu•tion (sə loo′shən) *n.* 1. The answer to a problem: *One good **solution** to the pollution problem is reducing the number of cars on the road.* 2. A mixture formed by dissolving a substance in a liquid.

som•er•sault (sum′ər sôlt′) *v.* To roll the body in a complete circle, head over heels: *The gymnast **somersaulted** across the mat, carefully tucking her chin down onto her chest as she rolled forward.*

sort (sôrt) *v.* To arrange according to kind, size, or other characteristics: *Be sure to **sort** the garbage into piles for trash pickup and recycling.*

spe•ci•men (spĕs′ə mən) *n.* One of a group of things that can represent the whole group: *The huge vegetables were not the usual **specimens** of broccoli, avocados, and peas.*

spon•sor (spŏn′sər) *n.* A person or organization that helps plan and/or pay for an event: *The **sponsors** of the contest provided the prizes and the refreshments.*

slouch

oi **oi**l / o͞o b**oo**k / o͞o b**oo**t / ou **ou**t / ŭ c**u**t / û f**u**r / th ba**th** / *th* ba**the** / ə **a**go, it**e**m, penc**i**l, at**o**m, circ**u**s

strengthen

strength•en (**strĕngk'**thən) *v.*
To make stronger: *Practicing every day for one hour has helped to* **strengthen** *my muscles.*

sus•pect (sə **spĕkt'**) *v.* To think that something is true without being sure: *He* **suspected** *that the water in the pond had already dried up.* (**sŭs'** pĕkt') *n.* A person thought to be guilty without proof: *We have questioned the seven* **suspects** *in the case of the missing map.*

T

territory

The Latin root *terra* is in *territory*. *Terra* means "land."

ter•rit•or•y (**tĕr'**ĭ tŏr'ē) *n., pl.* **territories.** A geographical area owned by a government: *The government set aside* **territory** *in central Oklahoma for the Native Americans.*

the•o•ry (**the'**ə rē) *n.,*
An opinion about what happened based on limited information or knowledge: *After studying the clues, Meg came up with a* **theory** *about who had broken into the strongbox.*

trea•ty (**trē'**tē) *n., pl.* **treaties.**
A legal agreement between two or more countries or governments: *Both governments thought the agreement was fair, so they signed the* **treaty**.

U

up•town (**ŭp'**toun) *adv.*
Toward the upper part of a city: *We took the train* **uptown** *after seeing the movie.*

W

won•der (**wŭn'**dər) *n.*
Something very remarkable or unusual; marvel: *How Charlotte wove those words into her web is a* **wonder**. — *v.* To want to know; to be curious.

won•drous (**wŭn'**drəs) *adj.*
Wonderful: *The sun reflecting off the spider's web made a* **wondrous** *sight.*

ă p**a**t / ā p**a**y / â c**a**re / ä f**a**ther / ĕ p**e**t / ē b**e** / ĭ p**i**t / ī r**i**de / î f**ie**rce / ŏ p**o**t / ō g**o**
ô p**aw**, f**o**r

ACKNOWLEDGMENTS

Selections

Selection from *50 Simple Things Kids Can Do To Save The Earth.*, by John Javna. Copyright © 1990 by John Javna. Reprinted by permission of Universal Press Syndicate.

"A Play," from *Childtimes*, by Eloise Greenfield and Lessie Jones Little. Copyright © 1979 by Eloise Greenfield and Lessie Jones Little. Reprinted by permission of HarperCollins Children's Books, a division of HarperCollins Publishers.

"Alice and Alex," by Deborah Sussman from *Storyworks* magazine, January 1994. Copyright © 1993 by Scholastic, Inc. Reprinted by permission.

"Ali Baba and the Mystery of the Missing Circus Tickets," from *Hurray For Ali Baba Bernstein*, by Johanna Hurwitz. Copyright © 1989 by Johanna Hurwitz. Reprinted by permission of Morrow Junior Books, a division of William Morrow & Company, Inc.

Selection from *California Kids,* edited by Jim Silverman. Copyright © 1992 by The California Kids History Catalog. Cover art by Rick Wheeler. Reprinted by permission of Jim Silverman.

Selection from *Classroom Peanuts,* by Charles M. Schulz. Copyright © 1982 by United Feature Syndicate. Reprinted by permission.

"Earth Day Kids," from April, 1993 *3-2-1 Contact* magazine. Copyright © 1993 by Children's Television Workshop. Reprinted by permission.

"Elliot's House," by Lois Lowry, from *The Big Book for Our Planet*, edited by Ann Durell, Jean Craighead George and Katherine Paterson. Copyright © 1993 by Lois Lowry. Reprinted by permission of Harold Ober Associates, Inc.

Encyclopedia Brown and the Case of The Disgusting Sneakers, by Donald J. Sobol. Copyright © 1990 by Donald J. Sobol. Reprinted by permission of Morrow Junior Books, a division of William Morrow & Company, Inc.

"The Flying Train Committee," from *Tales Of a Fourth Grade Nothing*, by Judy Blume. Copyright © 1972 by Judy Blume. Reprinted by permission of Dutton Children's Books, a division of Penguin Books USA Inc.

"Gluscabi and the Wind Eagle," told by Joseph Bruchac, from *Native American Stories*, by Joseph Bruchac and Michael J. Caduto. Copyright © 1991 by Joseph Bruchac. Reprinted by permission of Fulcrum Publishing.

"Gotcha," by John Shabe, from *Dynamath*. Copyright © 1993 by Scholastic, Inc. Reprinted by permission.

Grandfather's Journey, by Allen Say. Copyright © 1993 by Allen Say. Reprinted by permission of Houghton Mifflin Company. All rights reserved.

The Great Kapok Tree, by Lynne Cherry. Copyright © 1990 by Lynne Cherry. Reprinted by permission of Harcourt Brace & Company.

The Great Yellowstone Fire, by Carole Vogel and Kathryn A. Goldner. Copyright © 1990 by Carole Garbury Vogel and Kathryn Allen Goldner. Reprinted by permission of Little, Brown and Company.

I'm New Here, by Bud Howlett. Copyright © 1993 by Bud Howlett. Reprinted by permission of Houghton Mifflin Company. All rights reserved.

Selection from *Julian, Secret Agent*, by Ann Cameron. Copyright © 1988 by Ann Cameron. Reprinted by permission of Alfred A. Knopf, Inc.

Jumanji, by Chris Van Allsburg. Copyright © 1981 by Chris Van Allsburg. Reprinted by permission of Houghton Mifflin Company. All rights reserved.

June 29, 1999, written and illustrated by David Wiesner. Copyright © 1992 by David Wiesner. Reprinted by permission of Houghton Mifflin Company. All rights reserved.

Just a Dream, by Chris Van Allsburg. Copyright © 1990 by Chris Van Allsburg. Reprinted by permission of Houghton Mifflin Company. All rights reserved.

"Keepers of the Earth," by Joseph Bruchac, from the introduction of *Native American Stories*, by Joseph Bruchac and Michael J. Caduto. Copyright © 1991 by Joseph Bruchac. Reprinted by permission of Fulcrum Publishing.

Selections from "Kids Did It," February 1992 *National Geographic World*. Copyright © 1992 by National Geographic World. World is the official magazine for Junior Members of the National Geographic Society. Reprinted by permission.

Selection from *Koya DeLaney and the Good Girl Blues,* by Eloise Greenfield. Copyright © 1992 by Eloise Greenfield. Reprinted by permission of Scholastic, Inc.

"Leaving Home," from *All for the Better*, by Nicholasa Mohr. Copyright © 1993 by Dialogue Systems, Inc. Reprinted by permission of Steck-Vaughn Company.

"Look Ma! There's an Alligator in the Toilet!," from December, 1993 *3-2-1 Contact* magazine. Copyright © 1993 by the Children's Television Workshop. Reprinted by permission.

"Lucas Cott Does Raisin Bread Arithmetic," by Johanna Hurwitz from *Storyworks* magazine, November/December 1993. Copyright © 1993 by Johanna Hurwitz. Reprinted by permission of Scholastic, Inc.

"The Marble Champ," from *Baseball In April and Other Stories*, by Gary Soto. Copyright © 1990 by Gary Soto. Reprinted by permission of Harcourt Brace & Company.

Meg Mackintosh and The Case of the Curious Whale Watch, by Lucinda Landon. Copyright © 1987 by Lucinda Landon. Reprinted by permission of Little, Brown and Company.

"The Miracle," from *Charlotte's Web*, by E. B. White. Copyright © 1952 by E.B. White. Copyright © renewed 1980 by E.B. White. Reprinted by permission of HarperCollins Publishers.

Special thanks to the following teachers whose students' compositions are included in the Be a Writer features in this level:

Judy Thum, Paul Ecke Central School, Encinitas, California; Pamela Ziegler, Washington Elementary School, Fargo, North Dakota; Nancy Simpson, Friday Harbor Elementary School, Friday Harbor, Washington; Steve Buettner, Hammond Elementary School, Laurel, Maryland; Sandra Grier, Taylors Elementary School, Taylors, South Carolina; Cydelle Greene, Calusa Elementary School, Miami, Florida.

CREDITS

Illustration 18–33 John Dunivant; **43–57** Betsy James; **62–63** Charles Schultz; **84–87** Gregory Nemec; **88–89** Yvonne Brown; **93–105** Gil Ashby; **108–113** Will Terry; **146–155** Lark Carrier; **156–157** Piotr Kaczmarek; **158–159** Paul O. Zelinsky; **160–182** Lynne Cherry; **198–223** Chris Van Allsburg; **234–258** Lucinda Landon; **266–274** Larry Johnson; **280–281** Michael McParlane; **282–291** Michael Chesworth; **305–332** Allen Say; **344–355** Sheldon Greenburg; **358–359** Patrick Gnan; **360–370** Leslie Wu; **382–390** Ronald Himler; **391** Chris Costello; **399** George Littlechild; **407–417** Mike Reed; **428** Beatrice Brooks; **454–481** Ed Young; **488–505** Lloyd Bloom; **510–511** Steve Cieslawski; **518–545** Chris Van Allsburg; **550–556** Kenneth Spengler; **560–561** Shel Silverstein; **562–582** David Wiesner; **586–589** Ethan Long; **590–593** Eric Petersen; **594–603** Garth Williams

Assignment Photography 278–279, 394–395, 396–397, 420–421, 427 (TR), 546–547, 548–549 Banta Digital Group; **192–193, 194–195, 276–277** Kindra Clineff; **292–293** Dave Desroches; **506–507** John Lei/OMNI–Photo Communications, Inc.; **371** John MacLachlan; **183** (inset) Katie P. McManus/*Teaching K–8 Magazine*; **34–35, 58–59, 60–61, 80–81, 90–91, 106–107, 183** (background), **186–187, 188–189, 196–197, 226–227, 228–229, 230–231, 232–233, 260–261, 298–299, 300–301, 302–303, 304, 333, 334–335, 336–337, 338–339, 340–341, 342–343, 380–381, 392–393, 400–401, 402–403, 404–405, 448, 516–517** Tony Scarpetta; **36–37, 38–39, 40–41, 114–115, 116–117, 118–119, 190–191, 224–225** Tracey Wheeler

Photography 33 John Dunivant(tl); Johanna Hurwitz (t) **42** Mario Ruiz/Time Magazine (tl); Courtesy of Betsy James (tr) **60** C.A. Giampiccolo/FPG **79** Courtesy of Bud Howlett (bl) **82** Andrew Brusso **83** Beatriz Schiller (tl); Washington Post (tr); Cary Tolman (b) **90** Courtesy of Anthony Yengo **92** Courtesy of Eloise Greenfield (tl); Courtesy of Gil Ashby (bl) **120** ©Jerry Ferrara/Photo Researchers (background) **121** Robert Bower (mr) **122** Alan and Sandy Carey **123** Alan and Sandy Carey (t); Erwin and Peggy Bauer (m) **124–125** Boise Interagency Fire Center **126** National Park Service **127** Wyoming Travel Commission **128** Alan and Sandy Carey **129** Jeff and Alexa Henry (tr) **131** National Park Service **133** Alan and Sandy Carey **134** ©Robert Bower (l); Erwin & Peggy Bauer (tr, br) **135** Alan and Sandy Carey **136** Steven Dowell/Bozeman Chronicle **139** Wyoming Travel Commission **140** National Park Service **141** Courtesy of Carole G. Vogel (br); Courtesy of Kathryn A. Goldner (tr) **142–143** National Park Service (background) **144** ©Daniel R. Westergren/National Geographic Society (cover); ©Bill Moyer/National Geographic Society (inset); ©Micheal Yamashita/National Geographic Society (m) **145** ©Bill Moyer/National Geographic Society (m)

183 Katie MacManus/ Courtesy of Lynne Cherry **184–185** ©1994 Zefa Germany /The Stock Market **186** Courtesy of Megan Hunter **188–189** K.O.P.E. (t) **190** Courtesy of Melanie Essary **190–191** Intelligencer/ Record (tr) **196** Susan Lapides **259** Courtesy of Lucinda Landon (t) **262** Richard Gray Gallery **263** Greg Hiens/ Isabella Stuart Gardner Museum, Boston (t); Isabella Stuart Gardner Museum, Boston (l); Art Resource (r) **275** Das Anudas/Courtesy of Ann Cameron (tr); Courtesy of Larry Johnson **278** Courtesy of Bridget Hudson **282** Courtesy of Donald J. Sobol; Courtesy of Michael Chesworth (r) **294–295** Frank Micelotta/Children's Television Workshop **296** Barbara Nitke/Children's Television Workshop (tl); Michael Benabib/Children's Television Workshop (tm); Frank Micelotta/Children's Television Workshop (bm) **297** Don Perdue/Children's Television Workshop (br) Frank Micelotta/Children's Television Workshop (tr) **333** Courtesy of Allan Say **336** The Bettmann Archive (ml); The Granger Collection, New York (mr); Courtesy The Oakland Museum (bl); Wells Fargo Bank (br) **337** California State Library (bl); Courtesy The Oakland Museum (br) **338** The Bettmann Archive (tm); Wells Fargo Bank (tr) **340** Courtesy of The Bancroft Library (mr) **341** Courtesy The Oakland Museum (tl); Denver Public Library (tr) **342** Library of Congress (l); San Diego Historical Society, Photo Collection (mr) **343** Courtesy The Oakland Museum (ml) **344** Courtesy of Nicholasa Mohr; Mary Merrick/ Courtesy of Sheldon Greenburg (b) **356** The Bettmann Archive **358** Museum of the City of New York (tl) **359** Comstock (t); UPI/ Bettman (bl); Christian Kempf/Musee Bertoldi-Colma (bm); ©Bill Backman/Photo Researchers (br) **371** Courtesy of Patricia MacLachlan; Courtesy of Leslie Wu **373** ©David Scott Smith/Stock Connection **380** Sharon McElmeel/ Courtesy of Virginia Driving Hawk Sneve (tl); Courtesy of Ronald Himler (tr) **394** Courtesy of Briana Taylor **406** Courtesy of Mike Reed (r); Courtesy of Gary Soto (l) **420** Courtesy of Nathan Cox **422** The Boston Phoenix (t) **423** Peter Travers **424–425** Boston Athletic Association (t) **424** Jeffrey Dunn (b) **425** Boston Athletic Association (r) **426** Boston Athletic Association(l); Peter Southwick/Stock Boston (r) **427** Kathy Tarantola/The Picture Cube (b) **430** NAACP **431** UPI Bettmann/The Bettmann Archive **432, 435, 438, 440** Marshall Family Photo **433** Library of Congress **434, 436** Courtesy Moorland-Spingarn Research Center, Howard University **437** Library of Congress; UPI Bettmann (t) **439** AP Worldwide Photos, Inc.(r) **440** UPI Bettmann/ The Bettmann Archive (l) **441** AP Worldwide Photos, Inc.; The Bettmann Archive (l); UPI/Bettmann (bm) **443** AP/Worldwide Photos **444, 445** UPI/Bettmann **445** The Bettmann Archive (b) **446** Don Sparks/The Image Bank (m) **446–447** UPI/Bettmann (m) **447** U.S. Supreme Court Photo; UPI/Bettmann (tl) **447** AP Newsfeatures photo/AP Worldwide Photos, Inc. (b); ©Peter Chapman (br) **448** Courtesy of Sean Dolan (tl); Courtesy of Beatrice Brooks/PCI (r) **449** AP Worldwide Photos, Inc. (tl); Sandra Baker/Liason International (m); Virginia Blaisdell Photography (b); **450–451** Steve Dunwell/The Image Bank **453** Art Institute of Chicago **481** Courtesy of Ed Young (tr); Courtesy of Eleanor Coerr (tl)

483–484 Bruno J. Zehnder/Peter Arnold,Inc. **484** Gray Mortimore/Allsport (t); M. Greenlar/The Image Works (l); M. Greenlar/The Image Works (r) **485** Ronnie Fridthjor; Joseph H. Bailey/National Geographic Society **486–487** Uwe Lochstampfer/The Image Bank **506** Courtesy of Mavis Jukes **507** Courtesy of Mavis Jukes (b) **508–509** ©A.M. Rosario/The Image Bank **511–512** Tim Brown/Tony Stone Images/Chicago Inc. **514–515** Tony Stone Images/Chicago Inc. **516** Susan Lapides (tl) **548** Courtesy of Sophia Vilella **557** Courtesy of Lois Lowry (t); ©Susan Kennedy/Kenneth Spengler (l) **558–559** ©Ray Pfortner/Peter Arnold,Inc. **583** Len Irish/ Courtesy of David Wiesner (r) **603** Jill Krementz (t); Courtesy of Garth Williams (b) **604–605** ©Walter Bibikow/The Image Bank **608** David De Lossy/The Image Bank **609** Animals Animals **610** Jeff Hunter/The Image Bank **611** Paul & Karen Smith/Tony Stone Images **612** Terje Rakke/The Image Bank; Ulf Wallin/The Image Bank (b) **613** Steve Dunwell /The Image Bank (t); Louis Casteneda/The Image Bank (b) **614** Chris Hackett/The Image Bank (t); Mark Burnett/Photo Researchers (b) **615** Bob Daemmrich/Tony Stone Images **618** Ed Bock/The Stock Market

Special thanks **380–381; 392–393** Basket, doll, and skirt courtesy of Ah-Tha-Thi-Ki Museum, Seminole Tribe of Florida

Here's what visitors to our Web site said about stories in *Imagine.*

The story I read was *I'm New Here* by Bud Howlett. I like the story because it tells how Jazmin really felt. On my first day of school I felt the same way. I felt like no one liked me. I had no one to talk to or play with.

Roshonda Smith, Washington

The Great Kapok Tree shows you that the rain forest is a very special place. I learned that a tree is more than just a tree—it is a home to lots of animals. This book made me think of how I would feel if my home were gone. It made me care more about all living things.

Jaimelyn Beatty Seeman, New York

When you read *Grandfather's Journey,* you feel that you're in the place that it's talking about because it gives such good descriptions. The book made me want to go to California myself some day. I liked it because even though he loved to travel and go different places, after awhile he saw that Japan was really important to him.

Maggie Owens, Ohio

Post your reviews in the

Kids' Clubhouse

at

www.eduplace.com